INTERNET AS A MEDIA

INTERNET AS A MEDIA

Sudipa Gangopadhyay

KALPAZ

ISBN: 978-81-7835-968-7

Price: ₹ 900

First Published 2014

Published by

Kalpaz Publications
C-30, Satyawati Nagar,
Delhi - 110052
E-mail: kalpaz@hotmail.com Ph.: 9212142040

Laser Typesetting: Rajender Vashist, Delhi
Printed at: G. Print Process, Delhi

Cataloging in Publication Data--DK
Courtesy: D.K. Agencies (P) Ltd. <docinfo@dkagencies.com>

Gangopadhyay, Sudipa.
Internet as a media / Sudipa Gangopadhyay.
p. cm.
Includes bibliographical references (p.) and index.
ISBN 9788178359687

1. Digital media. 2. Internet. I. Title.

DDC 006.7 23

Contents

Acknowledgements

I gratefully and humbly acknowledge my esteemed research guide and supervisor, Professor (Dr) Tapati Basu, Head of the Department of Journalism and Mass Communication, University of Calcutta. For her supervision, advice, encouragement, patience and guidance from the initial to the final stage of the research that enabled me to develop an understanding of the subject and enriched my growth as a student and a researcher. Without her constant motivation, support and help it would not have been possible to complete my work and I am deeply indebted to her.

I would also like to acknowledge the love, encouragement and support of my parents, my husband, my young daughter and my extended family.

Lastly, I offer my gratitude to all those who helped me in any respect during the period of my research and apologise for not being able to thank each one of them individually.

Sudipa Gangopadhyay

List of Tables, Exhibits and Diagrams

Exhibits

Diagram

1

Introduction

The growing popularity of the Internet and the World Wide Web have since its inception generated an increasing interest in the new communication technologies and an ample impact on society and social systems. We are facing a new technology that allows decentralisation, multimedia and interactive communication[1] in a context of familiarity, ease of use and instant feedback over a global scale. Internationally, this revolution has facilitated the globalisation of the economy, business, finance and culture.[2] Today information and communication technology (ICT) constitutes the fastest growing component of the global economy, and the Indian ICT spending is expected to grow 14 per cent in 2010.[3] As an outcome of technological developments that enabled computers to exchange data through the regular telephone lines, a revolutionary medium of communication has emerged. Computers, connected to the global telecommunication network, have become powerful tools of instantaneous communication around the world. Two distinct functions, categorically, of this connectivity are: (1) online media—new agents of information and entertainment, that are similar to popular electronic media such as television and radio and print media such as books and magazines and (2) computer mediated communication (CMC)—new channels for interactive, two-way communication that rival telephonic conversations in their capacity to sustain conferencing and asynchronous communication.

The most influential dimension of this revolution is the worldwide escalation of access to the Internet. It is estimated that the number of Internet hosts increased from one lakh in 1988 to over 36 million in 1998; the number of Internet users rose from 26 million in 1995 to 143 million by mid-1998[4] and today it stands at 1.8 billion.[5] India has been a part of this revolution; 71 million users have used the Internet in 2009 registering a year on year growth from 2008 of 19 per cent.[6]

Internet technology has radically changed the nature of communication across the world. Now communication has become instant irrespective of distance and far less expensive. This medium has versatile uses and it can be used globally as an instrument for distribution of news and information, a medium for collaboration and a means of communication between people irrespective of the geographical division. The particular medium can provide mailing service, telephony, transfer facility of text, audio, image and video files and many other communication systems that have specific functions. The Internet through its technology therefore offers great opportunities in the delivery of basic services like information, education and health to far-flung regions. This contextual phenomenon, that has changed the nature of communication, human relations and public expectations, also represents a considerable challenge to the state in terms of public governance and various services to the society.

A new medium is considered a mass medium and a medium of choice for commercial reasons when there are a certain number of users for the same. The critical mass concept adopted from economists, physicists, and sociologists by researchers states that when ten to twenty per cent[7] of the population starts using a medium the critical mass necessary to spread to the rest of the social systems has been gained and in attaining this number the early users provide the necessary leadership. In India, for instance, the popularity of *Blogs* rose only when celebrities started creating and maintaining their *Blogs*. The story was similar with the social networking tool called *Twitter*.

There have been several criticisms about using Internet and Internet based social networking systems for providing information to the masses in India, though it has been more popular in the western countries. The Internet technology is an expensive medium in the Indian context and so it is difficult for common people to use this medium very often. The additional resources of skill, effort and education required by users for adoption and usage of this new interactive medium are also critical barriers to its common spread and usage. In the developing countries the use of Internet is not so popular because most people live at the poverty level, or below the poverty level. Hence they cannot afford an access to this medium. Added to that, there are very high levels of illiteracy amongst the general masses. The irony, however, is the advantage of this new communication system will never be exploited fully unless the number of users[8] of this medium increases. The e-mail has been considered a medium of mass communication in the west for quite a period of time, but in India Internet access came much later, and even after its arrival only a section of people was able to access it. However, from the year 2000, Internet has gained popularity among the young generation, service providing industries, software industries and others. Today, in metro cities, most of the young pupils and other educated individuals are conversant with e-mail and social networking systems. Through these social networking systems like *Facebook*, *Orkut*, *Twitter* etc., it is possible to contact friends, colleagues and relatives throughout the world and it is becoming a very popular and powerful medium not only for the general public but also for the political persons. It is interesting to note that some people residing in rural areas where Internet access is available are also developing interest in using Internet facilities.

The beauty of this technology lies more in its ability to create greater access to information and communication irrespective of the geographical distance in a fast and efficient manner than in the technology per se. The Internet is extensively, if not universally, viewed as a model technology of the emerging information era, with vast capability to restructure and alter the ways in which people organise their lives, interact with each other, contribute and join in the various spheres of society. Therefore, if this medium can be used in different situations and if it can offer diverse services to different people, through varied contents[9] then the chances of its greater appeal, wider acceptability[10] and better usability will be enhanced.

There are multiple applications on the Internet that are distinct and each gives rise to a discretionary database[11], which is a shared body of data and information to which several participants, if they choose, may separately contribute which emphasises the role of participants and users of the medium. There are different kinds of websites hosted by different kinds of people on the Internet. There are entertainment sites, knowledge sites, communication sites, game sites, e-governance sites, e-commerce sites, information sites, etc. All these sites do not attract the same set of people. If, for example, we consider the knowledge sites, then students and academicians will be expected to visit them. But within those sites, too, some may offer knowledge about Chemistry, while some will offer knowledge about History. Naturally the type of participant to these sites will be different, based on individual interests or discretion. Therefore, each site becomes an entity by itself.

In contrast, if we consider the radio, where interactivity and variety is less, but which is available all over the world, addresses a mass audience even in remote areas with a large illiterate population and serves the purpose of delivering knowledge, information, education, entertainment and health awareness messages, we see that its reach and acceptability are far more. The reasons being its affordability in terms of cost, skill and infrastructure requirement.

If Internet is eventually considered useful in a wide range of areas from healthcare services to news to entertainment to education to governance, trade, etc., and if it can be made accessible to a larger number of people, only then, will it be considered a mass medium. The concept of critical mass for the Internet will always be somewhat variable, rather than a fixed percentage of users because of the availability of a wide range of communication and other services.

The applications of the Internet can be broadly divided into two categories—public service applications, where it is used mainly for the development of society and welfare of the common people; or commercial applications in the second category, where it is an *entrepreneurial* activity, apart from its application in personal communication. A new category is also successfully emerging, where commercial applications are being used for the development of society. If the majority of people can get access to the Internet and if it can be considered a tool for communication and knowledge for all, then it can be used for development[12], which is a complex phenomenon[13] and where participatory communication[14] tools and knowledge play very vital roles.

With the changing scenario it is necessary to investigate the nature of changes and development that this medium has generated in the social, cultural and political arenas[15] through research.

Mass communication research has a very wide scope because it deals with print and electronic media like newspapers, magazines, television, cinema along with theatre, interpersonal and group communication, advertising, public relations, media technology, media management, media laws, etc. Today, the new media has also been included in the list. The effects and impacts of new media, cyber laws and their implications are also subjects of research in mass communication. Internet was initially considered merely a computer-mediated communication tool to aid in interpersonal communication and was used and researched in other fields such as education, management, information science and library science.

This research work focuses on the effect of Internet on certain development areas[16] like the news media, health, rural development and governance that are relevant to a developing country like India.

Internet as Medium of News

Communication is one of the most essential requirements of human society. Human beings have felt the need to communicate for thousands of years and for that they have used various means to reach the maximum audience. Every society institutionalises certain selected behaviours from a wide range of possible ones. Of this communication has been one—and its need has been wide. From communicating with the young for socialising them and making them acceptable to their society, to teaching them the language, tradition and culture and again to coordinating actions for accomplishing tasks for maintaining and preserving their society, it's been varied.

Traditional forms of mass media have been around for thousands of years and were more general. The communication was mainly face-to-face verbal communication using language and face-to-face non-verbal communication using body language. This term explores those performing arts, which are cultural symbols of people. Mass communication in which messages are conveyed to large groups of people have been around in traditional forms like sermons, plays, town criers, drama, puppet shows, musical concerts and the more long-distance medium of loud instruments such as horns, drums, flutes and smoke, etc. Traditional forms of mass communication have required both the presence of the individuals who communicate in certain situations and also on memory and retention beyond the moment of communication for conservation as in the *Sruti* method of learning the Vedas from the *Gurus* in *Gurukuls*.

The use of traditional mass media can be seen in Indian villages.[17] Folk-songs and lyrics were powerful means of propagating the ideas and experiences of the wise and learned to village people who could not read or write. In West Bengal, for example, the forms called *Kobi-gaan* (songs sung with actions), *Pala*, *Jatra* (folk drama performed in the open), dance and *mime* have been practised for ages to send different messages to the masses. In the south-east province of Andhra Pradesh *dandora's* were used to attract attention to public announcements. Drama, locally known, as *Natakam,* was very popular as well as a form of narration through songs called *katha*, which were based on epics and presented to an audience were well liked, too. The ancient Tamils classified literature under three heads—*Iyal, Isai* and *Natakam. Iyal* is in the form of prose or poetry, which either describes a thing or an event. *Isai* is music, which stirs the emotions and elevates spirits to rapturous delight and *Natkam* combines the effect of both *Iyal* and *Isai* and has thus been very popular down the ages.[18] This tradition of mass media has been observed in western cultures, too, where symphony music, church music, drama and plays long preceded any other form of mass communication. Influential after-prayer sermons have been observed in Muslim mosques and Christian churches and still continue to remain admired.

The invention of printing converted the printed word into a form of mass communication. With this technology it became possible to produce copies of messages economically, fast and widely, thus bridging gaps of numbers, time and space. Information was no longer the privilege of a certain section of society. The technology of printing led to various kinds of print medium—newspapers, books, magazines and journals to name a few. However, the barrier to this media has been its cost and literacy and these two factors have hindered its growth at times.

The development of the electronic media-film, telephone, radio, television and video provided the means for communication over space and time. This media could overcome the limitations of cost as it was not very expensive and further could be used by both the literate as well as the illiterate, rural and urban population alike. Additionally, this medium could *simulate* a face-to-face communication and thus had greater appeal. The media has diverse applications—news medium, soap operas, comedies, films, musical performances, documentaries, etc. to name a few.

Thus if we were to carry forward the social definition of communication together with the definition of mass as large-scale, we would see mass communication as, simply, communication on a large or mass scale. However, until very recently the accepted meaning of the term mass communication did not describe mass communication as communication taking place on a mass scale. What was, and still is, more often termed mass communication is the communication that happens by means of movies, large daily newspapers, and broadcasting. Tim O'Sullivan et al. (1983)[19] captured that type of mass communication quite well prior to the development of the Internet, cell phones, and CD-ROM games and so his definition does not encompass them:

"Mass communication is the practice and product of providing leisure entertainment and information to an unknown audience by means of corporately financed, industrially produced, state regulated, high-technology, privately consumed commodities in the modern print, screen, audio and broadcast media".

However, times and technology changed and the Internet arrived. Beginning from the early 90's, when Internet usage began to migrate from academic communication to the wider world, the possibilities for person-to-person communication on a mass scale expanded dramatically. Suddenly, it became possible to write e-mail to an e-mail address anywhere in the world. The transmission was both instantaneous and free and required no writing paper, envelope, postage stamp, mailbox or mail pickup. It was also much cheaper, convenient and faster than sending a telegram or a fax. As a chain reaction, a number of technologies were developed and became available to a large user base enabling easy digitisation and transmission of files of any type—text, sound, image from one computer to another at economical rates.

Sudden change, high competition, new forms of production, distribution and entirely new kinds of products has characterised the media industry in the last few decades.[20] Central to this is the availability of online news that is strongly influencing the industry, changing the existing market dynamics and requiring new strategies[21] to survive the competition. According to Picard, the development of the Internet has brought significant changes to audience behaviour that challenges the long-term survival of newspapers.[22]

Nicholas, Frossling, Martin and Buesing[23] have said:

> "What is even more worrying in the long run is that the young, for whom newspapers never played a big role in the first place–not being considered a sufficiently "hip" medium (and regarded as something associated with their parents generation)–have deserted the press."

With the Internet, it is possible to cater to both the larger as well as a small segment consumer base at the same cost and therefore makes it possible to cater to varied and special tastes and markets. It has become possible for anyone with a view or opinion to start a blog and make it available to a wide range of Internet users. A blog presents a personal view or an opinion of the creator of the blog. In that regard it cannot be considered an authenticated piece of information and is therefore considered only as a chat medium and not as a medium of information. On the other hand, editorials in the newspapers were considered earlier as an authentic view and till date some of the famous newspaper editorials are considered authentic news and their editors, valuable opinion leaders of the society. Sections like–Letters to editors, or 'Call-in' to radio shows, or TV shows, too, have always been subjected to a considerable degree of editorial control. Today, people regularly post pictures or video of events with a commentary, or even send their views, footage and other material to media agencies or other sites through the Internet for posting and publishing. This trend is further gaining popularity as popular news channels and newspapers are inviting personal videos, opinions or pictures of sensational events from their consumers.

In this sense, the contrasts with the print and electronic news sources are quite dramatic and these systems have expanded the very definition of mass media, from "one to many" to "many to many" communication. In these forms where the audience is both the primary source of media content as well as its receiver, represent a new and significant departure from conventional mass media forms and are being termed Collaborative mass media systems.[24]

This trend has gained momentum since Internet connectivity and Internet presence have become affordable. Most offices, educational institutions provide free access. People have connectivity at home or can use their local cyber-cafes and registering a domain, or setting up a site does not cost too much.

There are several criticisms about print media and electronic media, that they have played a vital role in making of a film star, or a politician, or a criminal. Some of the recent cases being the Jessica Lal murder case, the Dhanajoy hanging case and the Nithahari murder case. But media can only provide information regularly and it is finally the people who decide. It is not easy to be fool people with wrong information. If people realise that the reports are not true they will reject that source, but on the other hand it can also create mass opinion if the reports are found to be genuine. This has been observed on several occasions especially in election analysis and political campaigns. Therefore, even though the mass media is criticised for trying to control the society, it is seen that it is the people who do what they consider to be right.

Historically, there has always been speculation about the fate and death of existing media in the wake of a new media and the arrival of Internet was no different. Rupert Murdoch in his famous 2005 speech to the American Society of Newspaper Editors on April 13, 2005 had said that the perception of threat from this technology was fast increasing in the print newspaper industry.[25]

The scene in India is, however, different and the media is experiencing a boom amongst all age groups inspite of having an increasing Internet population.

Internet in Healthcare Services

Improving the health of individuals and communities, strengthening health systems, disease detection and prevention are crucial to development and poverty reduction in a country. Internet technology has the potential to impact almost every aspect of the health sector. In public health, information management and communication processes are pivotal, and are facilitated or limited by available Internet connectivity. Internet technology applied to the area of health has tremendous potential to provide and improve quality healthcare to an increased number of people regardless of geographical divide, since it can be used for medical training, information access, patient care and support, remote diagnosis, consulting, emergency, epidemic support as well as in preventive care. Using this tool can reduce the gap between the haves and have-nots in health[26] that is importantly influenced by wider information and communication processes, mediated by Internet technology.

It is necessary to examine how effective the technology has been in actually providing critical cardiac care to patients from impoverished communities, located in remote underdeveloped regions both in terms of geography and medical infrastructure, who previously had no direct access to such sophisticated medical intervention.

Internet in Agriculture

The agricultural sector suffers from poor communication infrastructure and weak institutional capacities. There is a growing consensus that knowledge and information are essential for empowering rural communities. Communication is central to this process. However, there are many other serious ills plaguing the population of which poverty and illiteracy are the most serious. Various projects undertaken by the Central government, or the different state governments, or non-government organisations like UNICEF have not been able to eradicate these two problems. *Students in most villages go to schools if there is one available for the mid-day meal that is offered.* This is a far cry from the level of education and skill that is required to be able to use computers and the Internet effectively. Convergence of technologies can help people share knowledge and information. Information intermediaries like social workers, educators and mass media can help rural communities access relevant information. Internet technology can be used for strengthening research and increasing farmer linkages through better agricultural marketing, disaster mitigation through forecasting, monitoring and early warning systems. Relevance of use of Internet technology in Agriculture lies in its ability to reduce isolation, facilitate dialogue, provide information and skills training and encourage orderly structure in the system.

Internet access is growing rapidly globally. However, the rural community in most countries is out of this growth map and Internet access in these areas is usually very marginal if at all. In a country like India, where the spread and use of information technology has been phenomenal in urban areas, the rural communities are still largely left out.[27]

Thus, it is necessary to research whether the usage of Internet technology in some parts of rural India has contributed positively to rural development.

Internet and Political Outcome

The relationship between adoption of Internet technology, related investments, their implementation, results and outcome are more about strategically administering the change, creating awareness and involvement than trying to force the technology on the people. The common expectation in scientific and public opinion is that intervention through Internet technology will change power relations in many, if not all domains in society. Some think that centralisation will occur, but most think decentralisation will take place. The most popular expectation is that it will empower users of all kinds: Citizens, consumers, workers, patients, students and audiences. It is also perceived that those in power reach more power in their control of design, investment and implementation of this technology. It is necessary to examine these perceptions and also try and understand how it changes the relations between governments and citizens. Further, the level of three types of access to this technology in the domain under consideration are: first, physical access to computers, the Internet and other digital media; secondly, digital skills and finally, the use that is the quantity and quality, or kinds of applications also need to be known as that may interfere with the perception of the technology itself.

It is necessary to find answers to these questions in a democratic country like India where governments are formed and broken based on the perceptions and reaction of people to changes brought in.

This research work tries to analyse the effect of Internet and its technologies in India in the specific development areas, namely—news media, health, rural development and governance. It is divided into ten major chapters.

This introductory chapter 1 tries to outline a general critique of the Internet and defines the dominant areas of focus in this study.

The second chapter outlines the objectives of the study.

The third chapter presents the chronological reviews of the previous research work. It is divided into three main sections, the first presents a brief summary of relevant research work conducted in India and abroad. The second section presents the grey areas that have been identified and the last section presents the research questions.

The fourth chapter presents the research methodology. This includes the theoretical framework of the research, a broad description of the tools used for the research and a description of the data.

The fifth chapter presents a content analysis of evolution and history of printing and print newspapers, Internet and Internet newspapers as well as the arrival of television in India. This is followed by a modest attempt to study the theories and uses of news, credibility perception and credibility components of media and media displacement theory. The existing literatures on telemedicine, infrastructure requirements, and telemedicine projects in India, cardiac diseases and their relevance as well as treatment techniques like *thrombolytic* therapy have been then reviewed. Next, the concept of social development has been researched along with democracy, use of technology by a government and it ends with a brief note on Andhra Pradesh.

The sixth chapter details the methods of analysis used for each of the four studies in four different sections.

The seventh chapter makes a modest attempt to present the results of the four studies in an organised and objective way. There are four sections related to the four different studies. In each section the results are followed by the related discussions and a summary of findings for each study.

The eighth chapter furnishes the summary of the research work conducted and presented in this thesis.

The ninth chapter presents the overall conclusions drawn from the complete research along with the implications of the study.

The tenth chapter states the limitations of the study and the final chapter mentions the future areas of research that this study has opened up for the researcher.

The lists of references used in each chapter have been appended at the end of the respective chapter for easy and quick reference and a bibliography has also been presented at the end. The questionnaire used in the study has been included in the appendix.

References

1. Gomez, R., 1997, *Information society and civil society: NGOs and computer-mediated communication in Latin America*, In J. Berleur and D. Whitehouse (Eds.), An Ethical Global Information Society: Culture and Democracy Revisited, London: Chapman and Hall, pp. 186–196.
2. Heeks, Richard, 1999, *Information and Communication Technologies, Poverty and Development, Development Informatics*, Working Paper Series, Working Paper No. 5, Manchester: Institute for Development Policy and Management, University of Manchester.
3. Gartner Says Indian ICT Spending to Grow 14 per cent in 2010, Gartner Press release: Mumbai, April 28, 2010.
4. UNDP, 1999, *Human Development Report,* 1999, New York: Oxford University Press.
5. Internet usage statistics, Miniwatts Marketing Group, Copyright © 2001–2010, accessed from http://www.internetworldstats.com/stats.htm on 01/03/2010.
6. 71 Million people claimed to have used Internet in 2009, Internet and mobile association of India, Press release, April 5, 2010.
7. Morris Merrill and Ogan Christine, *Internet as a Mass Medium,* In McQuail Denis, McQuail's Reader in Mass Communication Theory, Sage, 2002, pp. 135–145.
8. Valente, T.W., 1993, *Diffusion of innovations and policy decision-making,* Journal of Communication, Vol. 43(1), pp. 30 – 45.
9. Rafaeli S., and LaRose R.J., 1993, *Electronic Bulletin Boards and "Public Goods" Explanations of Collaborative Mass Media,* Communication Research, Vol. 20(2), pp. 277–297.
10. Rogers E., *Communication Technology: The new media in society,* 1986, Free Press, New York, p. 120.
11. Connolly, T., and Thorn, B.K., *Discretionary data bases: Theory, data, and implications.* In J. Fulk and C. Steinfield (Eds.), Organisations and communication technology, 1991, Newbury Park, CA: Sage Publications, p. 221.
12. Singhal, A., and Rogers, E.M., 2001, *India's communication revolution:From bullock carts to cybermarts,* New Delhi, Sage, p. 33.
13. Lent, J. A., 1979, *The evolution of development news: A brief history.* In J.A. Lent and J.V. Vilanilam (Eds.), The use of development news: Case studies in India, Malaysia, Ghana, Thailand and Singapore, Asian Mass Communication Research and Information Center, pp. 21–29.

14. Singhal, A., and Sthapitanonda, P., 1996, *The role of communication in development, Lessons learned from a critique of the dominant dependency and alternative paradigms*, The Journal of Development Communication, Vol. 7(1), pp. 10–25.
15. Porter, M.E., 2001, Strategy and the Internet, Harvard Business Review, Vol. 79(3), pp. 62–78.
16. ITU (International Telecommunication Union)/UNESCO (1995), *The Right to Communicate: At What Price? Economic Constraints to the Effective Use of Telecommunications in Education, Science, Culture and in the Circulation of Information*, Paris: UNESCO.
17. Hartman, P.B., Patil and Dighe A., *The Mass Media and Village Life*, London: Sage Publications, 1989, pp. 190 – 192.
18. Guha, B., *Media Development and Management*, Kanishka Publishers, New Delhi, 2006, p. 176.
19. O'Sullivan, Tim, Hartley, J., Saunders, D., and Fiske, J. Key Concepts in Communication, New York: Methuen, 1983, p. 131.
20. Chan-Olmsted, S.M., Competitive strategy for media firms. Strategic and Brand management in changing media markets, Lawrence Erlbaum Associates Publishers, Mahwah, NJ, 2006.
21. Doyle, G., *Understanding media economics*, London, Sage Publications, 2002.
22. Picard, R.G., 2003, *Cash cows or entrecote: Publishing companies and disruptive technologies,* Trends in communication, Vol. 11(2), pp. 127–136.
23. Nicholas D., Frossling I., Martin H., and Buesing P., 1997, *(Really) getting to grips with the Internet: what it has to offer in the way of newspapers, Vine*, Vol. 104, pp. 29–30.
24. Rafaeli S. and LaRose R.J., 1993, *Electronic Bulletin Boards and "Public Goods" Explanations of Collaborative Mass Media,* Communication Research, Vol. 20(2), pp. 277–297.
25. Speech by Rupert Murdoch to the American Society of Newspaper Editors, American Society of Newspaper Editors, April 13, 2005, available at http://www.newscorp.com/news/news_247.html, accessed on 12/10/2006.
26. "*WHO Director-General Highlights Potential of Telemedicine*", 1997 Press Release, WHO/65 accessed from http://www.who.org/inf-pr-1997/en/pr97-65.html on 10/1/2007.
27. Agarwal, S., May 7, 2009, *Connectivity, penetration keep IT away from rural India*, Financial Express.

2

Objective of the Study

Internet is a technology that can be used for various purposes. It can be used as a medium for providing knowledge, information, entertainment, communication and a range of services in the areas of health, agriculture and governance. In this regard its usage can reduce the disparities in the distribution and access of knowledge, information, entertainment, communication as well as health services, opportunities in trade and in services provided by the administration. This becomes more relevant in a country like India where there is a wide contrast in the availability of the above facilities between metro cities, towns, villages and remote villages.

The objective of this study is to investigate the use of Internet as a medium in these contexts. It will try to assess its use in certain parts of India as a medium of news, in providing healthcare services, in agriculture and rural development and in governance to examine the effectiveness and impact of this technology in a developing economy with such contrasts in the availability of services between regions.

This original research work will add to the body of existing literature in mass communication.

Internet technology has been able to open up new avenues in providing distribution of services, knowledge and information. Most of students and professionals living in cities of India have access to Internet and use the same very regularly for obtaining news, knowledge, entertainment, etc. It is not uncommon to find students using Google for their research needs. It is also not uncommon to find people accessing the net to find latest updates on news. It is, therefore, necessary to see how the population that has easy access to this new medium in India, is using it as a medium of news. It is also crucial to know the perceptions about this medium in the minds of this population. People have been exposed to various media for years and have certain experiences of using them and therefore expectations from different media. It will be interesting to learn whether those existing perceptions of media are influencing the perceptions about the new media and whether demographic and economic factors have a role to play in the usage of this new medium, when used as a medium of news by the population as described above. Finally, the study will try to analyse whether Internet news is displacing the print newspapers and TV news, or whether people are using it to complement the news provided by print newspapers and TV news.

In India, healthcare services available to villages in the interiors of the country are very limited inspite of the efforts of the Central government, various State governments and non-government organisations like the UNICEF, WHO, etc. The problems are many — limited access, availability of very few doctors and nurses, illiteracy, poverty, unavailability of infrastructure, etc., to name just a few. Internet technology has been used in some places to overcome the above stated problems. If this usage actually helps in reducing the problems of healthcare services, then it can be used more often to reduce the disparities in the availability of facilities between people based on their location of residence. Moreover, as this technology is neither very expensive, nor very sophisticated and can address many people at the same time, it can be considered for greater usage if it is found to be truly effective.

Thus, this study will focus on the area of critical heart care, which requires high level of monitoring and very sophisticated treatment to see whether Internet based treatment can be extended in such situations also.

Illiteracy and ignorance plague a large section of the society especially those who live in remote villages. However, it is these people who provide the agricultural support to India. These farmers are mostly short of information and knowledge about best practices of farming and even lack basic education in most cases. Further, the farmers are completely dependent upon middlemen for the trade of their farm produce and in most cases get into their clutches. The farmers frequently do not get the right price for their produce, there is plenty of wastage due to rotting and during transportation, or bagging and this vicious circle continues. Since information related to market trends normally do not reach villages, people are most often not aware of raising crops that could give them maximum returns. Moreover, these farmers mainly depend on the rains and other seasonal changes for their crops. In case, they are hit by drought or floods, the entire crop is lost. If weather predictions can be regularly and correctly made available to these farmers definitely some crops will be saved. If better marketing channels could be found for these farmers along with education regarding scientific methods of farming, their returns on yields could go up.

Internet is such a versatile medium that it can cater to these needs if used correctly. Commercial organisations are utilising this technology to bridge the above gaps in certain parts of the country.

Another objective of this study will therefore be to evaluate and assess the change that this technology has been able to bring in the livelihood and quality of life of even illiterate farmers who have been availing of these commercial Internet based applications. This will confirm another relevant use of Internet technology in the context of a developing economy.

Finally, we live in one of the largest democracies in the World. In the context, it is necessary to understand how the general public perceives the Internet in terms of its providing governance facilities. Making government documents, forms and tax returns available on the Internet is not enough. Since the spread of Internet has not been uniform across metro cities, town, villages and remote villages, the usefulness of this medium as a medium for providing government services has not been experienced by all. Because of the basic requirement of a computer, or a high-end mobile phone for this technology, it is still perceived as elitist and a luxury. Therefore, when a government tries to implement such a technology in a widespread manner people may not like it, they may not be able to access it and they may find it expensive. Further, the barrier of illiteracy may hinder even more.

This study will try to investigate the complex relationship through a case where Internet technology was brought in very early to see how and why the citizens had reacted to it.

The study will additionally involve review of previous research work to identify gaps and frame research questions for the study based on these gaps. Research works of other scholars will be read to gather necessary background knowledge about the areas of focus.

The study will be divided into four distinct areas of focus as described above for deeper investigation but the overall conclusions regarding Internet as a media in the Indian context will be drawn from the findings of all the four studies considered together.

3

Previous Research Work

The purpose of this chapter has been to summarise and explain what research has been earlier done on the topic, citing the sources as and when they are mentioned, to point out the different ways the researchers have treated the topic and to point out any connections between the sources, especially where one source built upon prior study. Surveys, scholarly articles, books and other sources (e.g., dissertations, conference proceedings, news articles) relevant to the topic of research have been reviewed and a description, summary, and critical evaluation of each work to explain, why the research question is significant, have been provided.

The literature reviewed ranges between publications in 1987 and 2010 and covers studies in the United States of America, different European and Asian countries, Africa, Australia as well as India. They have been presented chronologically, with the more recent studies placed first.

This chapter consists of three main sections. The first section provides a brief summary of other relevant research work conducted in India and abroad. This section has five sub-sections, the first deals with studies related to news media, where twenty one studies have been presented, the second centers around healthcare, where four studies have been presented, the third focuses on rural development having two studies, the fourth on use of technology by governments and has seven studies and finally, the fifth sub-section presents five studies on Andhra Pradesh. The second main section identifies the gaps and finally, the third section addresses the research questions.

3.1 This is not a reasonable content analysis but a modest attempt to identify few more dimensions to the impact of Internet on news media, healthcare, agriculture and political outcome. Brief summaries of other relevant research work conducted abroad and in India are stated below so that the present study can be assessed in that perspective.

3.1.1 Print Newspapers, TV and the Internet

An article entitled '*Passion for Print*' by K. Rothmer, published in the *Columbian Journalism Review,* Vol. 48(5), (pp. 17–18) in 2010, discusses the intense popularity of newspapers in Kenya, in comparison to the US where they are in the decline. The reasons cited are the recent expansion of literacy and limited Internet access. The article states that a copy of a newspaper is read on an average by 14 people in Kenya, and is available on rent for 30 minutes at local news shops where people discuss news. The article mentions that "The Star" daily newspaper, founded in 2007, has become profitable in this age of digital news.

Another study entitled '*News on the Net: Credibility, Selective Exposure, and Racial Prejudice*' by Debra Burns Melican and Travis L. Dixon, published in 2008 in *Communication Research*, Vol. 35(2), (pp. 151–168), that was based on an online survey found a wide disparity amongst people regarding their perceptions of Internet news credibility. Non-traditional Internet sources were perceived much less credible than all other news sources. The study concluded that those who view non-traditional Internet news sources as more credible than print and electronic media also score higher on a modern racism scale. The Internet according to the authors can be termed safe even for divergent, racist beliefs.

T.E. Patterson in his 2007, 18 pages report '*Creative Destruction: An Exploratory Look at News on the Internet*' published from the Joan Shorenstein Center on the Press, Politics and Public Policy, John F. Kennedy School of Government, Harvard University, examined trends in Internet based news traffic by monitoring traffic of 160 news-based websites over a yearlong period between April 2006 and April 2007 for the purpose of speculating the future of news in America. The sampling for this study was purposive and not random, based on preset characteristics. The major variable in this study was people count, which was used to compare the relative popularity of news sites and changes over the one-year period between April 2006 and April 2007. The month's chosen were typical. The data was essentially secondary in nature obtained from Complete snapshot, a feature offered by the Boston — based research company Compete Inc. The research suggests that websites of national brand-name newspapers are growing whereas those of local papers are not. The sites of national brand-name television networks were also attracting more traffic along with those of local television and radio stations. However, sites connected to traditional news organisations could not match the growth level experienced by non-traditional news outlets. The study has been centered on the process labeled 'creative destruction' by the economist Joseph Schumpeter where the technological disruption and change is being caused by Internet news. The study reports that online newspaper readership now exceeds the daily circulation of the hard-copy newspapers and observes that if this trend analysis is borne out, many newspapers will have difficulty even holding onto their online readers suggesting a tremendous competition in this segment.

This study has highlighted not only the traditional news outlets and disseminators, but also the non-traditional sources that are relevant to the new technology and media. However, the study is essentially based in the US where Internet penetration is far more than in countries like India where geographically and demographically the patterns are completely different. Another compelling observation has been that newspapers cannot succeed simply by replacing their hard-copy readers with online readers. According to Patterson (*op. cit.*), "it is estimated that a copy of newspaper needs to attract between two and three dozen readers to make up for in terms of advertising revenue the loss of a single hard-copy reader". It has also been reported that the web particularly threatens the daily newspapers. They have traditionally always been among the first to post the news on Internet but their initial advantage has almost disappeared in the face of increased competition from electronic media and non-traditional providers.

Authors R.S. Vyas, N.P. Singh and S. Bhabra in their research paper '*Media displacement effect: Investigating the impact of Internet on newspaper reading habits of consumers*' published in 2007 in Vision: The journal of Business Perspective, Vol. 11(2), pp. 29–40, tried to explore the impact of Internet on the changes in consumer behaviour with respect to reading news on the Internet. The study was conducted in six metropolitan cities in India, namely, Delhi, Mumbai, Chennai, Kolkata, Bangalore and Hyderabad with good infrastructure to support Internet access. The sample size was 101 respondents in three demographics—age, gender and profession. The data were collected in two phases—the first, through interviews and the second, through questionnaires replied over e-mail. The data were subjected to descriptive statistical analysis and frequency analysis. The study concluded that reading news on the Internet was complimentary to reading news on the newspaper. The authors predicted that there was no immediate threat to newspapers from the Internet. They found a positive correlation between years of Internet usage and longer hours of usage with likeliness to read news on the Internet. The study could not find any relation between factors like age, educational background, profession and reading news on the Internet. They did not have sufficient data to comment on the association between gender and news reading habits on the net. It was also found that Internet was more popular in case of business, stock, sports and international news.

Professors Kiran Thakur and U. Barve of Pune University in their UGC funded research project titled '*Readers prefer online newspapers in India*' in 2007 observed that the growth of online newspaper readership within India has been possible due to penetration of computers and easier availability of Internet connectivity even in small towns and cities. According to the study, which was carried out amongst 1,132 users of English newspaper websites, of whom 67 per cent were from cities and towns of India the profile of the readership of online editions had undergone a major change in the last eight years. In a similar study conducted in 1998, only 10 per cent readers were Indians residing in India, while 62 per cent were non-resident Indians residing in the US and 4 per cent in Canada.

The online survey was carried out through a questionnaire posted on the department's website and made available to surfers through banner announcements on the homepages of newspapers. The data gathered through the survey conducted between July and September 2006 was compared with the outcome of the 1998 study. The study found that the proportion of female Internet newspaper readers was 13 per cent and was considerably smaller than male readers of English Internet newspapers, but had still almost doubled since 1998. The majority readership was in the age group of 21–40 years, and more in states like Maharashtra, Karnataka, Delhi, Tamil Nadu and Andhra Pradesh. Most readers (60 per cent) were highly educated (Masters or Ph.D degree holders). Professionals from the fields of IT, education and media constitute almost half (48 per cent) the readership of English newspapers on the Internet, 95 per cent of the readers browse through online newspapers mainly for news, almost an equal number of users browse for the views expressed in the newspapers. The combined percentage of readers of *Op-Ed articles* was high at 97.7 per cent. A considerable proportion of the readership also reads book/film/theatre reviews. Advertisements were not among the top favorites with readers. However, their readership had still grown to 10 per cent from 4 per cent in 1998. The small percentage of users (7 per cent) reading women's columns was attributed to the fact that the percentage of women respondents was only 13 per cent. Almost 92 per cent respondents were interested in reading news about India. Interest in news from the hometowns also varied. 58.2 per cent Marathi readers were keen on reading news about their hometowns, against 33.8 per cent of English newspaper readers. Users seemed to be interested in reading more about business and economy (69 per cent), politics (60 per cent), science and technology (60 per cent) and 37 per cent of the users favoured for sports news.

A growth of almost 42 per cent was noticeable in the interest in news about social development and environment from 1998, 30 per cent readers showed interest in rural development, and 28 per cent in arts and culture. English newspaper readers had more interest in human-interest stories (44 per cent) and news about celebrities (21 per cent) than Marathi newspaper readers (32 per cent and 16 per cent respectively). Columnists, too, were read more by English newspaper readers (42 per cent) than Marathi newspaper readers (28 per cent).

Another striking finding of the study was that a large number of readers visit online editions to access archival material. English newspaper readers visit Web editions to participate in online polls and also to spend leisure time. Many readers, who are away from India or their hometowns, read Indian Internet newspapers to overcome homesickness. Further, most readers (about 60 per cent) reported higher level of satisfaction from the Internet newspaper/s that they read since 1998. Matrimonial advertisements in the online editions of newspapers did not seem to attract readers, even though youngsters dominated the readership. Cartoons, too, appeared to be less favoured by English website users.

This is an important study because it compares data obtained in 1998 with similar data in 2006. There has been a tremendous change in thc Indian Internet scenario in that decade. The study gives an interesting difference in the reason why people read English papers and why they read Marathi papers online. The study also provides an in-depth analysis of news type preferences.

However, it would have been interesting to learn whether non-newspaper sites also provided news to the respondents. No comparison was observed between blog sites and editorials in newspapers. Thc questions that arise from the study are: If homesickness is a reason for reading online newspapers, will it actually affect the readership, or circulation of local dailies; is there a natural bias towards the Internet as the study was conducted on all people who are already conversant with the Internet and since it has been reported that English newspaper readers visit the web editions to participate in online polls or to kill time, would that really affect the circulation?

Kara Chan and Wei Fang conducted a research in 2007 to examine the use of traditional media and Internet among young people in Hong Kong. The study entitled '*Use of the Internet and traditional media among young people*' was published by Emerald Group Publishing Limited in the Young Consumers: Insight and Ideas for Responsible Marketers, Vol. 8(4), pp. 244–256. A survey of 405 Chinese persons aged 15 to 24 in Hong Kong was conducted in February 2006 using a self-administered questionnaire.

The study found that the Internet plays a prominent role among the young people in Hong Kong as most respondents were online for one to three hours. Respondents listened to music and looked for entertainment, et al., while *online* as the Internet was the preferred medium of choice for information-driven activities and television was considered important for news and current affairs.

A. Nyugen and M. Western conducted a research on secondary data of a national survey of 4,270 Australian nationals in 2003 to study the complementary effect of online news and information usage on traditional news. The study was conducted to find a relationship between old and new media usage and was published as '*The complementary relationship between the Internet and traditional mass media: the case of online news and information*' in 2007 in Information Research, Vol. 11(3), p. 259. Most studies of media have been based from the perspective of the medium, which assumes that different media serve the same purpose and functions and therefore eventually old media will get replaced by new media. But in this study, Nguyen (*et al.*) argues the assumption and tries to investigate the way different media are used by different people to satisfy different needs.

The contention is that no single medium can be an absolute functional replacement of all medium and therefore even if people have to reduce time and resources spent on old media to be able to use the new media, they will not necessarily completely abandon the old. The study was based on the concept that every medium has its own distinctive features, which serve the users in different contexts, and hence they complement each other in their use.

This was tested by setting up four hypotheses, namely, *(a)* Internet users use traditional news and information sources more frequently than non-users of the Internet, *(b)* Internet news and information users use traditional sources more frequently than non-users of Internet news and information; *(c)* Frequent Internet news and information users use traditional sources more frequently than non-frequent users of Internet news and information; and *(d)* Internet news and information usage is more associated with news and information seeking from more information-intensive sources.

Testing was done employing hypotheses testing for the mean, partial correlations, and a linear regression analysis. The first three hypotheses were confirmed suggesting that even if a displacement effect does take place, a replacement effect is unlikely to occur. The authors have also stressed that traditional media will continue to exist and complement the Internet as a medium and serve people for different information needs.

A. Diddi and R. LaRose conducted a study entitled '*Getting hooked on news: uses and gratifications and the formation of news habits among college students in an Internet environment*' to explore the emergent news consumption patterns among future users. The research proposed a theory of news habit-formation based in the uses and *gratifications assumptions* and applied it to emerging patterns of news consumption among college students and was published in 2006 in the Journal of Broadcasting and Electronic Media, Vol. 50(2), pp. 193–210.

They conducted the study on 303 undergraduate students enrolled in an introductory communication class at a major midwestern university. The sample was 68 per cent male and 32 per cent female with a median age of 19 years, which was consistent with the demographic composition of the class from where it was drawn. Five distinctive patterns emerged: hometown newspapers, comedy news, cable news, Internet news and broadcast news.

It was observed that the campus newspaper was the most popular news source, followed by Internet portal-sites and late night comedy shows. There was, however, another consumption pattern, which included diverse sources specialising in-depth news coverage.

The hypothesis that surveillance needs will be positively related to consumption of all types of media like cable TV, broadcast, Internet and Newspapers was partially supported. The second hypothesis, that escapism and entertainment needs will be positively related to the consumption of television news forms was also partially supported. Escapism was correlated to depth coverage, which included both television, and non-television sources like journals, and supported the hypothesis that escapism needs will be positively related to the consumption of Internet news forms.

However, entertainment was not a significant predictor of consumption of news forms. The hypothesis that news habit strength will be positively related to all news consumption patterns was supported as was the final hypothesis that predicted that consumption of print-oriented news sources will be related to current events knowledge. Surveillance and escapism gratifications were the most consistent predictors of news consumption behaviour, but habit strength was the most powerful of news consumption across all. It was also observed that consumption of hometown newspaper and depth were related to current events knowledge.

An article titled *News Consumption and the New Electronic Media* by A. Douglas which was published in 2006 in Press/Politics, Vol. 11(1), (pp. 29–52), studies the hypothesised complete shift and migration of news consumption from the off-line media to the online news media and states that the facts do not support the theory of mass migration. The author analysed statistics related to the US adult population and has stated that only 12 per cent have migrated from offline to online news and 22 per cent of US adults have substituted some offline news with online news and yet for most of them the online medium still acts as a complement rather than a substitute.

Significantly, it has also been observed that two-thirds of the US adult population have not shifted to online news and are unlikely to do so. The author also explored the advertising markets of the print and electronic media and the online media and found that online advertising was not a perfect substitute in the eyes of the advertisers. Inspite of declining newspaper sales, television viewership, the revenue earned through advertisements by these media continued to increase and loyalty and faith towards these media could therefore be assumed.

Moreover, the Internet has opened up new opportunities in the area of online classifieds, and print and electronic news media companies were competing online to recapture a portion of the total online advertising revenues. The author reports that no major economic impact was being felt by the news industry due to the online news media even though certain pressures were certainly being felt but nothing to suggest that it was being replaced by the changes whose magnitude is not alarming.

M. Madden (2006) in her research paper '*Internet penetration and impact*' published by the Pew Internet and American Life Project asked Americans from the online community whether their lives had improved due to the Internet in terms of convenience to shop online and pursue their hobbies and interests. The study was conducted with data for the period March 2001 to April 2006. It was observed that the share of Americans who felt that their ability to shop because of the Internet had doubled in the period from 16 per cent to 32 per cent, for hobbyists the growth was reported from 20 per cent to 33 per cent, the share of online Americans who felt that the Internet had greatly improved their ability to do their job, had grown to 35 per cent from 24 per cent; and the share who felt that the Internet had improved the way they get their information about healthcare, had grown to 20 per cent from 17 per cent. It was also observed that daily and frequent Internet users were the ones to cite the biggest improvements.

In terms of gender, both genders noted the positive effects of the Internet in commerce and the workplace, and more women about 22 per cent than men around 17 per cent felt that their access to healthcare information had improved much more because of the Internet, even though younger shoppers reported bigger improvements overall, older users reported more growth overtime. It was also noted in this study that Internet penetration amongst the US adults had reached a very high level of 73 per cent, about 147 million adults that was never achieved before according to the study conducted between February and April 2006 and was up from 66 per cent or 133 million according to data on the similar statistics in January 2005. It has also noted the rise in the use of broadband to 42 per cent from 29 per cent in the previous year.

Another interesting observation was that the use of Internet still varied significantly across age groups. 88 per cent in the age group of 18–29 year old were online, compared to 84 per cent of 30–49 year old, 71 per cent of 50–64 year old and 32 per cent of 65 years and older. Also, comparable was the data on 12–17 year old, 87 per cent of whom were online.

The results of this report are based on data from a series of telephone interviews conducted by Princeton Survey Research Associates International. All data had a confidence level of 95 per cent with a 2-percentage point margin for error. The research concluded that Internet penetration had reached 73 per cent for all American adults. Internet users felt big improvements in their ability to shop, pursue hobbies, in their ability to do their jobs and personal interests due to the use of Internet.

W. Lee, T.M.K. Tan and S.S. Hameed (2005) did an empirical study entitled *Polychronicity the Internet and the Mass media: A Singapore study*, where the relationship between polychronicity, Internet skills,

Internet use and Internet perception were studied and the hypothesis that Internet use displaces other activities was tested. It was published in the Journal of Computer-Mediated Communication, Vol. 11(1), pp. 13–18.

Lee et al., in their research interviewed 1,048 adult Singapore citizens and permanent residents through a computer–assisted telephone interview. Of these only the 668 Internet users were included in the study where a two-stage *least square regression analysis* showed that polychronicity was not associated with Internet use but it predicted Internet perception. Further, Internet skills positively predicted Internet use and perception. It also found that Internet neither displaced nor promoted television viewing, radio listening or newspaper reading even though there was an indication that polychronicity suppressed television viewing.

According to this study television viewing, radio listening and newspaper reading are all positively correlated. However, there is no evidence that Internet use will displace or promote television viewing, radio listening or newspaper reading. Further, all participants in this study were Internet users with varying Internet skills and as such the sample was biased, as there should have been rational selection of sample characteristics. Also, the study examined only the home use of the Internet and did not explore the role of technology convergence.

S. Lehman Wilzig and N. Cohen-Avigdor (2004) in their article *The natural life cycle of new media evolution: Inter-media struggle for survival in the Internet age* (published in New media and Society, Vol. 6, pp. 707–730) have beautifully analysed the evolution of the Internet, with special emphasis on its impact on older media in their struggle for survival. They have designed a 6-stage natural life cycle model of the evolution of the new media. The stages are Birth or technical invention, Penetration, Growth, Maturity, Self-defense and Adaptation, Convergence or Obsolescence. They analysed several other models and have improved upon them by adding sub-theories like media constructionism, which suggests that constant interaction between new and older media is an important factor in the success or failure of the evolution of a new medium and the approach of 'diffusion of innovation'.

In the stage of its birth, the new medium draws on an existing technology or a medium, in most cases the inventors of the same may not have foreseen this use. In the next stage the new medium is introduced into the market, develops new users and attracts new users and captures between 0 per cent and 16 per cent of the market. In case it fails to achieve this mark they fade away. In the next stage the growth is 16 per cent 50 per cent of the market.

At this growth stage, developers and users are able to extensively put to use the new medium. The next stage is the stage of maturation when the medium has grabbed between 50 per cent and 90 per cent of the market. It is put to maximum use at this stage. When the next stage of defensive resistance begins, competition from the new medium forces the old medium to seek new directions to stay and preserve their traditional audiences. The market share begins to drop to about 50 per cent. In the final stage, if the medium adapts, it does so by developing different functions, preserving its old audience or gathering new audience. If it tries to converge because it cannot survive on its own, it merges or incorporates itself into another medium, otherwise it disappears as it becomes obsolete.

They applied this model to the Internet as a case study to understand the evolution of this medium and the survival chances of the older media against this medium.

In their research entitled *The Internet and Social Life*, published in 2004 in the Annual Review of Psychology, Vol. 55, pp. 573–590, John A. Bargh and Katelyn Y.A. Mckenna studied the Internet as the latest technology in interpersonal communication. The authors observe the Internet has features of its predecessors, such as bridging great distances and reaching a mass audience and again new features like the relative anonymity afforded to its users and the provision of group venues, where users can meet others with similar interests and values.

The Internet was placed in its historical context, and then the effects of Internet use on the user's psychological well-being, the formation and maintenance of personal relationships, group memberships and social identity, the workplace and community involvement were examined. The study confirms that while these effects are largely dependent on the particular goals which users bring to the interaction—such as self-expression, affiliation, or competition—they also interact in important ways with the unique qualities of the Internet communication situation.

Ingrid Volkmer outlines the new 'flow' of political information that enables us to become informed about issues of global, regional as well as local relevance in his research paper *The Global Network Society and the Global Public Sphere* published by Palgrave Macmillan in Development, Vol. 46(1), pp. 9–16. The new media infrastructure allows a more real view of events taking place in various locations all over the world. These global processes, in which information and knowledge, political values, ethics, aesthetics and lifestyles are exchanged, are becoming increasingly autonomous from nation-state contexts and are beginning to shape a politically relevant 'global' public sphere. The author discusses parameters of this new political space.

Another research work entitled *Impact of the high-speed Internet on user behaviors: case study in Korea* based in Korea by Cho Sungbin, Byun Jae-Ho and Sung Minje (2003) attempts to investigate the changes that are observed in Korea due to the development in network technologies. According to the findings published in Internet Research, Vol. 13(1), pp. 49–60, Internet users with a high-speed Internet service system enjoy various kinds of services, with greater convenience that include e-mail, and depend less on the traditional media, such as TV and radio, for information and entertainment.

Norman H. Nie and Sunshine D. Hillygus (2002) in their research entitled *Where does Internet time come from?: A reconnaissance*, on the displacement theory of time utilisation, found a negative relationship between the use of Internet and a number of activities, especially disproportionately from discretionary activities. The research published by the Stanford University publication indicated that time spent on the Internet came at the expense of social activities, hobbies, reading and TV viewing. However, time spent on the Internet has a small, but less substantive impact on time spent on work, childcare, housework and sleep. This displacement hypothesis according to the authors is because time is largely a zero-sum phenomenon. Since there are only 24 hours in a day, time spent on one activity must often be traded off against time spent on other activities. The researchers also argue that the more an individual is technologically advanced the more is he likely to be able to squeeze in other activities, thus as individuals use Internet more and more, they become increasingly abler to squeeze in more activities into the remainder of the day. While this is acceptable for people who spend a few minutes or hours a day it is less likely for people towards the limit. This study was conducted on the detailed time-use estimates of the diary approach through Knowledge networks' survey instrument for online survey administration conducted via the Microsoft Web–TV set-top box.

Respondents were asked about their activities on the previous day and instead of the 24 hour day the focus was on six randomly chosen hours of the day one in each six time blocks or strata—night, early morning, late morning, afternoon, early evening and late evening. The sampling design was structured to collect an even distribution of days of the week across the total sample and of hours over the course of the day for each respondent.

Alan Neustadtl and John P. Robinson conducted a research to study the media use differences between Internet users and non-users. The study was published in 2002 in IT and Society, Vol. 1(2), and pp. 100–120. Based on the General Social Survey data of 2000, which had questions on TV viewing and newspaper reading that was supported by bivariate data, the conclusion drawn was that, Internet users watch less TV than non-users, the difference being largely due to the demographic differences between the two groups. Again, it was observed that Internet users are more likely to read newspapers and significantly so after multivariate adjustments for demographic predictors are taken into account, but these differences are not monotonic with the duration of usage, which was based on certain questions asked regarding use of Internet versus other media for information on health and politics.

Analysis of these questions also provided little evidence of reduced use of traditional media by those who use the Internet for health and politics, especially for heavy Internet users for these purposes. Evidence in support of the 'Newtonian' model of increased use of other media by Internet users was obtained rather than evidence of any displacement effect. Interviewing took place between February and mid-June 2000.

The National Opinion Research Center (NORC) at the University of Chicago has conducted the GSS survey at one to two year intervals since 1972, and it is generally considered the premier social science instrument for monitoring social life and trends in the United States. The survey was based on personal, in-home interview that usually took about 90 minutes to complete with a national probability sample of 2,817 adult respondents aged 18 and older. In each selected household, one adult was interviewed at random, using certain sampling procedures.

According to the authors P. DiMaggio, E. Neuman, W. Russell and J.P Robinson in their research *Social Implications of the Internet* the Internet is a critically important research site for sociologists testing theories of technology diffusion and media effects, particularly because it is a medium uniquely capable of integrating modes of communication and forms of content. The Research was published in 2001 in the Annual Review of Sociology, Vol. 27, pp. 307–336. This research tends to focus on the Internet's implications in five domains: (1) inequality (the "digital divide"); (2) community and social capital; (3) political participation; (4) organisations and other economic institutions; and (5) cultural participation and cultural diversity.

A recurrent theme across domains is that the Internet tends to complement rather than displace existing media and patterns of behaviour. Thus in each domain, utopian claims and dystrophic warnings based on extrapolations from technical possibilities have given way to more nuanced and circumscribed understandings of how Internet use adapts to existing patterns, permits certain innovations, and reinforces particular kinds of change.

Moreover, in each domain the ultimate social implication of this new technology depends on economic, legal, and policy decisions that are shaping the Internet as it becomes institutionalised. Sociologists need to study the Internet more actively and particularly, to synthesise research findings on individual user behaviour with macroscopic analyses of institutional and political-economic factors that constrain that behaviour.

D.A. Ferguson and E.M. Perse carried out a study to understand the similarity of television viewing and world wide web surfing. In their research published in 2000 in the Journal of Broadcasting and Electronic Media, Vol. 44(2), pp. 155–175 as *The World Wide Web as a Functional Alternative to Television* they studied a sample of young adults with computer experience and Internet access going to colleges, which had Internet connectivity. The study focused on (1) the reasons why they go to the web, (2) on how much time they spend on the web, and (3) the kind of sites they visit. The study was centered on the World Wide Web and not on e-mail or newsgroups or other uses, because of the similarity it has in terms of multimedia content and the media-related industries that resemble other mass media.

The finding of this study suggests that "maybe" the World Wide Web is a functional alternative to television and that people visit the web quite frequently for entertainment. However, it also establishes that people watch television for relaxation, whereas in the case of web surfing it was not so probably because it involves more interaction like clicking the mouse to move around and also following links. The relaxation motive was endorsed significantly less by the sample population. The companionship motive was also rated low and did not establish that the World Wide Web can be a substitute for personal interaction even though the television offers a viewer a sense of pseudo-interpersonal interaction. The study also highlighted that a very small portion of the web-content is being used by the web audience.

The authors B. Wellman, J. Salaff, D. Dimitrova, L. Garton, M. Gulia and C. Haythornthwaite in their study *Computer Networks as Social Networks: Collaborative Work, Telework, and Virtual Community* published in 1996 in the Annual Review of Sociology, Vol. 22, pp. 213–238, have stated that when computer networks link people as well as machines, they become social networks. Such computer-supported social networks are becoming important bases of virtual communities, computer-supported cooperative work, and telework. Computer-mediated communication such as electronic mail and computerised conferencing is usually text-based and asynchronous. It has limited social presence, and on-line communications are often more uninhibited, creative, and blunt than in-person communication.

Nevertheless, these social networks sustain strong, intermediate, and weak ties that provide information and social support in both specialised and broadly based relationships, they foster virtual communities that are usually partial and narrowly focused, although some do become encompassing and broadly based. They accomplish a wide variety of cooperative work, connecting workers within and between organisations who are often physically dispersed. The networks also link teleworkers from their homes or remote work centers to main organisational offices.

Although many relationships function off-line as well as on-line, these networks have developed their own norms and structures. The nature of the medium both constrains and facilitates social control. Computer-supported social networks have strong societal implications, fostering situations that combine global connectivity, the fragmentation of solidarities, the de-emphasis of local organisations (in the neighbourhood and workplace), and the increased importance of home bases.

J.S. Quarterman in his chapter *The global matrix of minds* in the book 'Global Networks' edited by Linda M. Harasim published in 1993 from the MIT Press, Cambridge, MA, discusses the history and future prospects of computer networks from the perspective of technology as well as interpersonal communication. For the author, there is a distinct connection between the two. He feels that though networks may start as solely technological tools, they do not stay that way if they survive. They develop into places where people go, which turn into communities, which develop politics, economics, and legal issues which sum up to a society.

3.1.2 Delivery of Healthcare and the Internet

Karen E. Koch, Cathy Smith and McNeil T. Stanford in their research project entitled '*Application of Telemedicine to Home-Managed Congestive Heart Failure Patients in Rural Mississippi*' published in 1999 from the North Mississippi Medical Center aimed at improving the home-based management of North Mississippi's rural region's congestive heart failure patients. From July 2000 to March 2002, 44 homebound patients were managed via Telemedicine. Their average age was 75 years and 36 per cent were Phase-IV (most serious). There were

23 telemedicine units and 3 central units. The patients in the study were provided with a telemedicine monitor in their homes, which was manned by the patients themselves or by their caregivers. The study concluded that the program was successful in all three dimensions: Clinical, humanistic and financial.

In a prospective, non-randomised, intervention study, entitled *Long-Term Effects of Specialised Stroke Care With Telemedicine Support in Community Hospitals on Behalf of the Telemedical Project for Integrative Stroke Care (TEMPiS)'*, five community hospitals participating in the network were compared with five matched control hospitals without specialised stroke facilities, or telemedical support. The authors H.J. Audebert, K. Schultes, V. Tietz, U. Heuschmann, U. Bogdahn, R.L. Haberl and J. Schenkel published their findings in 2009 in Stroke, Vol. 40, pp. 902–908. All patients with consecutive ischemic, or hemorrhagic stroke admitted between July 2003 and March 2005 were evaluated. Outcome "death and dependency" was defined by death, institutional care, or disability. Multivariable regression analysis technique was used to arrive at the results. The study concluded that implementing a system of specialised stroke wards, continuing education and telemedicine in community hospitals offers long-term benefit for acute stroke patients.

Another study *Impact on Quality of Life of a Telemedicine System Supporting Head and Neck Cancer Patients: A Controlled Trial During the Postoperative Period at Home* reported by J.L. van den Brink, P.W. Moorman, M.F. de Boer, W.C.J. Hop, J.F.A. Pruyn, C.D.A. Verwoerd, and J.H. van Bemmel, in 2007 in the Journal of the American Medical Informatics Association, Vol. 14(2), pp. 198–205, investigated whether telemedicine could be beneficial to the quality of life of cancer patients. A prospective controlled trial evaluating the effects of a telemedicine application on the quality of life of patients with cancer involving the head and neck, by using quality of life questionnaires that covered 22 quality of life parameters were conducted between 1999 and 2002. This study confirmed that telemedicine may be beneficial for the quality of life of cancer patients.

The author Michelle Brear (2006) in her paper *Evaluating telemedicine: Lessons and challenges* in Health Information Management Journal, Vol. 35(2), pp. 23–31, feels that there is an urgent need for evidence about the clinical impact of telemedicine applications. Production of such evidence is complicated due to limited resources and wide range of research methods to identify and determine the nature and extent of both the intended and unintended consequences of an application and the context specific results that are obtained. Using a multi-method approach, which obtains qualitative and quantitative data and analyses it using various techniques while taking into consideration the evidence from other indicators, can overcome some of these complications.

Due to the nature and limitations of evidence, which can be derived from each type of data, it is necessary to use multiple methods of collection and analysis. In this way, it is possible to determine the presence or absence of changes resulting from a telemedicine application and explain the nature and reasons for these changes.

3.1.3 Rural Development and the Internet

The primary objective of the important study entitled *Impact of ITC's e-Choupal on rural India-A case study* by B. Garg, Mohita and S. Marwah, published in 2008 by the Indian Institute of Management Kozhikode was to understand the attitude of farmers towards concept of ITC *e-Choupal* and its impact on rural India, therefore a case study-cum-descriptive research design was found to be most suitable.

In another study entitled *Adoption of ICT in agricultural management in the UK: The intra-rural digital divide* by M.F. Warren published in 2002 in the journal Agricultural Economics, Vol. 48(1), pp. 1–8, the benefits from adopting ICT in farming businesses have been explored and the results show that the role of ICT in agricultural management is intrinsic, instrumental and fundamental. The study concludes that a great divide will be created in terms of competition and in overcoming geographical and sectoral disparities in case it is not used universally.

3.1.4 Governance, Democracy and the Internet

In the proceedings of National Conference on Information technology (2007), an article entitled *Leveraging governance in Africa through ICTs: Some policy directions* (pp. 724–736), by the author Wole Michael Olatkun concluded, greater use of Information and Communication Technologies (ICTs) is necessary to improve governance in Africa. Legislation for e-governance, appropriate policy changes and help of experienced individuals is necessary to ensure that African countries do not miss the opportunities of e-governance.

In the research work published in Digital review of Asia Pacific, 2006, *Social, political and cultural aspects of ICT,* the authors L. Green, E. Lallana, Z. Nain, and Ma hope that the improved communicative exchange will help build better understanding and bring down barriers of prejudice and fear as the Internet continues to offer new ways for people to communicate and reach out. With luck and commitment, the technology of communication will ultimately bring in necessary transparency and people will be able to engage in dialogue. This, the authors feel by itself, is a strong reason to work for the spread of digital communications throughout Asia Pacific and beyond.

R. Sudan (2000) in his study *Towards SMART Government: The Andhra Pradesh Experience,* published in the Indian Journal of Public Administration, (Special Number on Information Technology and Development) concludes that the successful induction of information technology in government requires a change of mindset amongst the employees and bureaucracy and a strong leadership of political will.

D. Elgin in his article *Revitalising Democracy Through Electronic Town Meetings* published in 1993 in the Spring volume of Spectrum, (pp. 6–13), opines that democracy is endangered unless citizens continuously involve themselves in setting policy direction, in this fast changing world. Modern technology offers the means to engage the public in decision-making, but runs the risk of being misused.

The author H. Henderson in his article *Perfecting democracy's tools* published in 1992 in New Perspectives Quarterly, Fall, pp. 22–24, provides a futurist perspective on the technological challenges facing democracy. The hardware requirements for electronic breakthroughs are available but not the rules of interaction, knowledge, values and ethics, which she terms as software. The author feels that Democracy runs the risk of losing the faith of the people unless it adapts to the new technological innovations that can give them a voice.

The book *The electronic commonwealth: The impact of new media technologies on democratic politics by* J.B. Abramson, F.C. Arterton, and G.R. Orren (Basic books, New York, 1998), provides a comprehensive and authoritative discussion of the new media technologies and their impact on American politics. The authors argue that revolutionary as the new communications technologies may be, there is nothing inherent in them that confirm whether they will be used to befriend or belittle democracy. Their vision of America as an 'electronic commonwealth' composed of diverse communities served by heterogeneous programming and participating in a variety of electronic town meetings is counterpoised to the prevailing trend toward 'electronic plebiscitary democracy,' which the authors believe would impoverish the public debate on which democracy thrives.

If used instead to remove the obstacles of distance and time, the new media would prove an ally of democracy. The authors' primary concern throughout remains the tension between using the new media to 'quicken' democracy through electronic polls, home-centered voting and other instant feedback schemes *versus* using their congregating and conferencing capacities to slow down and enhance it.

F.C. Arterton's pioneering work *Teledemocracy: Can technology protect democracy?* (Sage Publications, Newbury Park, CA, 1987), explores the results from experiments in electronically mediated forums, and what they may suggest about the future of democracy. The author concludes that there is 'little support for the notion that citizens have the interest necessary to sustain near universal participation.... Most citizens, probably around two-thirds, will not participate.' He also provides a very useful conceptual model of four different applications for electronic forums.

3.1.5 Studies Centering around Andhra Pradesh

A. Grondeau in her article *Formation and emergence of ICT clusters in India: The case of Bangalore and Hyderabad,* published in 2007 in GeoJournal-Springer Science and Business Media, Vol. 68, pp. 31–40, analysed the nature of Information and Communication Technology clusters, the policies that encouraged the growth of these clusters and the birth of Hyderabad and Bangalore as the major hubs. She analysed the impact on the population and concluded that this development did not benefit the entire population. The research was based on a substantial amount of literature review in English and French along with digital reports from India. She also carried out field study in Bangalore to understand the layout of ICT activities in the city. This study, therefore, seems to be focussed mainly on Bangalore, which is not in Andhra Pradesh and mainly based on literature review.

In another study, by N. Kshetri, entitled *The Institution-ICT-Economic Development Nexus: Two Cases* published in 2005 in the conference proceedings of the Americas Conference on Information Systems (AMCIS) 2005 named as Proceedings: Association for Information Systems, pp. 491–499, tried to address the nature of institutional factors that interact with an ICT project in a developing country along with the mechanisms by which these factors influence the success of the project. The author also explored ways of introducing ICT projects in developing countries to boost economic development. The study is based on a multiple case study design that investigates using two cases to provide insights. These cases varied widely in terms of institutional settings such as law, beliefs, norms, rules, conventions and economic factors. The cases selected in this paper are ICT projects in the Andhra Pradesh state of India and Operating Systems Software project in China.

The case studies are based on secondary data and some semi-structured interviews and there is no use of inferential statistical methods. The study concludes that the success or failure of an ICT project depends entirely on the institution. In the case of Andhra Pradesh, the cause of failure and barriers to success of the project have been attributed to incompatibility with social norms and thus perceived as an elitist, top-down project. The study concludes that projects perceived such normally never succeed. However, due to the exploratory nature of the study no concrete theory could be built upon.

B. Powis (2003) in his study *Grassroots politics and Second wave of decentralisation in Andhra Pradesh,* published in Economic and political weekly, June 28, pp. 2617–2622, sought to find whether community based development could be exploited for realistic political objectives. He purposefully sampled 18 villages in Andhra Pradesh in 2002 based on contrasting political relations at the village, *mandal* and assembly constituency through structured and semi-structured interviews of the rural electorate and well reputed leaders.

The study concluded amongst other findings that the electorate voted mostly on party lines due both to an ideological commitment to parties and to the political biases in benefit allocations like loans, or house sanctions, for their *sarpanch* elections. Development promises of any kind of village development works (schools, roads) were also equally important reasons. However, the determination of the unit of analysis is not clear in this study.

G.K. Reddy (2002), in his study entitled *New Populism and Liberalisation, Regime Shift under Chandrababu Naidu in AP* (Economic and Political Weekly, March 2, 2002, pp. 871–883), focuses on the impact on economic reforms due to political compulsions of a government and tries to analyse whether the compulsions spring up from the economics of the regime, or its electoral politics.

The study concludes that through ideologically oriented populist programmes such as *Janmabhoomi*, Naidu's regime sought to create supporting ground for liberalisation policies.

P. Chakravartty (2001) in her paper entitled *Flexible Citizens and the Internet: The Global Politics of Local High-Tech Development in India* discusses her findings based on discussions on five popular translocal websites mainly targeting Indians in the United States on high-end technology developments in India, with special emphasis on Hyderabad or Cyberabad in the Emergences, Vol. 11 (1), pp. 69–88. The study period is for two years and other commercial and non-commercial websites that targeted a similar NRI population were also studied. The study concluded that the problems and realities are generally overlooked in such discussions and the commercial communications thus only erases the divide between the first and third worlds, urban and rural India and also the state's failure in terms of social infrastructures and these reassuring stories written on the web binds the transnational population together.

3.2 Gaps Lapse Identified

To strengthen the area and focus of research a citation based literature review was done as presented above, but it is seen that there is no study in the Indian context that covered holistically the complete impact of Internet on the four major areas of society—news, health, agriculture and politics. Moreover, no study was found that has combined the three media-print newspapers, TV news and Internet news in a single study. Again, it has been observed amongst the studies reviewed, that researchers have focussed on either the Internet as a whole, or on online newspapers but not on Internet news in particular.

None of the studies reviewed has tried to combine the uses and gratification of the three media, the credibility perception of the three media, the mutual displacement effect and the utility perceptions of the three media in a single study. It was also observed, the displacement effect of Internet as a medium on the traditional media have been researched, but the effect of traditional media on the growth of Internet news has not been studied. Hence, the present study will try to fill these gap (lapse) areas in this research.

Further, it is necessary to see the impact of using telemedicine in the emergency critical cardiac care units and as such very few studies could be found on the use of telemedicine in the Indian context. The present study will therefore try to address this gap.

Research on the use of Internet in a rural setup with a huge illiterate population and minimal infrastructure is necessary to judge whether use of Internet has contributed to the social development and to see whether it is a sustainable model. Some studies in this area exist but it would be necessary to contribute in greater detail.

In a democratic country like ours, the impact of Internet and its technology on the fate of a political party is necessary to study. Very few studies could be found that focused on this aspect. The present researcher wishes to fill in some of the gap in knowledge regarding the political outcome rather than the technological outcome of use of such technology in politics as was felt necessary by certain researchers.[1]

3.3 Research Questions

The use of the Internet in India, with only a short history but with such rapid development, is certainly useful for researchers trying to determine Internet use patterns and the social impact of the Internet on Indians. The Internet has many uses as a medium, and therefore, it will be necessary to examine its impact on various sectors of society. This study will focus on the four major areas—news media, healthcare, agriculture and rural development and political outcome to arrive at a conclusion about the impact of this medium on the Indian society.

In the context of news, Internet will be observed as a medium of news only, to explore its impact on the news gathering habits of people, since its general usage would include several unrelated and unecessary uses. Drawing upon this argument, this study examines the Internet as a new medium of news against the backdrop of two traditional media-print newspapers and TV news, whose basic functions are very similar to the ones provided by the Internet-information and entertainment to see whether the new media competes, or complements the traditional media.

The current study utilises the theories of uses and gratification of media and media displacement, blending it with media credibility perception in the context of the Indian audience who have access to print newspapers, TV news and Internet to gauge the extent to which this new medium has evolved as a distinct medium of news in India and what factors have impacted this through the following research questions.

R1: Is there a difference in the news acquiring habits of the Indian audience from the three media, namely, Print newspapers, TV news and Internet news?

R2: Is there any difference in the news-gathering habits of people from print newspapers and TV news between the groups who read Internet news and those who do not read Internet news?

R3: Is there any difference in the news-gathering habits of people from Print newspapers and TV news, within the group of non-readers of Internet news?

R4: Is there any difference in the news-gathering habits of people from Print newspapers and TV news, within the group of readers of Internet news?

R5: Is there any impact of news-gathering habits from traditional media (Print newspapers and TV news combined) on the news gathering habit from Internet?

R6: What is the effect of gender, age, education, profession, Internet usage patterns, credibility perception of Internet and credibility perception of traditional media on the news-gathering habit from traditional media and what are the relative influences of these variables on it?

From literature-review-based background information it has been observed that the relationship between traditional media and Internet news is very complex as there are various kinds of research findings: displacement, no confirmed displacement and also a complimentary relationship. Hence more research is required in this area. Subsequent to an extensive literature review and validation by an exploratory research with a few renowned academicians, it has been confirmed that not too many studies in this area have been conducted in India. Therefore, very little is known about the different relationships amongst the traditional and new media and more so about the impact of the utility perceptions of the traditional medium of news (print newspapers and TV), on the gap between the perceived and observed utilities of Internet news. However, the managers of Internet news portals should be responsible to ensure that the gap in the expected and observed utility perceptions of their users is minimised, based not on subjective but objective methods.

On the basis of the above findings, the following two managerially relevant research questions have been identified:

R7(a): Is there any difference between the perceived and observed utilities of Internet news?

R7(b): What is the impact of the perceived utilities of print newspapers and TV news on these identified gaps amongst the Indian audience?

It has been argued that the above research questions need to be addressed through a statistical analysis since there were not many studies that dealt with these issues in India.

A second study will be necessary to examine the impact of Internet as a medium of delivery of critical healthcare in India. This is relevant since most of the people residing in semi-urban and rural parts of India do not have access to quality medical care. Further, it is well known that prompt medical attention is desirable in cases of strokes to be able to reduce the rate of mortality amongst patients. Studying a real case to assess the impact of active use of Internet technology in the delivery of these services in providing clinical care will be necessary to answer the following research question:

R8: Has the use of Internet technology positively impacted the stabilisation of acutely unwell patients in the telemedicine cardiac care units at the three active telemedicine centers connected to the Rabindranath Tagore International Institute of Cardiac Sciences (RTIICS), Kolkata?

The objective of this research also includes an examination of the use of Internet technology in social development and agriculture. Internet in India like in other developing countries has not spread much to the rural areas, where people are poor, illiterate and marginalised. Participatory development and a sustainable commercial model in rural India can serve as a starting point for community development. This medium that can inherently be used for democratisation of information flows, increase in accessibility of information, increase in participation of the marginalised population and in the creation of a scalable, sustainable and profitable business model could be useful as an intervention.

This medium has been put to use in some areas. It is necessary to investigate how its use has contributed in the development of the agriculture sector through a case based study to answer the following research question:

R9: Has this medium been able to bridge the gap in opportunities and bring global resources as well as best farming practices to the Indian farmers and thereby contribute to the alleviation of their poverty and marginalisation?

In spite of all the uses that we may find of the Internet, when a government tries to utilise it in administering better governance to its citizens, it needs to bring in plenty of changes in terms of infrastructure, human resource, and government spending. It also needs to educate its citizens through effective communication. In a democracy like ours, where people ultimately decide what they want from their government it is necessary to investigate the issues of trying to introduce this medium. From the above studies, it emerges that none of the researchers have addressed the principal research question that the current researcher would like to address.

R10: What was the political outcome of Internet in a democratic process?

To be able to answer the above question better, the focus of the study will be in the following areas:

1. Economic development under Chandrababu Naidu;
2. Contributions of the Naidu government towards development of IT facilities and IT industry in the state;
3. Did over emphasis on Internet have an impact on the way the electorate voted;
4. Did the electorate benefit because of the introduction of Internet based services;
5. Did this new technology bring in opportunities for employment; and
6. A summary for the reasons of failure.

Reference

1. Haque, S.M., 2002, *E-governance in India: Its impacts on relations among citizens, politicians and public servants,* International Review of Administrative Sciences, Sage Publications (London, Thousand Oaks, CA and New Delhi), Vol. 68, pp. 231–250.

4

Research Methodology

This chapter consists of three sections. The first section provides the theoretical framework of the research. The next section states the tools used for the study. The last section describes the data.

4.1 Theoretical Framework

The research has been divided into four independent studies based on the objectives of this research. The studies are:

- Internet as a medium of news;
- Internet in healthcare services;
- Internet in agriculture and rural development; and
- Internet and politics.

This is a scientific research work based on different information gathered from various authentic sources. Social research is *theoretical*, meaning that much of it is concerned with developing, exploring, or testing the theories, or ideas that social researchers have about how the society operates. This is a social research based on systematic and scientific techniques aimed at (1) discovery of new facts, testing and verification of established facts, (2) finding the inter-relationship and causal relationships within an applied theoretical frame of reference, and (3) developing new concepts which would be based on reliable and factual data and its analysis to see the impact of Internet as a media in the Indian context.

This research is an original contribution to the existing collection of research. It is a *descriptive research* work as it consists of surveys and fact-finding enquiries of different kinds. In this research the responses of the different respondents have been reported. This research is also a *relational research as it investigates the relationships between* different variables. This research is certainly a causal research as it has described both the cause and effect variables and shown they are related to each other. Causal studies are more demanding than the other two–descriptive and relational. This is in addition a qualitative research work as it is designed to find what people think about the Internet as a medium in comparison to print and electronic media like print newspapers and television news in particular. This study is furthermore focused on qualitative research, as it is important in behavioral science and through such research the impact of the utility and credibility perceptions of the respondents towards print and electronic media and Internet news have been analysed. It is necessary to note that application of quality research in practice is a difficult task. This research is empirical in nature as it is based on observations and measurements of reality—on what the respondents perceive. This is data based research work, where statistical tests have been applied, that can be verified by observation and experiment before arriving at conclusions. This research is also exploratory in nature, as various experts have been interviewed to gain a better understanding of the different linkages in the areas of delivery of healthcare services, agriculture and rural development and also in politics. Exploratory research tools have been used to study perceptions. This research is probabilistic as most contemporary social researches are based on probabilities. Statistics was very dominant in this research as it allowed probabilities to be estimated. This research is nomothetic as even though individuals were studied, the objective was to generalise more than just the individual, specially when the focus group was considered. The research is formalised research with specific structure and hypotheses to be tested. A part of this research is historical in nature as it was based on historical documents, etc. It was important to research this literature to be able to gain an understanding about media in general and print newspapers, TV news and Internet newspapers in particular. A part of this research is *ex-post facto* research as the researcher has reported what has happened, or is happening.

For this research work, different libraries, speciality hospital, district hospitals, metropolitan cities and small towns, government offices, private offices, Internet kiosks, *e-choupals* and *Mandis* have been visited to collect data, observe events, conduct surveys and interviews, record notes, perform data analysis and statistical compilation, content analysis as well as obtain references and abstracts. Tape recorders, telephones, video conferencing tools and cameras for partial observation have been used for field research in addition to the questionnaire based survey method, where techniques like established and new scales have been used. The process of personal interviews was also conducted in a structured manner with a detailed schedule and open and close questions. This was used extensively to research on the impact of Internet on health and on agriculture and rural development. The focus group-interview method was further adopted to focus attention on the impact of Internet on politics. Three cases have been considered for intensive analysis and collection of relevant data.

4.2 Tools Used

4.2.1 *Statistical Tables*

Statistical tables have been used to present data statistically because of its advantage of being self-explanatory. Some of these tables are general and some have a specific purpose.

4.2.2 *Testing of Hypotheses*

A hypothesis may be defined as a proposal intended to explain certain facts or observations. In the context of statistical analysis, a null hypothesis and an alternate hypothesis were taken. The null hypothesis and alternate hypothesis were chosen before the sample was drawn. This was necessary in the studies entitled "Internet as a medium of news" and "Internet in healthcare services" as these are empirical in nature.

4.2.3 *Case Study Method*

The case study method is a reliable form of qualitative analysis and involves a detailed intensive study of a unit such as a corporate division, or a corporation with a focus on the factors contributing to its success, or failure. Three cases have been considered to analyse the reach and impact of Internet in society. The case study places more emphasis on the complete analysis of a limited number of events and the mutual inter-relationships of the causal factors. In this research, case studies have been conducted in the areas of health, agriculture and rural development and politics. The objective of the case study method in this research work was to identify the effect of Internet in the chosen sectors.

In this study the concerned units have been studied directly. Case study method based research in social sciences is widely accepted. Dr William Healy considers the case study method to be better than using statistical data and used it in his study of juvenile delinquents. This method has been applied to study the impact of Internet on health services, rural development and in outcomes of political processes.

This method facilitates intensive study of social units, which would not be possible if either the observation method, or the method of collecting information through schedules was used. Further, this method allows use of different methods to the researcher–like depth interviews, focus groups, study reports of individuals, questionnaires, correspondence and other documents. This method is well suited to understand the social impact of Internet in the various sectors of the society.

4.2.4 *Empirical Models, Statisitcal Tests and Tools Used*

ANOVA has been considered for research question R1 and *t*-test for research questions R2, R3 and R4. Paired *t*-tests were considered for the research question R7. The logistic regression model was considered for the research question R5 and multiple regression models in the cases of research questions R6 and R8.

Principal component analysis with Varimax rotation was used to summarise most of the original variance, or information in a minimum number of factors for prediction purposes. Cronbach alpha measures were used as a test of reliability of constructs.

4.3 Types and Sources of Data

There are various methods that can be used for collecting data from the respondents. Whether data are primary, or secondary, we normally think of three basic ways of gathering data, including:

(1) Survey;

(2) Observation; and

(3) Experimentation.

Among these three methods, the survey has been the dominant data collection technique in marketing research. Observation techniques are also practised in exploratory research. The present study also makes use of these methods because of its versatility and limited scope for experiment in this case.

Two types of data have been used in this study. They are—(1) time-series, or secondary and (2) cross-sectional and primary data. Time-series data have been collected from unpublished sources, namely, documents and records, various public records and statistics, historical documents, publications of associations. Analysing documents and records for obtaining time-series (secondary) data is a very useful method. It is worth mentioning that for empirical study, it is the most widely used source of data.

Cross-sectional (primary) data have been gathered through a primary survey of respondents. For this purpose detailed questionnaires have been prepared, which have been subjected to pilot survey for final selection of items (on the basis of reliability and validity tests) and correct framing of the questions. The data have been classified and put in tables. The analysis of data after the tabulation is based on the application of various established statistical formulae.

Statistical tests have been used to see whether the results of the outcome are real or the result of a fluctuation, and therefore, tests of probability have been used to measure the same.

It is not possible to evaluate a medium without knowing about the historical development and evolution of the social system in that context. For that previous research work on the early history and origin of printing, newspapers, Internet and Internet newspapers have been studied to learn about the evolution of different media of news. Further, the studies centering on various uses and theory of news have been also considered.

To gain a better understanding of telemedicine, telemedicine projects in India, cardio-vascular diseases and their relevance, infrastructure requirements of telemedicine, case fatality rate and the thrombolytic therapy related research work of previous researchers were studied.

To gather knowledge about social development, participatory social development and Brown's theory on social development have been studied. Further, theories of democracy, use of technology in a government and a background study of Andhra Pradesh through previous research work have been also considered, as they are relevant to the scope of study.

5

Content Analysis

5.1 Print and Media

The purpose of this chapter is to study the circumstances and events surrounding and leading to the evolution and history of printing and newspapers (section 5.1.1), Internet (sections 5.1.2-5.1.3) and Internet newspapers (sections 5.1.4-5.1.5). For a reasonable explanation of when a society adopts a new technology and why there may have been delays, we need to identify not just the factors that may have obstructed change in some technologies, but also those that have facilitated the swift adoption of technological advancements in other areas. In that context, the above study was considered necessary. The arrival of television to India has been presented in section 5.1.6.

A modest attempt has been made to study the perceptions of news, different angles of media, credibility perception and credibility components of media and media displacement theory (sections 5.1.7.1-5.1.7.5). Finally, the relationships between media, society and culture have been highlighted (section 5.1.8).

The research has further focused on existing literature on telemedicine (section 5.2.1), infrastructure requirements (section 5.2.2) relevance of telemedicine in India (section 5.2.3) and telemedicine projects in India (section 5.2.4), cardiac diseases and their relevance (section 5.2.5-5.2.7) as well as the treatment technique of thrombolytic therapy (section 5.2.8).

Next, the concept of social development has been researched (section 5.3.1) along with democracy, use of technology by a government and a brief note on Andhra Pradesh (sections 5.4.1-5.4.3). This knowledge was essential as the key to an understanding of the social phenomenon that has affected millions of people across the globe. Familiarity with this knowledge was also necessary to create awareness about the multi-dimensionality of social science analysis.

5.1.1 Evolution and History of Printing and Newspapers

The history of print media and written communication trails the development of civilisation in different cultures and cannot be actually treated chronologically. As early as 25,000–30,000 B.C. the first human civilisation painted pictures on the walls. These pictures depicted their day-to day lives, their religious and spiritual beliefs, fears and their own way of communicating with their predecessors. The pictorial communication found in caves of Pompeii, Southern France and Spain are believed to be the beginning of written communication for the human kind.

The change in the livelihoods of civilisations from hunter-gatherer societies to more permanent agrarian settlements where they needed to count their property led to the advent of a writing system that took communication to a different level. One of the earliest examples of pictorial writing was found in the excavation of Uruk in Mesopotamia, dating 3500 B.C.[1] The Sumerians developed *cuneiform* or pictographs writing on wet clay tablets, which are over 3500 years old.[2] Later, the Egyptians developed hieroglyphic writing during the era of the Pharaohs.[3] Around this time communication also became a tool for making profit and earning as Egyptian priest class who obtained tax from the population employed special scribes to keep the records. These records were written using pigments and were less durable and permanent as they were maintained on *papyrus*.

Initially stone and clay tablets were used to express thoughts and ideas. Gradually new writing surfaces like papyrus rolls in Egypt and early parchment paper made of dried reeds in China were used around 500–170 B.C. It has been recorded that printing had existed in China almost from the middle of the second millennium. The Chinese would rub the sheets on a converted image of a single unit made of hand carved wooden blocks. Later, movable types made of porcelain, wood, or cast in bronze were also known to have been used in China and then in Korea.[4] Tsai Lun an official at the Chinese Imperial Court at the Han Dynasty of China is credited with the invention of the paper that we know today, about 1800 years ago. In, or about the year 105 A.D., he presented Emperor Han Ho Ti with samples of paper.[5] In eighth century China, handwritten news-sheets appeared as the first newspapers in Beijing.[6]

With the invention of paper, writing became more common. By sixth century A.D., Chinese engravers mastered the art of wood-block printing, and by 11th century A.D., Pi Shung of China started using movable clay type.[7]

A minister of state in China–Foong-taon, who was a learned man, first accomplished the art of making copies of a book that he liked in the tenth century by using the concept of an engraved tablet with the face of the letter cut-out unlike in a typical engraving where the letters are cut in like an inscription.[8] This style was also used in Japan, but the method generally used was what is known as 'block-printing', the carved wood-block being used to print a single page of a specific text.

This method was suitable to cultures, which used thousands of ideograms rather than alphabets of twenty, or thirty letters. It was probably because of this that the Chinese invention of the movable type in the eleventh century had few consequences.[9]

Prior to Johann Gutenberg's invention of the printing press, books were produced and supported only by monasteries and were hand written by scribes. Since it was always a very slow and laborious process it neither spread fast nor much. This remained the status until the discovery of the movable metal type by the German inventor Johann Gutenberg of Mainz in 1450[10], which was probably influenced by the wine presses of his native Rhineland, which used movable types.

This revolutionary invention brought in the first mass medium and allowed for free spread of ideas in a completely unprecedented fashion. The practice of printing spread through Europe and by 1500 A.D., presses had established in more than 250 places in Europe–80 of them in Italy, 52 in Germany and 43 in France. *Basel* had its first printer by 1466, Rome by 1467, Paris and Pilsen by 1468,Venice by 1469, Leuven, Valencia, Cracow and Buda by 1473, Wesminster and not London by 1476 and Prague by 1477.[11] Between them about 27,000 editions were produced by the year 1500 in an Europe of 100 million people. The Protestant reformation might have happened because of the thousands of copies of Luther's theses that were printed for public distribution.

Even though the practice of printing spread to most parts of Europe very fast, it was slow in penetrating Russia and the Orthodox Christian world, essentially because the alphabet was usually Cyrillic and literacy was confined to the clergy. Essentially there was also resistance, so when a white Russian trained in Poland set up a press in Moscow in 1564, it was soon destroyed by a mob. During the rule of the Tsar

Peter the Great (1686–1725), the scene changed and he founded a press at St. Petersburg in 1711, followed by the Senate presses in Moscow and Petersburg in 1719, the Naval Academy Press in 1721 and the Academy of Sciences Press in 1727.[12] It is perhaps not the technology alone that helped spread the printing revolution as any other technological revolution, but also the social and cultural ambience of the area. The first newspaper to appear in Russia was the 'Military and other matters Gazette' in 1703.[13]

The Muslim world which is considered to have stopped the flow of printing from China to the West resisted the print throughout the period between 1450 and 1789 which historians call the 'early modern' period. It has been recorded by an imperial ambassador to Istanbul, that it was a sin to print religious books. Sultan Selim I who ruled between 1512 and 1520 had issued a law that printing would result in the death penalty. They also resisted Western learning by giving a religious deterrent to it. It took more than 200 years after the first *Hebrew* press in 1494 and 150 years after the first Armenian press in 1567 and finally, a Hungarian convert to set up a press in 1726 with the permission of the sultan to print only secular books.

The first Ottoman gazette was founded in 1831 and the first unofficial newspaper in Turkish launched by an Englishman appeared in 1840[14]. But newspapers were not new. Civilisations have used some form of the print media to spread news and information to the masses.

The earliest recorded newspaper is the *Acta Diurna*, which appeared around 59 B.C. in the Roman civilisation. *Julius Caesar* used the *Acta*, which used to be written on large white boards and displayed in popular areas like the *Baths* in major cities to inform citizens about the important social and political happenings, upcoming events, military campaigns, trials, executions and scandals. The concept of writers (*Actuarii*)[15] was prevalent.

In the East, the Chinese had a spoken newspaper,[16] where the news was composed in verse and chanted in the streets by the writer himself more than 2300 years before Christ.The oldest continuing newspaper at Peiping was the court Gazette.[17] The King, Pan, literally meant 'Capital sheet' known as the Peking Gazette began to appear from 911 A.D. It was irregular then, but from 1315 A.D. became regular, every week then in three editions the morning edition-Hsing-pan; or Business Sheet on yellow paper containing commercial and industrial news of the previous week; the midday edition; Shuen–pan, or official sheet also of yellow paper, giving orders of council, court circulars and other official news; and the afternoon edition; Tilani-pan,[18] or Country sheet in red paper with all the general news of the week. It was edited by a council of six members of the Academy of Science.

However, it was the printing press, invented by Johann Gutenberg in approximately 1450[19], that ushered in the era of the modern newspaper. Gutenberg's machine enabled for the first time the free exchange of ideas and the spread of knowledge-themes that would define Renaissance Europe. Samuel Hartlib, an East European exile in Britain who fought for social justice had written in 1641 that 'the art of printing will so spread knowledge that the common people, knowing their own rights and liberties, will not be governed by way of oppression'.[20]

That is exactly what happened. Most commentators wished this had never happened, writers and scribes lost business to printers, to the clergy it meant that people of lower gentry and social status had access to religious texts and therefore would not follow them blindly and for the government, Hartlib's prophecy was bad news. The rise of newspapers in the seventeenth century[21] increased these fears about the effect of print.

In 1556, the Venetian government had published *Notizie scritte*, for which readers paid a small coin, or "Gazzetta." [22] Even though this was an insignificant newspaper in terms of size, information and influence it has left its mark through its title Gazette. This name may have been derived from the Latin word *gaza* which means a treasury, or store; or from the Italian *gazza,* or *gazzara* which means a magpie, or chatterer, or perhaps more significantly from the name of a coin, *gazzetta* whose value was between a farthing and a half penny, now out of circulation, which one had to pay as a reading fee, or price for the sheet in manuscript.

Printing received a further fillip, when in 1714 Henry Mill an Englishman received the first patent for a typewriter.[23] Then in 1737 Pierre Simon Founier[24] invented the point system in type, which was later modified and standardised by Ambroise Didot. Fournier and Didot designed the system of use of 72 points to an inch, which is still used by present day computers.

The presentation of news took a visual turn when in 1839[25] wood-cuts and lithograph from *daguerreo* types decorated pages of magazines and around 1890[26] the first photographs appeared in books and newspapers; much of it was due to the development of the *halftone* press[27] around that time.

By the first half of the 17th century, newspapers began to appear as regular and frequent publications. The first modern newspapers were products of western European countries like Germany (Relation[28] in 1605[29]), France (La Gazette[30], May 30 1631, founded by Theophraste Renaudot[31]), Belgium (Nieuwe Tijdingen[32] in 1616[33]) and England (The Oxford Gazette[34], later renamed the London Gazette appeared as a semi-weekly single sheet in 1665 and is still published as court journal).

The 'Daily Courant' a daily newspaper, began to be published in England from 1702.[35] Sweden was the first country to pass a law in 1766[36], protecting the freedom of press.[37] The first daily publication was Einkommende Zeitung (Incoming News)[38] started by a bookseller Timotheus Ritzsch in Leipzig in 1650.[39]

Theophraste Renaudot who is credited for starting the first newspaper in France[40], was a journalist, doctor and a philanthropist. He started his newspaper to combat the slanderous, scandalous news that would normally get circulated through leaflets at that time in France. It initially printed news from abroad, with variety and truthful stories and though it started as a four-page paper, by 1631 it became an eight pages paper with two sections.

The first newspaper that was in circulation in England had started in the sixteenth century but it had plenty of malice, gossip and a lot of distorted reporting. To correct the same, during the reign of Queen Elizabeth, The English Mercurie[41] was started by Burleigh with an intention to publish only true information. Several similar newspapers followed this newspaper but they all suffered from malicious reporting prevalent at that time. During the rule of Queen Elizabeth, there was great news censorship and she thwarted free printing of news and pamphlets. So even though some of the gentry did have access to news that resulted in them getting educated, aware and liberated, the majority of the masses continued to remain in the dark.

It is also recorded that around this time a new profession of 'news writers', or correspondents started, who collected small scraps of information and for a small fee sent them every post day to their employers. However, this profession continued but the status and the faith in these correspondents reduced a lot over the years. In the reign of Queen Anne, the English Press revamped itself. Sir Richard Steele in an attempt to introduce literature in newspapers started The Tatler, but it was Addison[42] who could finally do away with all reporting that spoke of specific interest groups.

The first newspaper to be published in America was The Boston Newsletter that was issued in April 1704 by John Campbell, who was a postmaster by profession at Boston. However, Benjamin Harris had made an earlier failed attempt to launch a newspaper on September 25, 1690, called the 'Publick Occurences both foreign and domestic'. The first daily newspaper in the USA came from Philadelphia when the tri-weekly 'Pennsylvania Packet, or General Advertiser' appeared in 1784.[43] Historians such as Emery and Emery have called the *Boston News-Letter* which published regularly from 1704, the 'first genuine American Newspaper.'[44]

The *New York Gazette* was the first newspaper published in the state of New York on November 8, 1725. Frank Luther Mott in his *American Journalism, A History: 1690–1960,*[45] writes that it was a "small two-page paper, poorly printed, and containing chiefly foreign news from three to six months old, state papers, lists of ships entered and cleared, and a few advertisements."

The first African-American newspaper called *Freedom's Journal*, was published in New York City on March 16, 1827. A weekly New York publication of the American Anti-Slavery Association *The Emancipator*, started in 1834.[46]

During this time the paper underwent a lot of change and newspaper publishing became big business.

The New Yorker Staats-Zeitung[47] issued on January 7, 1868, was the first New York newspaper made entirely of ground-wood pulp.

In early 19th century, the industrial revolution brought major innovations in printing technology. In 1814, Friedrich Koenig applied steam power to printing press. Rotary steam presses replaced hand operated machines, doing the same job in a small fraction of the time. The type moved horizontally printing 1000 impressions per hour.[48] Typesetting was transformed by the introduction of line-casting machines; first Ottmar Mergenthaler's Linotype (1884),[49] and then the Monotype machine.

Line-casting allowed type to be chosen, used and then re-circulated back into the machine automatically. The age of industrial revolution made transfer and interchange of written information between cities as well as continents readily available.

In 1831, Joseph Henry[50] invented the first electric telegraph, seven years later, in 1838, Samuel Morse patented his Morse Code, and is also credited for the first long distance electric telegraph line.

Around the same time, in 1846, Alexander Bain[51] patented the first fax machine then known as the electro-chemical telegraph. In 1867, Thomas Edison patented his mimeograph, which was the first office-copying machine, which might have inspired Chester Carlson[52], almost a century later, to invent the photocopier machine.

In 1878, Remington[53] came into the market with its first typewriter capable of printing both large and small letters. This changed the face of business life and also journalism. When Howard Krum introduced the Teletype in 1914[54], the Morse code started becoming less popular. These inventions also made it possible for news to travel faster over long distances. These allowed faster typing, greater range of fonts and styles and mostly allowed variable line and character spacing. The World War II made these mediums even more popular.

By the middle of the 19th century, newspapers were becoming the primary means of disseminating and receiving information. The period 1890–1920 marked as the 'Golden Age' of print media, saw the rise of media barons like William Randolph Hearst, Joseph Pulitzer and Lord Northcliffe. These men used their enormous power and influence on the media industry to build their publishing empires.

The other role that newspapers played during that period was that of a propaganda vehicle. *Iskra* (The Spark) published by Lenin in 1900[55] is one such example. Started by members of the League of Oppressed People, Vietnamese section, especially Nguyen Hai Than, the *Thanh Nien* made its appearance in Vietnam in 1925[56] and brought in Marxism and information on the revolution's strategic policies.

The *Sydney Morning Herald* is the oldest newspaper in Australia owned and managed by the Fairfax family that started in 1831.[57] They pioneered the use of steam machinery for printing newspapers in Australia.

Although printing from movable type was introduced in Japan in the late 16th century, Japan's first daily newspaper, *Yokohama Mainichi Shimbun*, appeared only in 1870.[58]

In India, the first forms of journalism was through *Akhbar* or *Akhbrat* which contained special information from the royal court, provinces and other important matters related to the province. This practice was started by emperor Akbar in 1574.[59] Under the Mughal emperors; newsletters were important public institutions, meant primarily to supply news and sometimes views.

There were two kinds of dispatches, *Waqia* and *Akhbar*. The *Khabarassan* collected news, the *Waqayi-nawis* wrote the news and the

Harkaras, or postal runners dispatched the news[60]. But as was the custom in the other parts of the world then, these news were meant only for the rich and the gentry. However, some news did leak and trickle down to the public.

Aurangzeb had in his court two kinds of reporters[61]–the *Waqia-nawis* who were the public reporters and the *Khufiya-nawis* — who were the secret reporters. This practice has been recorded also in the courts of the Maratha chiefs in Upper India, in the Sindhia court, in the Nawab of Banda's court[62] and a few others.

The manuscript newsletter system, which was always true reports, was present even around 300 B.C.[63] in the northern part of India.

Foreigners imported the printing press to India. Christian missionaries had installed the first presses in Bombay, Madras and Calcutta by 1556,[64] essentially to print Christian doctrines to spreading the religion. The first printed book in Marathi, which was a grammar and translation of Matthew's *gospel* was printed in the Serampore press in 1805.[65]

The first Indian newspaper in English was brought out by James Augustas Hickey and was called the *Bengal Gazette* or *Calcutta General Advertiser*. Hickey was a printer and a member of the Stationer's company and came to India as an employee of the East India Company. The first issue appeared on Saturday, January 9, 1780, announcing itself as a 'weekly political and commercial paper open to all parties but influenced by none'.[66] This information had other support.[67] It "consisted of two sheets about 12 inches by 8–a miserable 4 pages with three narrow columns of smeared Letter-Press on every page. It contained advertisement, correspondence from local and distant contributors and occasional extracts from the news last received from Europe".[68]

This newspaper was politically harmless but was known more for its notoriety and thus went through a lot of turbulent times. Within a year of its launch, in November, 1780 the *India Gazette*[69] was launched under the leadership of Peer Reed who was a salt agent and B. Messinck,[70] the owner of a theatre. The newspaper was printed properly on good paper of about 16 inches in length and was divided into three columns.

As Persian was the official language in India for a long time, it was used for newspaper printing as early as 1784, or even earlier. The *Calcutta Gazette* in its first issue dated 4th March, 1784 had a Persian column named: *Khulasai-Akhbar i Darbar i Mo'alla ba Dar al Khilafat Shah Jahanabad*[71] (Summary of news from the exalted court at the capital of Delhi). F. Galdwin a civilian published the *Calcutta gazette* under the sanction of the Government under Warren Hastings.

It was a semi-official weekly published on Thursdays. It carried official notifications, reports of social parties, reports from Supreme Court cases, editorial comments, news and extracts from other papers, including from England and some advertisements. However, in June 1815 it became the Government Gazette, retaining some features of a newspaper. It became a bi-weekly by 1823 but shutdown in 1832.[72] It is also considered the first printed newspaper in a local language.

The *oriental magazine,* or *Calcutta Amusement* started in April 6, 1785 and the *Oriental Journal,* or *Oriental Advertiser* first appeared in 1785. Then, there was the quarterly journal for the sophisticated society called the *Asiatic Miscellany*, which started in 1785 and had a run of only two years. It started again in 1789 in a new form, with a distinct literary flavour and was sold at a Gold *Mohur* per volume in Calcutta. It was run by W. Chamber, William Jones[73] and others from the literary circuit in Calcutta. Other newspapers that were available in the eighties and nineties of the 18th century were the *Asiatic Mirror, Oriental Star, Calcutta monthly journal* and the *Bengal Hurkaru*. The *Telegraph* was started in 1790.[74]

The *Madras Courier* was started by Richard Johnston, who was a Government printer in Madras on October 2, 1785. Then in January 1795, a weekly, the *Madras Gazette* was started by R. Williams who wanted to introduce Persian and other Oriental types. In 1791, Boyd started *Harkaru* after he quit his job as editor of the *Madras Courier*, but it was short lived as it ended with the death of its founder in 1792.

The first magazine to come out without the Government sanction was the *Indian Herald* that was established by the Humphrey's at Madras on April 2, 1795. The Government did not take it lightly. Government took action against the paper; Humphrey was deported to England, though he managed to escape on the way. The government introduced censorship[75] and the facility of free postage[76] that had been prevailing for circulation of newspapers was withdrawn.

In 1789, the *Bombay Herald* was published in Bombay as the first weekly newspaper and the *Bombay Courier* published by Luke Ashburner in 1790[77] was the second. Even though the *Bombay Courier* was an English newspaper it published advertisements in Gujarati. It faced opposition from the government over certain reporting, however, it managed to survive and became a government paper thereafter. The *Bombay Gazette* appeared in 1791 and it adhered to all government norms. In 1792, the *Bombay Herald* and the *Bombay Gazette* were amalgamated.

Henry Mckenly started the *Telegraph* newspaper in 1796 and soon after in 1797 he started the *Bengal Directory* and *Almanack* from the Telegraph office. In 1799,[78] Lord Wellesley published a set of eight censorship regulations.

The pattern of evolution of newspapers has been almost the same across the various cultures. The hunger for news has been the driving force behind every type of newspaper. Newspapers have been used and misused as a propaganda vehicle and have also been used to preserve and record events. People, to exchange private information through advertisements and have helped people gather information for various kinds of commerce, have used newspapers.

The practice of sailors unloading news from distant land was taken care of by technology–through telegraph, facsimile and now through Internet. Newspapers in the past, owing to smaller community sizes focused less on local news as people usually knew what was happening around them and therefore such news did not interest them.

It has been observed throughout history that print and newspapers were cause for a lot of anxiety amongst the clergy and the privileged classes, because when information filtered and knowledge spread it became difficult to exert and coerce. Almost every culture tried to impose some form of censorship on the press, with the basic intention of suppressing news from traveling.

As with any new media, there were several speculations about the harm that it would do to people, but it survived and survived so well. This medium generated over the years plenty of new professional opportunities and provided employment to many. It has supported causes, created opinions, discussed private lives and above all has brought the world to the common man's table.

5.1.2 Evolution and History of the Internet

"The Internet is an international network of networks that are both commercial and publicly owned."[79]

The Internet originated through a project by the US military agency called Advanced Research Projects Agency (ARPA) which was set up on February 7, 1958.[80] This was a mission to keep the US military ahead of its rivals by conducting advanced research in areas of defence. This agency was small with no laboratories of its own,[81] so even though it initiated and managed these projects, researchers and academicians in various universities who were able to develop new knowledge and technology, which could be used by the military as well for commercial gains, did the actual research and development work.

In 1962,[82] the Information Processing Techniques Office (IPTO) was set up and ARPA became a major funding source to universities for research in Computer Sciences, which till then was not very advanced. This initiated advanced research in computer graphics, artificial intelligence, time-sharing operating systems and networking. President Lyndon Johnson issued a memo in September 1965[83] urging the federal funding agencies to encourage development of centers of creative learning, where scholars and researchers would be encouraged to research beyond defined parameters.

IPTO had created large research centers in various universities, like the MIT, Carnegie Mellon, UCLA and many more. ARPA had funded several time–sharing computers as well on these campuses. The idea of joining these computers and sharing resources between them was the reason for the need for ARPANET. A computer scientist, Lawrence Roberts from MIT's Lincoln laboratory, who was well versed in the technology of networking,[84] managed this project.

According to some sources, this was a time when the cold war between the US and USSR was at its peak, USSR had launched the Sputnik satellite and the US military felt an urgent need to develop a robust communication system that could withstand a nuclear war.[85] Other sources, however, deny this.[86] The Advanced Research Projects Agency (ARPA), changed its name several times over the years and is now referred to as Defense Advanced Research Projects Agency (DARPA).

The concept of the Internet came from J.C.R. Licklider's *Galactic network* in 1962.[87] Licklider formerly from MIT and later the head of DARPA created the concept in his pioneering work on social interactions through networking, which was described as a globally connected network of computers, which could be accessed by anyone, from anywhere for data and programs. Licklieder was able to convince his successors at DARPA—Ivan Sutherland, Bob Taylor and MIT researcher Lawrence G. Roberts of the concept of networking, while Leonard Kleinrock of the MIT who had published the first paper and a book on packet switching theory in 1961[88] convinced Roberts of the theoretical feasibility of communications using packets rather than circuits. These two moves were very significant towards computer networking.

After networking, the next step required computers to talk to each other. For that an experiment was conducted in 1965 by Lawrence

Roberts along with Thomas Merrill who set up the first widearea network by connecting a TX-2 computer in the Lincoln laboratory at MIT, Massachusetts to a Q-32 in System development Corporation, Santa Monica, California [89] with a low speed dial-up telephone line. The result of the experiment supported Kleinrock's contention for the need for packet switching.

Lawrence Roberts went to DARPA in 1966 and developed his plan for a computer network, later named the ARPANET. Roberts met two other researchers at a conference—Donald Davies and Roger Scantlebury, who were working on packet networks, from the National Physical Laboratory, UK and the RAND research project for the military, on packet switching networks for secure voice transfers. All these researchers came together to devise a communication system called 'packet switching', that would work even if one, or more nodes of the system were destroyed, since transmitted data was broken up into small packets of data, sent to its destination, and reassembled at the other side.

This meant that a single signal could be routed to multiple users, and an interrupted packet could be re-sent without loss of transmission. Packets could also be compressed for speed and encrypted for security, resulting in a kind of communications web, where if one link of the web was broken, information could still flow around the broken link to get to its final destination.

The research resulted in the creation of ARPANET in 1969[90] when four host computers–the Network Measurement Center at University of California at Los Angeles (UCLA), Doug Engelbart's project on 'Augmentation of Human Intellect' at Stanford Research Institute, Glen Culler and Burton Fried's project on mathematical functions to deal with the problem of refresh over the net at UC Santa Barbara and Robert Taylor and Ivan Sutherland's investigating methods of 3-D representations over the net at University of Utah, on incorporated application visualisation projects got connected to the initial ARPANET and the first Internet started. After the initial work to complete the host-to-host protocol was completed and the necessary network software developed, the Network Working Group under S. Crocker finished the original ARPANET Host-to-Host protocol called the Network Control Protocol in December 1970. All ARPANET sites began implementing the protocol between 1971 and 1972[91] and thereafter network users started developing applications.

The ARPANET used NCP, or Network Control Protocol[92] as its transmission protocol between 1969 and 1982.[93]

In October 1972, Robert Kahn made a large and successful demonstration of the ARPANET at the International Computer Communication Conference. In that conference representatives from various projects around the world—UK, US, Canada, France, Japan, Norway and Sweden had gathered and discussed the need to start working on establishing agreed protocols. The InterNetwork Working Group (INWG) was created to begin discussions on the subject with Vinton Cerf, as its first Chairman.[94]

In March 1972, the most popular application on the Internet, the electronic mail was introduced for the first time by Ray Tomlinson at Bolt, Beranek and Newman Corp.(BBN).[95] He wrote the first basic e-mail sending and reading software, to assist the ARPANET developers with an easy management device.

The *Ethernet* technology still widely used, was developed in 1973, by Bob Metcalfe at Xerox PARC.[96] This technology contributed greatly to the advancement from the ARPANET model that had a few networks with low number of time-shared hosts to a model which supported an open architecture networking, where the option of any individual network technology was not dictated by a particular network architecture but could be selected freely by a provider and made to work internally with other networks through a meta-level 'Internetworking Architecture'. This also led to the classification of the networks based on their range of built-in networks into Class A, Class B and Class C.

The increase in the number of hosts meant that their associated names and addresses also increased and management of that became a challenge. Hosts were now assigned names instead of numbers to make it easier for people to remember. The Domain Name System, or (DNS) was invented by Paul Mockapetris[97] of USC/ISI, Craig Partridge and John Postel. Craig Partridge who was a programmer at BBN also developed the Mail Exchanger, or MX,[98] which allowed non-IP network hosts to have domain addresses.[99]

The DNS allowed a scalable distributed mechanism for resolving hierarchical host names into an Internet address. It was also introduced to identify the type of institution, which represented the host. Seven large domains were named: *.edu* for education, *.gov* for government, *.mil* for military, *.com* for commercial, *.org* for organisation, *.int* for quasi-governmental organisations and *.net* for network resources.[100] In

1985, the Information Sciences Institute (ISI) at the University of Southern California was given the responsibility for DNS root management by the Defense Communications Agency and Stanford Research Institute for DNS Network Information Center Registrations and on March 15, 1985, *Symbolics.com* was assigned as the first registered domain. Other first domains registered were *.edu,gov* and *.org.*[101]

Another milestone in the history of the Internet was in 1983, when the host protocol of ARPANET was changed from NCP to TCP/IP, which was a standard developed at BBN (Bolt, Beranek and Newman Corp.) under the leadership of Kahn and Vinton Cerf and widely used today.

Research communities were convinced of the usefulness of computer networking by the 1970's and several computer networks like the US (DoE) Department of Energy's MFENet for its researchers in Magnetic Fusion Energy and DoE's High Energy Physicists HEPNet were started. NASA Space Physicists started SPAN in 1983 and Rick Adrion, David Farber and Larry Landweber established CSNET for the academic as well as industrial computer science community with an initial grant from the US National Science Foundation (NSF). The European Academic and Research Network, JANET was formed with funding from IBM in 1984.[102]

Mike Lesk created another protocol, the Unix-to-Unix-Copy protocol, or UUCP in 1976 at ATandT Bell labs as part of a research project. Three researchers–Tom Truscott and Jim Ellis of Duke University and Steve Bellovin of the University of North Caroline, improved the original version which was released along with the Unix version 7[103] in 1979.

One of those early networks was Theorynet, which was started by Lawrence Landweber, Richard DeMillo and Richard Lipton at the University of Wisconsin in 1977 and it provided e-mail facilities for over 100 computer science researchers. In May 1979, Lawrence Landweber convened a meeting, with participants from DARPA, the National Science Foundation (NSF) and several computer scientists from different universities with the goal of establishing a Computer Science Department research computer network and it eventually led to the establishment of the Computer Science Research Network, or CSNET. CSNET[104] was established mainly for two reasons—the UUCP, modems and telephone lines provided an easy means for data-transportation and also because many large computing facilities like the one in the University of Wisconsin were not part of the ARPANET and wanted to have the advantage of being linked with other systems.

In 1980, Vinton Cerf from DARPA suggested a plan for inter-network connection between CSNET and ARPANET, where they wanted to use the TCP/IP communication protocol and to conceive the CSNET as a logical network containing a number of physical networks. For the user, working on ARPANET, or CSNET would appear to be the same because of the standard protocols to be used. The connections between the networks would be through a gateway called the Value-added-network, or VAN. In 1982, Defence Communication Agency (DCA) and DARPA established the Transmission Control Protocol (TCP) and Internet Protocol (IP) as the standard for ARPANET. In the same year DOD also declared TCP/IP as a standard, thus creating the first definition of Internet as a connected set of networks, specifically those using TCP/IP. In Europe, European UNIX Network Group for e-mail and USENET services with the Netherlands, Denmark, Sweden and the UK formed the European UNIX Network in 1982.[105]

Usenet was established in January 1980, as an open system focusing on e-mail communication by Jim Ellis and devoted to 'newsgroups' and is still in use. USENET grew out of AT and T's Unix computer operating system's built in communication protocol the Unix-to-Unix-copy-protocol or UUCP. Usenet used UUCP and a client-server architecture. A user had to connect to a machine, which would connect to another machine (server), which contained postings for the past few days on it. It also had the concept of newsgroups and users could issue commands to search for a particular article, which he could read, store or reply through electronic mail.

By 1988, a group of system operators at a number of important ARPANET sites had established an administrative body for Usenet, dedicated to providing stable news feeds and electronic mail. This group began to be referred to, as the "backbone cabal." Typically, Usenet newsgroups are created using a quasi-democratic system in which Usenet users have the opportunity to vote on whether or not a new group should come into existence.

In 1987, two groups, which dealt with the recreational use of drugs and sexual techniques, had been proposed and accepted, but the backbone administrators refused to allow them on their sites. As an act of protest, the 'alt' distribution was set up, using alternative routes that were separate from the backbone and theoretically avoided traversing the ARPANET. It was then that the first group on sex –*alt.sex*, and the first group on drugs –*alt.drugs*[106] were created, as was a newsgroup dedicated to rock and roll.

Gene Spafford is credited as the creator of the original Usenet backbone in 1983 to rationalise the retransmission of Usenet news. Spafford formalised the backbone subsequent to this event termed as Great Renaming in 1986–1987. This was done primarily since large number of groups were difficult to manage without reorganisation and it also became easier for administrators who wished to remove such groups from their newsfeed to do so and was considered more desirable and practical than attempting to eliminate controversial newsgroups.

UUCP networks spread quickly as costs of connectivity were low and could be used over existing leased lines, X.25 links and also over ARPANET connections. By 1983, the number of UUCP hosts had grown to 600 and then to 900 in 1984. Early versions of Usenet used the 'A' release. At Berkeley an improved version called 'B News' was produced by Matt Glickman a high school student and Mark Horton a graduate student at the University of Berkeley, California, in 1981. Between 1982 and 1984 several revised versions appeared. It had a message format that was compatible with Internet mail that improved its performance and was used as the Server software.

Geoff Collyer and Henry Spencer at the University of Toronto further developed 'C News' a much faster version of 'B News'. Usenet continued to expand. In 1981, Ira Fuchs and Gleydon Freeman devised the BITNET that connected academic mainframe computers. BITNET, the "Because It's Time NETwork,"[107] was started as a co-operative network at the City University of New York (CUNY). BITNET use electronic mail systems and mechanism called a "listserv" to distribute information. There are more than 4,000 discussion subject areas provided by BITNET, or BITNET-style. When a message is sent to a BITNET list, it gets replicated and sent to all the subscribers on that list. A person can subscribe, or unsubscribe to a list automatically by sending a mail to a certain address.

BITNET is presently administered by the BITNET Network Information Center, or BITNIC, under the auspices of EDUCOM. BITNET addressing and mail delivery systems[108] are different from the domain-style addressing of Internet and modern UUCP addresses. Regarding the management of lists, some are open, or unmoderated and others are moderated and administrated by one, or more moderators who approve postings before they are "exploded", or mailed out.

All the early networks except BITNET and USENET were built with the purpose of connecting defined closed communities of scholars and hence the need for compatibility between networks was less. In the commercial sector, alternate technologies were being used, namely XNS from Xerox, DECNet and IBM's SNA. The British JANET (Joint Academic Network), that provided links to British Academic Institutions and US NSFNET were conceptually different in that they started with a mission to serve and connect entire higher education communities regardless of their disciplines. A condition was created that a US university would receive National Science Foundation funding for an Internet connection only if it was made available to all qualified users on the campus.

In many ways, the administrative decentralisation of the network preceded its technological decentralisation. While packet-switching technology avoided the client-server relationships of other networks, ARPA encouraged developers of the networks to organise themselves through tools like RFC, or Request For Comments, which were a series of numbered electronic documents which formed the basis for determining network standards and acted as early distributed conferencing as one could read ongoing discussions on network protocols, new innovations, interviews, details of Network Working Group meetings and also informal histories.

The constant mediation between authority and individual needs, central to the development of the Internet, can be seen within the networking community itself.

In the 1980's, before the Internet was popularised, bulletin board systems became increasingly popular as a base for communications between geographically dispersed users who accessed the BBS over telephone lines. Ward Christianson is credited for the invention of the first computer bulletin board system, or BBS, in 1977–1978.[109] Christianson was also the author of the X-modem file transfer protocol, the first widely available file transfer method for personal computers.

In 1989, the first commercial services emerged with CompuServe, through Ohio State University and the first relays between a commercial electronic mail carrier and the Internet were established through MCI Mail and the Corporation for the National Research Initiative.[110]

On February 28, 1990, ARPANET was formally decommissioned and the remaining hardware was dismantled, Dr Vinton Cerf in his 'Requiem for Arpanet' lamented:

"And so, at last, we knew its course had run,
Our faithful servant, ARPANET, was done,
It was the first, and being first, was best,

But now we lay it down to ever rest.
Now pause with me a moment, shed some tears.
For auld lang syne, for love, for years and years
of faithful service, duty done, I weep.
Lay down thy packet, now, O Friend, and sleep."[111]

The FTP protocol, enabling file transfers between remote systems, was first published as a "Request for Comments", RFC 114 (a collection of technical and organisational notes about the Internet) on April 16, 1971. Since it's inception FTP has been the standard protocol used to transfer files between remote computers. RFC 959, File Transfer Protocol (FTP), was published in October 1985 with revisions and additions and became the base specification for FTP. Since that time a number of other standards have been published that define other extensions such as better security measures. This set of standards is still what is used today.[112]

In 1989, Peter Deutsch, Alan Emtage, Bill Heelan and Mike Parker from the McGill University in Montreal created Archie, which was a selective index of files that were considered important and interesting by those who submitted them and of the ftp servers that hosted them. Archie was a huge index hosted on one computer. It had three components—the data gatherer, the index merger and the query protocol. Bunyip Information Systems depended only on licensed and reliable Archie server operators across the world to run a data gatherer that indexed local files by searching each local site.[113] These local gatherers passed the partial index upstream and they merged into a full index that had a single-level alphabet sorting. This process increased the speed and minimised the bandwidth required. It was also possible to for clients to query the full index to identify the FTP server that contained the requested file.

In 1991,[114] Paul Lindner and Mark P. McCahill from the University of Minnesota introduced Gopher a search engine and navigation system that could search in pure text only. Gopher was developed as a protocol for viewing remote files on local computers. The Gopher browser allowed viewers to click and read other pages outside the current page whenever there was a reference required. To overcome certain limitations in Gopher's central search facility a central search aid facility for Gopher files was created in November 1992 by Fred Barrie and Stephen Foster of the University of Nevada System Computing Services Group. This was named Veronica[115] which was an acronym for Very Easy, Rodent-Oriented, Net-Wide Index to Computerised Archive. This software could search the Internet to collect and index information using robots and was the forerunner of today's search engines.

In 1993, the Jughead software an acronym for Jonzy's Universal Gopher Hierarchy Excavation and Display was created by Rhett 'Jonzy' Jones at the University of Utah computer center. This software was an improvement over Veronica as it could use keywords and Boolean search and thus refine the search. The next landmark in the history of internet navigation tool was the Wide area information server, or (WAIS) which was capable of searching documents on the Internet based on strings of words given to the query by searching the word indices and returning a list of documents that it estimated to be of relevant importance to the user. WAIS did not index the entire database but upto 600 databases globally. It was used by Dow Jones amongst others to create a fully indexed online file of its publications. WAIS built upon known information retrieval methods and standards like the Z39.50, search and retrieve standard. It was developed between 1989 and 1992 at Thinking Machines Corporation by a team led by Brewster Kahle.[116]

Tim Berners-Lee and Robert Cailliau, while working at CERN (the European Organisation for Nuclear Research), made proposals for hypertext systems. In 1990, they joined forces and wrote a joint proposal in which the term "World Wide Web" was used for the first time (originally without spaces). And in late 1990 and early 1991, Tim Berners Lee wrote the first web browser. It was CERN's (Conseil European Pour La Recherche Nucleaire) contribution that the hypertext data structure on the Internet could be practically implemented on the Internet and the World Wide Web, or WWW was born on May 17, 1991.[117] The WWW was made available to the public in 1992.[118] The Web structure, which is hypertext, was conceived as 'associative indexing' by Vannevar Bush in a famous article entitled 'As We May Think'.[119]

Many of the concepts that form the bases of the Web, existed in Gopher as well, but the Web was more advanced in its interface features and was designed explicitly for linking information across sites which were written in a common language called the Hypertext markup langauge, or HTML. With the release of the Mosaic browser, the first browser with a graphical user interface in 1993 for the PC and Apple environments by the National Center for Supercomputing Applications (NCSA) at the University of Illinois, Urban-Champaign and later its commercial counterparts the Netscape's Navigator and Microsoft's Internet Explorer, viewing HTML formatted documents and images on the net became possible and more appealing to users than Gopher's text-oriented system. It had an immediate effect on the widespread adoption of the Web by the non-research community. Marc Andreessen one of the developers for Mosaic, later became a co-founder of Netscape. Mosaic was released in 1993 by the National Center of Supercomputing Applications. Matthew Gray of the MIT, created the World Wide Web Wanderer[120] to count Web servers and create a database, Wandex, of their URLs.

5.1.3 Arrival of Internet to India

Internet access was initiated in India in November 1986 through the Education and Research Network (ERNET), with assistance from the Government of India and the United Nations Development Programme (UNDP). Eight institutions were involved: the five Indian Institutes of Technology (IIT), the Indian Institute of Science (IISC) in Bangalore, the National Centre for Software Technology (CST) in Bombay and the Department of Electronics (DOE) in Delhi.[121] The project ERNET was started in the Seventh five year plan (1985–1990), when computer networking was identified as a thrust area by the Department of Electronics. The initial plan was to set up a computer network for leading academic and research institutions. ERNet started as a low-bandwidth, unreliable, shell and UUCP based Internet service under Dr S. Ramakrishnan as its Director and grew to become the first project to be able to provide full TCP-IP access to dial up modem customers through accounts. The ERNET project brought Internet through VSAT technology to the country in 1995. This was followed by an upgrade to a nationwide V-SAT network and high-reliability services by 1996. NICNet was designed to provide V-SAT and dial-up Internet access primarily to Government departments under Dr Sheshagri as its first Director. Initially it could provide only shell access, at 2400 BPS and then started high speed TCP-IP access through 64 Kbps V-SAT links. ERNet and NICNet are considered India's first ISPs.

Three other internal service providers SOFTNET by Software technology park (STP), National Information Center (NICNET) and Gateway Internet Access Services (GIAS) were also soon available.[122]

The Software Technology Parks of India (STPI) Internet service was a service that was permitted only for the software exporters falling under the STP scheme of the DoE. STPI has been providing high-end Internet services through leased lines and dial-up links through its respective SoftNET networks in Bangalore, Hyderabad and NOIDA.[123]

On 15th August, 1995, VSNL launched the Gateway Internet Access Service, for providing public Internet access. Initially, DoT allowed VSNL the license to operate this service only in the 4 metros. According to the VSNL charter, VSNL can only provide international telecom gateways, not end-user services. Hence the name "Gateway Service" was used so that it could provided direct service as well. VSNL started initially in the four metro cities with dial-up and PPP access. For the first four years, VSNL was the sole provider of Internet Services in the country.

On October 7, 1998, the Government ended VSNL's monopoly and allowed provisioning of Internet Services by Private Operators. The terms and conditions of the ISP's License were unusually liberal with no License Fee and allowed unlimited number of players. ISPs could set their own tariffs and even their own International Gateways.[124]

By September 1996, India had more than 100,000 Internet users of which 70,000 were ERNET users, 15,000 SOFTNET users, 2,000 NICNET users and 8,000 users of GIAS. The education and research community had maximum penetration with 65 per cent followed by business users of 25 per cent and other users of 10 per cent in the government and private household.[125]

By 1999, there were already 132 Internet service providers regsitered with the government.The cost of using the Internet had dropped by half and the number of users doubled to 300,000 from 150,000 in the previous year.[126]

In 2001, there were 1.12 million Internet subscribers that was up by 215 per cent from the previous year.[127] By September, 2006 Internet users in India had reached 37 million up from 33 million in March 2006.[128] This figure has grown dramatically to 71 million in March 2010 which is a growth of 42 per cent from the previous year.[129]

5.1.4 Evolution and History of Internet Newspapers

The need for experiments with publishing newspapers electronically arose when the stagnation was felt in the various mature media markets of the west.[130] In countries with high newspaper penetration, the newspaper as a product was mature and in the long run on the decline due to a shrinking base. This was because they were not able to attract sufficient new and young readers to compensate for the natural reduction in the older audience.

Moreover, they had also started losing their market share to other multimedia advertising markets.[131] A study based in Britain carried out to determine the present state and the future of the British newspaper on the World Wide Web showed that newspapers, to a certain extent, are still using their hard copy content for the Web. However, online newspapers are making some advances by maximising their content and by developing discussion forums and feedback mechanisms but the conclusion was that newspapers needed a fast makeover to overcome the competition from the web.[132]

The growing use of Internet amongst the new generation reinforced that threat by creating an easy market for competitors with new online products. However, online newspapers also suffer from financing problems as well as the continued preference of many readers to have the printed version of the newspaper rather than the web version.[133]

On the Internet news market, newspaper publishers face competition from established media companies as well as new Internet startup portals. These companies could be domestic or international. Most of these would be providing information for free. The same or similar companies may also use this technology to create electronic markets in the classified sections bringing in more competition. Newspaper publishers thus get threatened in both their core business of sale of news and the sales of reach or access to audiences.

On the other hand, Internet empowers newspaper publishers to innovate their products and target new audiences. They can use the same medium that threatens them to reach new and young audiences. They can also use it to strengthen their ties with the existing audience by offering new services like breaking news or classified advertisement sites, collect reader information and establish a two-way communication channel.[134] They can furthermore expand their market by serving foreign customers cost effectively.[135]

Some researchers feel that the Internet requires that newspaper publishers should change their business models completely. According to them the media-logic now demands that news sources be more interactive, immediate, personalised and multimedia oriented. Online editions will now make this content available in realtime[136] and package the text with multimedia elements like video and audio.[137]

Electronic newspapers have been available since the early 1970's using Videotexts.[138] On May 17, 1991, CERN (Conseil European Pour La Recherche Nucleaire) released the World Wide Web standard by Tim Berners-Lee and it merged the techniques of networked information and hypertext. In May 1992, the Chicago Tribune in the United States[139] launched the first newspaper service Chicago online on America Online.

Since the emergence of the Internet, many newspapers have arrived on the World Wide Web. These newspapers are going online with an intention[140] of reaching a larger audience, greater income generation through advertising, as a means of publicity for their print products, to protect their monopoly as a distributor of news, to have an advantage over their competitors, and to stay ahead in terms of technological development.

Internet newspapers are special as they are able to update content more than once a day and add several multimedia features to the text. These online versions are not necessarily designed any more to be mirror images of their print versions instead they are supposed to offer something extra, such as interactive features or information that could not fit in print versions to target local readers.[141] The early versions faced a lot of criticism,[142] but today they are known for their sophistication and attractiveness in delivery and presentation. The difference between print and Internet newspapers is that the former is restricted to a geographical area and distributes the same information to one and all in a given set, however, in the case of Internet newspapers, this is possible, but along with that customisation of news, addition of audio-visual content, interactivity, archival links and links to other resources or interpersonal communication and distribution across the globe can also be very easily made possible, thereby reducing the barriers of entry and creating sub-markets and niche markets. The major difference between print and online editions of a newspaper is the delivery system. A study on German online newspapers found that seventy-five per cent editors-in-chief favored shortened articles, because readers gathered the information by reading just a little, thirty four per cent desired an abbreviated "news item" style, twenty nine per cent wanted the article to be linked and only eighth per cent saw no need for revision from the print version, further articles were revised "seldom", or "never" in almost two-thirds of German online newspapers.[143] According to the study of Peng et al. (1999)[144] half of the US online newspapers updated their online edition only once a day. Further 43 per cent of the US online newspapers differed in their online version from the printed version either by giving an expanded indepth coverage or limiting the number and length of stories displayed. The attitude of the bureau is also relevant in the design and delivery of an online newspaper.

The cost of delivery of Internet newspapers is also far less than that of the print version. The other advantage of online newspapers is that they are less bulky, can be stored much longer and can be easily archived for future searches and content can be updated several times in a day.

Notionally, it is possible for any person or organisation to become a publisher on the Internet. It is now an avenue for unheard voices to be heard. For example, there was an Internet campaign by Chinese students and academicians demanding justice for the Chinese- Indonesian women raped during the May 13–15, 1998 riots in Jakarta;[145] or publishing news of corruption in India's defense procurement by Tehelka.com through indepth investigations.[146] But, it has also been established, that organisations and media companies that have reporters, news bureaus, and writers and have a brand image enjoy a greater advantage from being online.

Moreover, these bodies can take larger risks as they have other sources of steady income and can thus afford to be online without worrying about advertising revenue.[147] Web sites produced by larger newspapers perform better in terms of structure, content, presentation and interactive features[148] and the borderless nature of the Internet changes the characteristics of their readership, they are able to reach additional and new audiences both national or international who do not read their print editions.[149]

The previously quoted study of German online newspapers shows that almost one quarter (22 per cent) of the users of online newspapers were residing outside of Germany, half of these in the USA or Canada (12 per cent). For these people, online newspapers are often the only means of obtaining up-to-date information about what is happening in their home country.[150]

The trend for publishing on the Internet caught on fast and by 1992 itself; NAA reported that 11 newspapers had an online presence in the US and in Canada.[151]

In the year 1993 several important newspapers and magazines made their online debut. The *Forbes Magazine* launched its online version in June 1993 and *Times online* was launched in September 1993.[152] In September 1993, book publisher O'Reilly also launched *Global Network Navigator*, a popular web magazine.[153] In 1993, a collaboration between the Atlanta Journal-Constitution and Prodigy services company of the Cox Newspaper led to the launch of the *Access Atlanta.*[154] This site contained a variety of news and advertisements and soon became very popular.

In Spain, a Spanish language daily newspaper from Barcelona, *El Periódico de Catalunya* offered its content through *Servicom*, the first consumer online service in Spain launched publicly on November 8, 1993.[155] Of all the Internet newspapers launched in 1993, the most innovative was from the local paper of San Jose, *California-The San Jose Mercury news*. It was the first Internet newspaper to offer a news archive, an electronic bulletin board for readers to communicate between themselves and with the staff as well as a personalised news service.

By 1994, there were more than 3 million hosts on the Internet. Editor and Publisher reported that there were about 20 newspapers existing worldwide.[156] On January 19, 1994, the *Palo Alto Weekly* in California that regularly published on the web, began bi-weekly postings of its full content and made it available for free and around the same time *Raleigh News* and *Observer* started a bulletin board system on the Internet aimed at public-school children called *Nandoland*.[157] Salt Lake Tribune also opened a Bulletin Board System called *Utah online*.

In Singapore, *The Strait Times* installed an ISDN link from newspapers to advertising agencies.[158] On June 9, 1994, *The New York Times* launched *@times on America Online* (AOL)[159] which was a global internet company and the content was mostly arts coverage, and was quite interactive. However, it was widely criticised. By July, Raleigh News and Observer went to the net launching *Nando Times* and the *SportsServer*, both Web-based news services.[160]

The Casper, Wyoming and Star-Tribune in the United States launched a web-based newspaper called *Electronic Signpost* in April 1994.[161] The weekly magazine *El Temps* began offering its content on *Servicom*. *Times Mirror*, *Los Angeles Times* and *New York Newsday* launched their online editions on *Prodigy*. In November, when a Guild struck work and shut down *San Francisco's* daily newspapers, the strikers and management created rival dailies on the Web, the *Free Press* and the *Gate*.[162] *The Seattle Times* announced a BBS—based electronic newspaper. The *Washington Post* offered an online service called *Washington Post online* in 1994, whose format, look and feel were very similar to its print version.[163]

In Europe, BBC launched its Internet service on April 13, 1994.[164] The online edition of the British *The Daily Telegraph* produced its first web edition in 1994.[165] *The Irish Times* also launched its website in 1994.[166] In Spain, *El Mundo* started an edition on the Internet in October 1994 with two of its weekly supplements from the newspaper.[167] In Luxembourg, *Europe Online* came into being by the initiative of three European publishers.

In February 1995, *St. Petersburg Times* was launched on the web. In March of 1995, *Chicago Tribune* launched its first website as a classified advertising service called *Career Finder*. CERN in Switzerland held a two-day web seminar for reporters in 1995, which was attended by almost 250 European Media. In Spain *Avui* from Barcelona written in *Catalan* became the first Spanish daily to publish on the Internet.

After the Oklahoma City Bombing, the potential of online-journalism was observed on April 19, 1995, when the world turned to the Internet for current information on the incident. Web sources included statements from the Government, photos of the damage, victim lists and regular updated reports. Die Welt in Germany was launched on the web in May 1995 and Yomiuri Shimbum and Asahi Shimbum in Japan in June and August respectively.[168] In Israel, *The Jerusalem Post* launched its web version in 1995.[169] By May 1995, more than 150 newspapers had online editions.[170] In the same year *La Vanguardia* a Barcelona daily written in Spanish from Spain launched its Web edition *La Vanguardia Electronica de Barcelona* in June followed by *El Diario Vasco,* a weekly edition of the daily in August.[171] By the end of the year in Asia, *The China Daily*, *Utusan Malaysia*, *Kompass of Indonesia* and *Asahi Shimbum of Japan* were all available on the net. The statistics of online newspapers in 1995 showed 208 in the US, 56 in Europe, 16 in Latin and South America, 16 in Canada, 11 in Asia, 5 in Australia/New Zealand, 2 in Africa and 1 in the Middle East.[172] According to certain researchers like Beamish[173], Carveth et al.[174] Garrison[175] and Molina[176] the period from 1995 was crucial as newspapers started opting for Internet as their medium of choice for delivery of digital news content.

On August 24,1995, Singapore's *New Strait Times* reported that several Asian newspapers like the *Singapore Business Times*, *Melbourne Age* and *Sydney Morning Herald* were available on the web indicating that Asian newspapers had also joined the race. In January 1996, the *New York Times* opened on the web with a requirement for registration. However, it was made free for residents of the US. In March the *Washington Times* and the *Chicago Tribune* both started their full-newspaper website. *Le Monde*, France's largest daily launched its website in 1996 and in May of the same year, *Wall Street Journal* launched its interactive edition which was a pay site.

In July, Microsoft and NBC in the US partnered and launched a cable TV channel and online news service called MSNBC and in October the Associated Press launched AP online, a wire service to provide content to online newspapers. In April 1996, the National Newspaper Association reported that 175 North American dailies had online presence and 775 globally.[177] By the next year the number rose to 820 in the US and 1600 globally. By mid 2003 a review of three online newspaper directories—*American Journalism Review*, *NewsLink* and *NewsDirectory.com* stated the population of daily online US newspapers as 1,279.

In 1997, *BBC news* launched its Web news site *news.bbc.co.uk* in the UK. In E and P's Interactive Newspapers '99 conference, it was reported that 25 per cent of US Newspaper web sites were profitable. *The Washington Post, New York Daily news* and *South China Morning Post in Hong Kong* all started their web editions in June, October and December of 1996 respectively. It was reported that approximately 230 North American newspapers had Internet sites, or dial-up services. By 1997 the number of newspapers with websites rose to approximately 2600 as reported by Editor and Publisher and to 3250 by 1998.

Also according to the Carlson's, 'The online timetable'[178] and Shedden's 'New media timetable'[179], between 19 and 43 per cent journalists were using search engines like Yahoo, Altavista and Netscape very regularly for their work and only 15 per cent were still not accessing search engines.

The number of US dailies that were publishing online in 1995 was 175 and that rose to 750 by 1998.[180]

In 2000, Oh Yeon Ho founded *OhmyNews* in Seoul, South Korea. During the country's election, the free online news service registered 20 million page views per day in a country of 40 million. In July of 2003, The Manchester based *Guardian Unlimited* in the UK claimed to offer a subscription service for ad-free content and in March 2004, it had 7.5 million unique visitors, of which more than two-third viewers were non-residents of the UK.[181]

The Iraq war of 2003 propelled the popularity of online news, 56 per cent of all online users had accessed news of the war online and 14 per cent or one in seven Internet users had said that they were going online more to get news on the war.[182]

According to the World Association of Newspapers report in the Asian Media (2006), the global readership for online newspapers rose by almost 9 per cent in 2005 and by more than 200 per cent since 2001.

5.1.5 Online Journalism in India

The history of online journalism in India is also over ten years old. *The Hindu* of Chennai is the first Indian newspaper that launched an Internet edition, in 1995. The digital edition of the *The Hindu* has the same format as its printed version. Thus all reports, graphics, pictures, advertisements are similar to its print counterpart and the importance, relevance of news and its positioning are maintained in the same way. Three editions of the newspaper–Chennai, Hyderabad, and Delhi–are available in digital form for viewing at 6 am, Indian Standard Time (IST) every day. A search engine is provided for easy search along with a facility for news tracking. Further a weekly issue of the digital *Hindu* is available in archive mode on the website. It also provides links to the group's other newspapers and magazines like the *Business Line*, *Sportstar* and *Frontline.*[183]

The Gateway Internet Access Service was launched on 15th August 1995, by VSNL for providing public Internet access in India. *The Hindu* launched its online edition in the same month, followed by Rediff.com, a news portal which does not have a print form, in February 1996. *Udayavani* started their e-edition on April 8, 1996. *The Indian Express* pubished its first online edition on July 8, 1996, followed by *The Economic Times* on July 23. In December of the same year, the Hindusthan Times launched its online edition.

Times of India launched its web edition in January 1997, followed by the launch of *The Telegraph* on February 6, 1997.[184] On February 17, 1997, *Dainik Jagaran* was launched on the Internet followed by the *Kesari* and *The Business Standard* in August. In October, *Nava Bharat* launched its e-paper followed by *Malayala Manorama* on November 17. On January 14, 1998, *Dinakaran* was launched, followed by *Lokmat* on July 02 and *The Tribune* on July 31.

By 1998, there were at least 48 newspapers in India that had launched their Internet editions which was less than one per cent of the total 4719 dailies registered with the Registrar of Newspapers of India as of December 1997. In a research conducted on comparing the language-wise break-up in numbers of Indian online newspapers with their print counterparts, with data upto December 1997, it was found that there were 19 online papers in English against 338 print newspapers, 5 in Hindi against 2,118, 5 Malayalam e-papers against 209 printed ones, 4 in Gujrati against 99 printed newspapers, 3 in Bengali against 93 print dailes, 3 in Kannada against 279 printed newspapers, 3 in Tamil against

341 printed dailies, 3 also in Telugu against 126 dailes, 2 in Urdu against 495 printed dailies and 1 in Marathi against 283 printed ones.

The Daily Pioneer, The New Indian Express, The Belgaum Tarun Bharat, the Dinamani and the *Tarun Bharat* from Nagpur were all launched on the net in 1999. In 2000, on January 26, *Sakal* launched their online edition, followed by the launch of *Maharashtra Times* in March. On May day, *Pudhari* was launched online followed by *Ananda Bazar Patrika* on May 6, 2000. *Navabharat Times*, *Trinabhoomi* and *The News Today* also launched their e-newspapers in the same year. *Amar Ujala* started its online edition in 2001 along with *Rashtriya Sahara*. In October 2003, *Punjab Kesari* was launched and in March 2004, *Hindusthan* was launched on the web.[185]

Just as the Iraq War and the Oklahoma bombing in the US had initiated a quantum leap in the popularity of online journalism in the US for regular updates, live feeds, video reports and citizen interactions, in India amongst other reasons the investigative journalism conducted by Tehelka in 2000 helped in the rise of the popularity of online journalism.

Today, there are Indian websites like the *Indiapress.org*[186], which provide free online newspaper links to all Indian language newspapers and also World newspapers. There are online newspapers in several languages like English, Bengali, Assamese, Gujarati, Hindi, Kannada, Konkani, Malayalam, Marathi, Oriya, Punjabi, Tamil, Telegu and Urdu.

Online newspapers had started off as 'little more than static boards displaying weather, tourist and civic information, or telephone numbers of editiors at the newspaper' according to Noack (1997)[187] but by 2003 it was observed by Outing, that the Iraq war news coverage was 'Web-centric, well-planned, compelling multimedia content (with) breaking–news headlines and video delivered at nearly the speed of television-(at least for broadband users).[188]

5.1.6 Arrival of Television to India

Television arrived in India in 1959 on a restricted scale with the help of the United Nations Educational Scientific and Cultural Organisation (UNESCO), the USA, West Germany, Yugoslavia and Japan. These countries along with UNESCO helped India establish, extend and program its television network. The first Indian TV station was inaugurated in New Delhi on September 15, 1959. The service was operated by the *All India Radio*. The programs were telecast, twice a week for one hour each, covering a distance of 25 km. The objectve of this experiment initially was to study the use of TV as a medium of education, rural upliftment and community development. But pressure from the urban elite began to increase. By 1965, it was converted to a regular daily service. Simultaneously, entertainment elements began to predominate along with feature films, light music and plays. By 1970, the duration of the telecast was increased to three hours.

This success prompted the setting up of the second centre in Bombay in 1972 and within three years five more centres in Srinagar (1973), Amritsar (1973), Calcutta, Madras and Lucknow (all in 1975) were set up. Additionally relay centres were set up in Mussorie from Delhi and in Pune linked to Bombay. All these seven centres began telecasting programes of entertainment, including commercial feature films, song clips of films, news, sports and plays. Advertisement was introduced from 1976.

In 1975, India initiated its SITE programme (Satellite Intructional Television Experiment programme) using the US-loaned satellite. This experiment was the first of its kind in the world. It linked 3000 villages in six Indian states and beamed television progammes for four hours everyday. This experiment emphatically underlined the potentials of the medium as an aid to development.

After this, the scene of TV changed completely by the 80's and more and more homes started installing TV sets with low power transmitters. The ASIAD games that was held in New Delhi 1982, ushered in a new era for Indian TV wih the introduction of colour. Doordarshan took a big leap forward with an unprecedented expansion scheme. In 1984 alone 126 relay transmitters were set up.

Introduction to satellite technology and its use by Doordarshan was a major step in its rapid growth. Since 1982, Doordarshan also started transmitting daily the national progamme from Delhi. To cater to the local interests and languages, *Doordarshan* started its INSAT service in six states—Andhra Pradsh, Orissa, Maharashtra, Gujarat, Bihar and Uttar Pradesh. Doordarshan introduced the second channel of transmission in Delhi from September 1984, followed by commissioning of the second channels in Bombay, Calcutta and Madras.

Gradually, this medium transformed from a medium of education to a medium of primarily entertainment and viewers started demanding greater variety. In 1991, the first Gulf war started and CNN which had a satellite based telecasting service started beaming live pictures of the war to individual homes. This was the beginning of the arrival of satellite TV to Indian homes. At that time people had to use the services of a cable operator for a fee to find access to these new TV channels. This facility was expensive initally and therefore restricted to urban localities. Gradually with the economies of scale it became more affordable and spread to smaller towns and even villages. Other popular channels in those days were STAR-TV, BBC and Pakisthan TV.

Today, the scene has changed even further, with Satellites beaming directly into the dish antennas at homes bypassing the cable system. In India there are hundreds of channels catering to a wide variety of programmes in different languages—news, films, music, religious, entertainment, sports, mixed. The list is endless. Huge revenues are earned by these companies through advertisements. There is immense competition to catch the interest of the viewers and this media has exceeded all imagination in terms of its present volume, growth rate, popularity and affordability.

5.1.7 Empirical Research

The literature survey has been done on perceptions and uses of news to understand why and how audiences seek and consume media content, including news. The various credibility parameters of different kinds of news media and different credibility measures used have also been explored. When a new medium emerges some displacement in terms of functions, usage, dependability and utility are observed. The present researcher has tried to search relevant studies in these areas.

5.1.7.1 Perception of News

All audiences are not the same and therefore they use[189] and respond to media in a manner, which is influenced by their social and psychological background. Audiences seek and consume media content including news for various reasons. They are active, know the media content and also which media to use to meet their requirement.[190] Almost any perception of media unequivocally asserts as its central maxim the idea of an active, rational, goal-seeking audience[191]. In the Internet environment, users are more actively engaged communication participants, compared to other print and electronic media.[192]

Audiences consciously and rationally choose a certain media over others, based on their needs and thus there is competition in making media choices to satisfy individual needs[193]. Further, the media compete with other information sources for audience's need satisfaction.[194] Print and electronic mass media and new media continue to provide people with a wide range of media platforms and content and therefore it is necessary to investigate why audiences choose to be exposed to different media channels.[195]

There are different kinds of audience with different kinds of needs and media preferences and have varied reasons for using a certain media instead of others. Gratifications are utilities that can explain choice of media by its users.[196] Perceptions and past experiences regarding utility in a particular situation,[197] exposure as well as social and cultural contexts.[198] Media-centric theory places a lot of emphasis on cultural influence on users choice.[199] Media is also used by individuals for satisfying their need for self esteem, social utility functions from a need for social affiliation and escape function to release tension,[200] and all of this all play an important role in media selection.

The audience based on their interest,cognitive, affective and social needs select and find information and content in various ways. This is suuported by studies on TV and newspapers.[201] The more an audience is interested in a news item from a certain media the more will be his retention of that news.[202] The expectations and satiation of those obtained from media are dependent upon media effects like knowledge, dependency, attitudes, perceptions of social reality, agenda setting, discussions and politics.[203] The news audience wants their news to inform, explain, persuade, interpret and entertain and thus media has to provide the news narrative.[204]

Audience also choose media based on the various needs that are met by the media or based on individual social and psychological requirements.[205] Information needs are not primary needs but basic needs that can be defined as physiological, cognitive or affective.[206] The rise of a particular need is influenced by the context, which can be the person per se, or the role the person plays in work and life, or the environments like social, political, economical and technological.[207]

Further, psychological characterisitics and demographic attributes, also play a role in creating media preferences.[208] The audience can have two orientations towards news—an instrumental orientation, or a ritualised orientation.[209] When it is associated with an instrumental tendency it reflects a media-use process that is motivated by more specific cognitive needs and goals like excitement to find new news or entertainment and requires more involvement and affinity towards the medium. Whereas, audience activity related to a ritualised orientation implies a media use process that is motivated more by habit and satisifies more diffusive and affective or emotional needs and goals. In such cases there is less selectivity[210] or intentionality in the minds of the audience.[211]

Media use patterns after adoption of a new communication techology is also dependent on the uses and satisfaction of needs that it brings to its user.[212] Moreover, within the communication channels using new technology, there is competion. TV for instance is more likely to replace other activities in children's time use but demographic factors play a role.[213] Channels having similar content and satisfying similar communication needs but having greater utility are more likely to replace alternatives with fewer utilities.

5.1.7.2 Uses of Media

There are several angles related to news use.Newspapers are judged mainly as a learning resource that can satisfy informational needs in the larger context and not in specified personal affective contexts.[214] Newspapers are perceived as being able to satisfy specific needs like understanding, knowledge and credibility associated with information gathering but not emotional needs like beating loneliness.[215] Another utility provided by newspapers is surveillance of the environment needs.[216] Besides, the above people rely and read newspapers more for interpersonal discussion related to political information and public affairs.[217]

The news consuming audience view telelvision news and print newspapers similarly in terms of their motives such as parasocial interaction,[218] ability to satisfy their interpersonal communication utility and surveillance needs,[219] entertainment needs, information needs.[220]

There is also a diversion aspect of news consumption, where the motive could be entertainment, passing time and information gathering.[221] Apart from surveillance need satisfaction and entertainment, escapism is also an important factor[222] and habit strength is the most consistent predictor of news consumption.[223]

The reasons and motives between Internet news surfing and TV viewing are also very similar.[224] Providing entertainment and information are two important functions of the Internet medium.[225] However, Internet news is viewed more as a source of entertainment.[226]

Internet as a medium has three attributes of data not commonly associated with traditional media: interactivity, demassification, and asynchroneity.[227]

Interactivity is the most special feature of the medium and strengthens the concept of uses. Interactivity is "the degree to which participants in the communication process have control over, and can exchange roles in their mutual discourse".[228]

Demassification is the ability of the user to select from a wide variety. Of choices with greater control over the medium that likens the new media to face-to-face interpersonal communication.[229] This technology makes it possible to tailor pick certain portions from a large selection, which was previously available on a shared mass media platform[230]. According to some scholars, the most useful basis of inquiry for interactivity would be one grounded in responsiveness where interactivity means three pertinent levels: Two-way (non-interactive) communication, reactive (or quasi-interactive) communication, and fully interactive communication,[231] such that the value of a focus on interactivity is that the concept cuts across the mass versus interpersonal distinctions usually made in the fields of inquiry. It is also helpful to consider interactivity to be variable in nature, increasing or decreasing with the particular Internet service in question. The interesting observation by Chamberlain[232] in this regard is that in future mass messages will lose their preferred status to individual, one-on-one dialogue mode.

Asynchroneity of a medium is the ability of the user to manipulate its use as per convenience. In the case of e-mails, asynchroneity enables people to send, receive, save or retrieve messages at his or her convenience.[233] In the case of TV, ansynchroneity would allow the user to record a program and view it later and in the case of print newspapers it is the ability to carry and read it anywhere and at anytime. Similarly, the Internet news can be read in an updated way anytime of the day.

5.1.7.3 Credibility Perception of Media

Information obtained via the Internet is abundant, easily available and also comprehensive and it differs from news and information from other media sources in this. Moreover, this is still a new media and so several people are presently experimenting with strategies. One of the outcome of this is that the Internet can become a source of inaccurate, biased or misleading news. In addition to Internet becoming a popular information and news source, issues of the credibility of these news have also risen.

The information freedom that is enjoyed by the Internet is not enjoyed by any other medium as they all undergo certain levels of factual verification, analysis of content, and editorial scrutiny. One way in which media users learn to distinguish among various sources of news is by experiencing and using them. Over time, people become familiar with the media, its delivery mode and also its credibility and develop their own perceptions that affect future use. In the case of traditional news media, users identify the genre of the medium to interpret information, its credibility, sensationalism and objectivity, which guides the users interpretation of the content.

Editorial processes provide a certain level of security to the veracity of news through mass media sources. Moreover, the use of multiple media sources for obtaining news, helps in rating the standards of reporting, fact-checking and judging the reliability of the medium and source.

The early public perception of the precision and accuracy of computers led to a common belief of their being reliable and dependable. Computer users tend and want to trust their systems, based on—presumption, reputation, surface inspection and first hand experience, but the trust is often lost and damaged when the system fails.[234]

Familiarity of use has an impact on the credibility perception of a medium.[235] People, who have had some experience in using Internet technology find print and electronic media to be less interactive than computer communication in the case of news. This may not be able to predict mass media credibility in general, but does positively influence the perception when interactivity is treated as a feedback mechanism.[236]

Information can be uploaded by anyone in the Internet. Therefore the authenticity of the news or information can be an issue and could ultimately affect the credibility of the medium; however, Internet information is perceived to be as credible as television, radio and magazines but not newspapers.[237] Internet has also been found to have similarities with telephone, newspapers, TV, books and magazines based on its functions of information retrieval, information giving and conversation abilities. However, it is its ability to deliver updated news more often that could set it apart from the other communication media.[238]

Regardless of Internet exposure, users rate the credibility of the Internet very similarly to that of TV and newspapers and that perception is influenced by their own experience, media coverage and personal narrations which may be different. The spread and diffusion of Internet as a medium is also positively affected by its credibility.[239]

In some cases, online news media, print and electronic news media are all perceived as somewhat credible in terms of believe ability,[240] fairness, accuracy and being in-depth, but online media is found to be more credible.[241] People find similarity in their credibility perception of print newspapers and TV news but find online news credibility to be different from them.[242] Newspapers are judged more credible than online news or TV news and online news is ranked more credible than

TV, when credibility perceptions are influenced by media use and interpersonal discussion of news.[243]

Journalists rate Internet news and information as moderately credible overall but online newspaper journalists rate Internet news information as significantly more credible than the print journalists and Internet reliance is a strong positive predictor, where as an adversarial or competiveness between the two roles is a negative predictor of credibility, across all demographic characterisitcs.[244] Amongst the audience in India reading news on the Internet is complementary to reading news from the newspaper and the likeliness to read news on the Internet is positively correlated with longer years and hours of Internet usage.[245]

Research on credibility of print and electronic media versus Internet information has produced inconsistent findings. A study on the delivery of political messages via the Internet versus more traditional sources found the Internet users judged online political information sources as more credible than their traditional counterparts. However, the study included only users of Internet and moreover the credibility ratings of all media were low.[246] Another study on Internet users found that news sources were not judged as significantly more credible than traditional sources.[247] Only a few people agreed that online news was more credible. Contrary to these, a study found that print and electronic media sources were fairer and more unbiased than the Internet counterparts for political information.[248] Thus previous studies have not demonstrated any clear pattern and it would be necessary to study this in the Indian context.

5.1.7.4 Credibility Components of Media

Credibility of a medium has several components. Trustworthiness[249] of a medium is a traditional component of credibility. If readers or viewers feel that the information that is being provided by the media of their choice is incorrect then overtime the audience will begin to discard the media. Flanagin and Metzger[250] observed that while newspapers, books, and television undergo a process of information verification before they reach the public, Internet sites do not always use such measures.[251] However, it remains one of the most important qualities for a user. In a study conducted in Texas,[252] to assess people's attitudes toward the three media channels it was found that users are generally skeptical of the news from all media, but find newspapers the most credible, followed by online news and lastly television.

Fairness, unbiased ness, accuracy and trustworthiness[253] are other important credibility factors. News needs to be unbiased and representative. Reporting needs to be fair, accurate and true. The job of the mass media is to report and not create opinions based on intentional misrepresentation of news. That is why people associate readership of a particular newspaper with the person's political alignment. Being branded as biased is not good for news media. Once branded it may find favour amongst the section towards which it is biased but will be rejected by the remaining section of the society. There is a distinct correlation between the use of print and electronic media and its perceptions.[254]

Authenticity,[255] which is a combination of trustworthiness and expertness, is another quality expected by users of a media. These two qualities can also be treated separately.[256] Earlier editorials were considered authentic pieces of information and editors often became thought leaders. This still remains in the case of some famous newspapers. However, that is not a quality that all Internet news sources can demonstrate. *Blogs*, or the *Wikipedia* available on the Internet do not contain authenticated news. Credibility of a medium is influential[257] since readers learn not only about a given issue, but also how much importance to attach to that issue from the amount of information in a news story and its position. Readers decide on the importance and significance of the news or event based on the coverage it receives.

Trustworthiness of a medium can be based on honest-dishonest, trustworthy-untrustworthy and sincere-insincere[258] and is associated with the reliability of a medium.[259] Trustworthiness is thus an important dimension[260] of credibility.

Timeliness and currency of reporting[261] an event are both positive contributors of credibility for all the three news media. News reporting is about time and relevance. If a particular incident is not reported on time then it loses its relevance and significance and a story is lost. In this day and age, readers want to have constant updates of news that interest them. This is why people are getting attracted to both TV news and Internet news. The news audience cannot wait for the next day's print newspaper to learn about the latest development. This is where Internet news has an advantage. It can update news very often. Timeliness is considered by some as an important measure of credibility for Internet news.[262]

Fairness[263] has been used as an indicator and a dimension to assess the construct of credibility.[264] Fairness has been used in other scales of measurement of credibility too, by Rimmer and Weaver[265] as well as by Meyer.[266] The scales of Gaziano and McGrath as well as by Meyer have been validated.[267] Early credibility research[268] on media communication and persuasion found that the "trustworthiness" of a source significantly affected acceptance of the message and changes in opinion. Significantly, related to trustworthiness were reactions to "fairness" of presentation and "justifiability" of the conclusions.

The reporting of a news media is expected to be fair and nonaligned. Fair reporting adds to the credibility of the medium, be it print newspapers, TV news or Internet news.[269] Hence fairness is a desirable dimension of a medium.

Another important and traditional dimension of a news media is its believability and has been used by several researchers in the past in their scales. In a study to measure perceived credibility of the message with three commonly identified items oriented toward the content of the information: accuracy, believability, and factualness, it has been suggested that the variables used to measure credibility influence perceptions.[270] Meyer used it in his scale, too.[271] These indicators were measured with Likert-type items ranging from a score of 1 (e.g., not at all believable) to a score of 5 (e.g., very believable). Believability is a factor in the credibility of a source, or medium.[272]

Balance in reporting is another important credibility dimension for news media, especially print newspapers as shown in previous research.[273]

Accuracy[274] refers to the degree to which a news item is free from errors, when the information can be verified elsewhere. Accuracy of reporting has always been an important factor in judging credibility of a news medium. It has therefore been used by several researchers.[275]

5.1.7.5 Other Theories of Media

Whenever a new media emerges, there is a concern that it might bring an impact on existing media.[276] Whether it was radio,[277] in response to a valid concern that broadcasting would mean the end of print media or television by Mendelsohn[278] and then Williams.[279] However, Belson found a positive impact of TV on existing print media[280] and Lazarsfeld found that radio did not decrease newspaper reading maybe because radio and newspaper serve different functions.

The displacement theory is based on the concept that users have a limited time available to spend on the various types of media and other activities. Therefore, the basic model of time displacement assumes a zero-sum relationship for amount of time invested in various activities.

Therefore if a new media activity is introduced into their scheduled lives, it starts taking up time from the set schedule, and there will be a corresponding reduction in the time spent with other media activities and/or non-media tasks. In a study based on time-diary data, it was found that Internet use at home has a strong negative impact on time spent with friends and family and also social activities, but Internet use at work had no such effect; similarly, Internet used over weekends indicated a displacement effect[281] and so the displacement theory was supported, but indicated that the location and timing of use mattered.

In another similar study it was found that time spent on television viewing, newspaper reading, telephone usage and family conversations were affected by online use; the study[282] concluded that there was a functional displacement of television by online media. An early study[283] had reported that the introduction of television into people's schedules reduced the amount of time they spent with most other media. Similarly, in 1981, it was reported that those who spent more time watching television spent less time with other media such as radio and non-media activities such as social visiting.[284] Further, greater use of Internet in studies[285] has also been associated with increase in loneliness and depression as well as decline in communication with family members and social circle.

Displacement effect[286] of Internet on print and electronic media has also been recently observed. A recent study[287] suggested entertainment and information are two of the functions of online media and spending time on it also negatively impacted other media and social activities. If the new media serves the same functions or provides similar facilities and uses to the users then the existing media suffers a displacement at the onset of the new medium. This theory has been supported by research.[288]

Inspite of the logical appeal of the theory, there are contradictory studies to the theory. Studies have indicated a complimentary relationship or a more-more relationship between new and print media and between new and electronic media. Complementary relationship[289] between cable television and television has been reported; additionally it has been shown that cable television actually increased television use. Similarly, evidence of a "symbiotic or supplemental relationship"[290] between computer mediated communication and print media where each seems to reinforce the use of the other has also been found.

Some researchers[291] have disputed the more-less relationship and have said that the data is biased to sell the new products. It is also not established[292] that there is the expected displacement of print and electronic media by Internet; rather there is evidence Internet users read more newspapers.[293] According to a study based in India[294] reading news on the Internet is complementary to reading news from the newspaper and the likeliness to read news on the Internet is positively correlated with longer years and hours of Internet usage.

This indicates that people who are more inclined towards gathering information gather information from all the available sources. Moreover since the formats, modes of delivery, content as well as time of reporting vary between print media, electronic media and Internet news these media do not always act as absolute competitors.

When we talk of competition between media, it is necessary to mention that the competition can arise in the area of loyalty to a medium, if a user feels that a new medium of news is being able to provide far more satisfaction than the one he has been using then the user may shift his loyalties towards the new medium. Again, if too many media choices are available with the user, then there will be competition between the media for time. The user will have to sacrifice some media to incorporate a new media habit.

In some cases people are found to alter their daily routines or sacrifice some chore to find time for a new activity–for example people addicted to the *Suduku,* or *Crossword puzzles*. Finally, we also have to consider the competition amongst media in terms of cost to the user. People will opt for the less expensive media in case he feels there is no significant difference amongst them. However, people will be willing to pay higher prices in case they feel that the medium is worth spending on.

Research[295] has shown that Internet use does not impact daily routines. That is because people are able to do their regular work more efficiently and faster using technology thus saving time. This raises questions as to whether Internet acts more to enhance communication behaviours[296] rather than displace it. Another study[297] has confirmed that using Internet can increase the efficiency and therefore even allows greater free time. Studies[298] have found that Internet users are more likely than non-users to be newspaper readers and concluded that the Internet is not the cause of the decline in use of the other media.

Further, it has also been found[299] that Internet users led more active social lives than non-users and reinforces the conclusion that working on the Internet can be rather time-enhancing. Research has also shown that people who like to do several activities simultaneously are more inclined towards using Internet even though their skill level[300] may be a barrier.

Therefore, it is clear that there is a more complex nature to the issue than that meets the eye. This leads us to the theory of niche, based on the principles of competition and coexistence that found its origin in bio-ecology[301] but has been used by researchers in the field of media studies.[302] Niche has been defined as "the function or role of a form, or population within the community".[303] In the case of media it is the competition to reach the maximum audience. Therefore, when a new media emerges it starts competing in the functional niche in trying to provide similar utility to that population.

When the new medium is able to provide functional alternatives, then the competition emerges and either of them can become irrelevant. Functional displacement would occur when the established resource is displaced by the new resource. These functional alternatives that are provided by the new medium always develop over time and are in the context of its use. Therefore it is necessary to also see whether there is a displacement effect in terms of reduction of time spent on the print and electronic media,[304] or a similar effect of the print and electronic media on the use of new media.

5.1.8 Media, Society and Culture

Media has been a cause of both wonder and alarm due to its influence since the beginning. Inspite of all the changes that the science of communication or society or media institutions have undergone the terms of debate regarding the potential social significance of media have changed very little. Three issues have always been associated with mass media. The first concern was the power of the new means of communication; the second, the question of social integration or disintegration that they may cause and the third, the question of public enlightenment which they might either increase or diminish.

The idea about the power of mass media was based on the observation of their great reach and obvious impact, especially in the cases of newspapers and television. The spread, or popularity of a media is not uniform across countries at the same time. Newspaper circulation had been highest around the early twentieth century in the USA but its popularity rose much later in Europe and other parts of the World.

The popular press has mainly earned its revenue from advertisements, sensational news stories and has often been controlled by powerful press barons. Just as we observe the great impact that media had during the First World War and the reason why print newspapers became so popular, we see a similar event—the First Gulf War catapulting the Internet as a medium of news in the west.

The power of media has also been reinforced by the events of Soviet Union and Nazi Germany, where they were used as a medium of propaganda. When mass media is used for entertainment and propaganda simultaneously then it can have very strong impact on international alliances and relations, too. Mass media have been able to generate public opinion and so have been used by companies for advertising and politicians for campaigning. Politics is, therefore, regularly conducted and reported on the assumption that if it is presented skillfully it is sure to succeed. The conditions for effective media popularity have been a national media industry capable of reaching most of the population, a degree of similarity in the messages regardless of the direction of the message and a certain measure of credibility and trust in the media on the part of the audiences.

As the pace of life changed in the late nineteenth and early twentieth century in most parts of the world due to the start of urban living and greater expansion and exposure to social activities, crime, poverty, prostitution and other social ills increased because people were in new environments where they were relatively anonymous and isolated. Further, there were a lot of uncertainties of modern life that were bothering them. While these changes were happening in the social and economic arena, these were also being reflected in newspapers, films and other forms of popular culture like music, books, magazines, etc. The perception of media due to this change started becoming negative and responsible for the declining morality amongst the population, loneliness and loss of collective beliefs of the more moral nature.

The modern and forward-looking view of the twentieth century saw a new role of media in society. This view was more positive—that the media could be a potential institution for public enlightenment, where it could supplement schooling, library and popular education. Politicians and social scientists also held this positive view and the media itself felt that it was making a positive contribution to progress by spreading information and ideas, exposing political corruption and crimes and providing harmless entertainment to the masses. Journalists began to evolve, too; they became more professional and developed their own codes of ethics and good practice.

The press has always had a democratic task—be it the radio, which has had a cultural, educational and informative mission along with the task of promoting national unity and identity, or the newspaper that has been able to reach out to all kinds of people.

With the Internet joining the media, fears and hopes are all being voiced. Internet has been feared to spread and encourage paedophilia, pornography, violence and hate and various forms of international crimes and terrorism. Moreover, the media is now trying to make greater profits in a highly competitive market place by selling more of entertainment that has more market value than education and knowledge. Ironically, these views are also being highlighted and amplified by the media, perhaps because they confirm the power of media or because they are already popularly believed and also newsworthy.

Thus media and society are entwined. People require media for their information, knowledge and entertainment needs. People use it in a manner that they find suitable, be it in opinion forming, or otherwise. The task of media remains the same-continuously presenting facts and events to the general public.

5.2 Internet and Cardiac Healthcare

5.2.1 Telemedicine

The telemedicine applications are applications, which enable the practice of medicine at a distance. Its use has increased globally since the early 1990s. Rapid technological advances, most notably the emergence of high bandwidth connections and Satellite connections for the Internet, have created new and significant opportunities for telemedicine use. There is a need to improve the efficiency and equity of health service delivery, in response to the increasing specialisation and shortage of medical professionals and centralisation of health facilities and for that telemedicine presents itself as a possible solution. Technologically advanced telemedicine applications are now used in a wide range of healthcare settings both in hospitals and general practices and medical specialties like radiology, oncology and neurology.

They enable access to specialist expertise at previously unavailable times, for example by transmitting images to computers and other devices; and from previously inaccessible locations. Telemedicine applications have the potential to reduce patient travel requirements and also other costs incurred. Emergency telemedicine applications can enhance the timeliness of treatment and care delivery. They are also being implemented in order to provide previously unavailable health services to remote areas.

5.2.2 Definitions of Telemedicine

Telemedicine may be defined as 'the use of electronic information to communicate technologies to provide and support healthcare when distance separates the participants.'[305] In this case the participants are the patient, the medical professionals—doctors, nurses and technicians of the local hospitals as well as specialists from the nodal hospital.

According to Puskin et al. (1995),[306] Telemedicine is "the use of modern telecommunications and information technologies for the provision of clinical care to individuals at a distance and the transmission of information to provide that care."

Grigsby et al. (1993)[307] defines telemedicine as "the use of telecommunications technology as a medium for providing healthcare services for persons that are at some distance from the provider".

"Telemedicine involves the use of modern information technology, especially two-way interactive audio/video communication, computers and telemetry, to deliver health services to remote patients and to facilitate information exchange between primary care physicians and specialists at some distances from each other."[308]

5.2.3 Infrastructure Requirement for Telemedicine

The use of telemedicine applications has increased[309] especially with the advancement of technology, namely, Internet and high bandwidth connections and these have significantly contributed to increasing the scope of telemedicine.[310]

Telemedicine systems consist of customised medical software integrated with computer hardware, along with medical diagnostic instruments connected to the commercial VSAT (Very Small Aperture Terminal), ISDN, or telephone lines at each location. Generally, the medical record/history of the patient is sent to the specialist doctors, who study and provide diagnosis and treatment instructions using video-conference between his and the patient's end. These systems essentially use Internet technologies for transferring data and communicating between centers. Therefore, telemedicine equipment does not need to be very sophisticated[311], expensive or high end.[312]

5.2.4 Relevance in the Indian Scenario

One of India's largest sectors is Healthcare, in terms of revenue and employment, and the sector is expanding rapidly. During the 1990s,

Indian healthcare grew at a compound annual rate of 16 per cent. Today the total value of the sector is more than $34 billion. This translates to $34 per capita, or roughly 6 per cent of GDP. By 2012, India's healthcare sector is projected to grow to nearly $40 billion.[313] In this the private sector accounts for over 80 per cent of total healthcare spending in India and the chances of significantly higher public health spending is unlikely as there are deficits both in the central and state budgets.

One reason for this boom in the market is the rapidly rising population of India and according to projections India will soon emerge as the world's most populous nation. One of the reasons for this growth is reduction in infant mortality and better healthcare facilities combined with the government's initiative to eradicate diseases like polio amongst infants and TB amongst adults.

Further, there is an emergence of a strong middle class with better education and income. Women are joining the workforce in large numbers and literacy and awareness due to various technologies, and government efforts are increasing. Therefore, people can afford better medicines and treatment and are desirous of that as well. Another reason that is pushing the healthcare market is the increase in both infectious as well as degenerative diseases. While some ailments like polio and tetanus may soon be eliminated, new ones like dengue, malaria, hepatitis are returning with stubborn resistance to different drugs. These can be attributed to sub-standard housing, inadequate water supply, poor sewage and waste management systems, ill managed public health systems as well as increased travel.

Over and above all this is, a new set of diseases termed lifestyle diseases are spreading like epidemics. These diseases like blood pressure problems, diabetes, heart related problems, bones and obesity related problems result in much higher cost per treatment. Wellness programs targeting companies and employees involved in sedentary desk jobs are becoming very rampant. Moreover, cardio-vascular diseases that are life threatening in most cases are spreading very fast, both for genetic as well as lifestyle reasons. Unfortunately, the public healthcare facilities are woefully inadequate both in numbers and quality and there is a huge gap amongst the people who have access to healthcare and those who do not. India can be split into two on this. There is one India that provides high-quality medical care to middle-class Indians and medical tourists, and the other India in which the majority of the population lives—a country whose residents have limited or no access to quality care. The sophisticated and good facilities–both in terms of infrastructure and specialists are all bundled in the urban areas. For the majority of Indians, who live in rural areas there is hardly even the basic healthcare centre and the ones that do exist, perennially lack in qualified doctors and nurses; therefore, most people are treated by quacks and under qualified people.

In a country like India, where there is such diversity and disparity amongst citizens, geographical terrain and facilities, the delivery of proper healthcare to all has not been possible. Some of the major hurdles in delivering proper healthcare have been lack of adequate infrastructure facilities in hospitals, very large population to serve most of whom reside in rural, or semi-urban areas and are affected by poverty and illiteracy, very low doctor-patient ratio and very few rural practitioners along with lack of both infrastructure facility and knowledge updating facility for medical practitioners in rural areas. Tele-medicine under these circumstances could be an effective low-cost solution[314] to provide healthcare to the under served population.

According to the Medical Council of India, the allopathic doctor-patient ratio at present is 1 per 1634.[315] The nurse-patient ratio in India is 1 per 2250.[316] Doctor-patient ratio is currently one per 500 in wealthy countries of the west[317]. Moreover, according to the 1981 census of India,[318] 73 per cent of the doctors are located in cities, that, too, mainly in metropolitan cities. As per the last census there were only 69 doctors to one lakh population in 2010 (mospi.nic.in).

In this situation, some of the obvious advantages of telemedicine from the patients perspective could be – improved access to quality and specialised healthcare, better access from underserved rural, semi-urban and remote regions, access to medical experts' services, reduced clinical travel and unnecessary patient transfers, cost effective care[319], prevention of costly health complications resulting from delayed treatment[320] and timely intervention.

Potential benefits for practitioners could be, linkages with doctors and centers of excellence-education benefits, appropriate referrals and reduced professional isolation, ability to retain their local patients, access to comprehensive patient's data–offline and online, quick and timely follow up of patients after treatment, training, retraining, educational facilities[321], and ability to cater to patients from a wide and varied geographical region or territory.

Other benefits to government and institutions from employment of telemedicine applications would be enhancement of timeliness, effectiveness and efficiency of healthcare delivery, which could produce cost savings to both the health system and individual patients. Telemedicine applications can bridge the gap in health service facilities between rural, or remote and urban areas[322] and commercially create a wider care base–therefore increasing viability of investments. The other benefits include low capital investment to create a facility, increased utilisation of hospital resources, maintaining continuous relationship with old patients, introducing a new model in healthcare–nurse and technician led clinics.

5.2.5 Telemedicine Projects in India

The Department of Information Technology (DIT) has spearheaded telemedicine programs in India. Some of the other organisations that played a key role are the Indian Space Research Organisation (ISRO), the NEC Telemedicine program for North-Eastern states, Apollo Hospitals, Asia Heart Foundation, Ministry of Health and Family Welfare (MoHFW), World Health Organisation (WHO), Indian Medical Association (IMA), Indian Council of Medical Research (ICMR), Indian Space Research Organisation (ISRO), WIPRO Healthcare IT, Insurance Regulatory and Development Authority (IRDA), law firm Amarchand Mangaldas Shroff and Sons (AMSS), Apollo Health Street Limited, all India Institute of Medical sciences (AIIMS), Sanjay Gandhi Post-Graduate Institute of Medical sciences (SGPGIMS), General Insurers Public Sector Association of India (GIPSA), Centre for Development of Advanced Computing (CDAC) and certain State governments.[323] Since DIT has the role of facilitator, it has taken the initiatives of development of technology, testing out pilot schemes and standardisation of telemedicine in India. It has established more than seventy-five nodes across the country and has supported research and development of software and applications.

The DIT has facilitated initiatives to implement telemedicine projects in the states of West Bengal, Tripura, Kerala, Tamil Nadu, Himachal Pradesh and Punjab.

In Himachal Pradesh, the Centre for Development of Advanced Computing (CDAC), Mohali is the implementing agency for the project 'Customised development and implementing of telemedicine application for rural ad remote areas of Himachal Pradesh'. The referral centers have been created in IGMC, Shimla and PGIMER, Chandigarh. The nodal centers were started in zonal hospitals at Mandi and Dharamshala, civic hospitals in Pooch, Jhanjeli, Tissa, Banjar, Nerwa, Karsog, Rohru, at district hospitals in Recong Peo, regional hospitals at Kullu, Hamirpur, Chamba, Nahan, Keylong and at the community centres at Shillai, Sangra, Bharmaur and Rampur. These centers use ISDN connectivity.

In Tamil Nadu, with the referral centre at Royapetah hospital, the telemedicine centers were started at the government hospitals at Thiruvanamalai, Kancheepuram, Thiruvallur, Krishnagiri, Ooty and Rameswaram. These centers also used ISDN connectivity.

A telemedicine facility for cancer treatment and follow-up, 'Cancernet–an online cancer detection and patient follow up system, has been setup in RCC, Adyar, Chennai, with nodal centers in Chennai, Ghandhigram, Nellore, Bhimavaram, Coimbatore and in Kanyakumari district. Another project entitled 'ONCONET-Cancer care for rural masses-Development of a Tele-Oncology System' was also set up in Tamil Nadu. Both these projects were implemented and completed by CDAC-Trivandrum.

A nodal centre at Andaman has also been set up. The connectivity is through ISDN and VSAT.

In Kerala, CDAC-Trivandrum and IITM Kerala have set up the Telemedicine and Tele-education facilitites in Kerala. The referral centre has been set up in RCC, Thiruvanthapuram, with nodal centers in Kannur, Kochi, Pallakkad, Kozhencherry and Kollam. The centers use VSAT connectivity.

With help from the Sanjay Gandhi Postgraduate Institute of Medical Sciences, Lucknow (SGPI-Lucknow) a project entitled 'Application of Telemedicine technology to provide Tele healthcare during Mela/Festival and Disaster' was set up by the department to provide emergency and preventive healthcare at religious festival sites like the Kumbha Mela.

In the North-East, a project called 'Setting up of Telemedicine in the Capitals of North-eastern States (Mizoram and Sikkim), was implemented by CDAC-Pune and Apollo Telemedicine Network Foundation (ATNF), Hyderabad. A Telemedicine solution to provide specialty health services to remote areas of north-eastern states of India at Naga Hospital, Kohima and remote states of Mizoram and Sikkim with support from Marubeni India Ltd., Government of Nagaland and Apollo Hospital, Delhi has also been commissioned.

In Tripura, two referral centers in Agartala–one at the Govinda Ballav Pant Hospital and the second at Indira Gandhi Memorial Hospital with nodal centers at the sub-divisional hospitals in Amarpur, Kanchanpur,

Chailengta, Gandachera and at Kathalia have been set up using 512 kbps leased line. IIT, Kharagpur has been involved in this project.

In West Bengal, a project entitled 'Development of Telemedicine for Diagnosis and Monitoring of Tropical diseases over low speed WAN' was completed with the help of IIT– Kharagpur. The referral centre has been set up at the School of Tropical Medicine, Kolkata and nodal centers at Habra State General Hospital and MJN Hospital, Coochbehar, the telemedicine project was completed using 512 kbps leased line connectivity on the WBSWAN.

In another project, 'Deployment of Telemedicine in West Bengal Government Hospitals', referral centers were set up at NRS Medical College and Hospital, Kolkata and the Burdwan Medical College and Hospital, Burdwan. The nodal centers were started in Purulia District Hospital, Purulia, Suri District Hospital, Birbhum, Baharampur District Hospital, Murshidabad, Midnapur Medical College and Hospital, Midnapur using a 512 kbps leased line on the WBSWAN.

In a third project for Government hospitals of West Bengal, entitled, 'Development and Application of Telemedicine for Radiology cases referral centers were set up at Calcutta Medical College and Hospital, Kolkata, North Bengal Medical College and Hospital, Siliguri and Chittaranjan National Cancer Institute, Kolkata using 64/128 kbps leased line and WBSWAN as the backbone. The nodal centres were started in Darjeeling District Hospital, Darjeeling, Raigunj District Hospital, Uttar Dinajpur, Tamluk District Hospital, Midnapur (East), Arambag Sub-Division Hospital, Hoogly, using an ISDN link for Arambagh and 512 kbps leased line on WBSWAN for the rest.

Telemedicine has been used quite widely in West Bengal. It has been used in dermatology, hematology, general medicine, orthopaedic cases, ENT, cardiovascular medicine, neurology, psychiatry, obstetrics, urology, leprosy and paediatric cases.[324]

5.2.6 Cardiovascular Diseases

A group of diseases of the heart and vascular system, namely, ischaemic heart disease, hypertension, cerebro-vascular disease, or strokes, congenital heart disease and rheumatic heart disease are together called cardio-vascular diseases[325]. In ischaemic heart disease there is a shortage of blood supply to the heart muscles. In initial stages the patient suffers from breathlessness, or chest pain called angina after an activity, stress, or exercise. Taking rest and avoiding such activities help in some cases. This is caused by blockage in the arteries of the heart due to deposition of fats, triglycerides and cholesterol. When the heart muscle is starved of oxygen and nutrients it is called ischemia. It can be hereditary and chances increase if the patient has high blood pressure, diabetes, or cholesterol. Depending on the symptoms and risk, the treatment may be using mediation, angioplasty, or coronary bypass surgery. When this condition worsens the coronary arteries become thicker and harder from a build up of the fat and cholesterol and other substances that are together called plaque. This happens over time and this process is known as atheroschlerosis.

When a plaque in a heart artery breaks, a blood clot forms around the plaque. This blood clot can completely block the artery and shut off blood flow to the heart muscle. When the flow of blood is severely reduced, or stopped due to the blockage, a coronary attack, or heart attack is likely to occur. Once a heart attack occurs there is damage, or death of part of the heart muscle as a result of the ischemia. This is also known as myocardial infarction. Emergency treatment requires dissolving this clot by the minimally invasive procedure called thrombolytic therapy.

5.2.7 Relevance of the Disease

Cardio-vascular diseases (CVD) are the cause of over half the deaths caused globally by non-communicable diseases. According to 2003 statistics, 16.7 million deaths occurred due to this.[326] More than one-third of all deaths in developing countries are caused by these diseases. In India, around 2.27 million people died owing to these diseases in 1990 and more than 2 million people have died in 2010.There were more than 5 million people suffering from CVD in India in 1999 according to the World Health Organisation (WHO).[327]

5.2.8 Case Fatality Rate

This is a method of measuring the damage by coronary heart disease. The International Society and Federation of Cardiology have defined sudden deaths as deaths 'occurring instantly, or within an estimated 24 hours of the onset of acute symptoms, or signs'. It has also been recorded that about 55 per cent[328] of all cardiac related deaths occur within the first hour. Therefore, timely diagnosis and treatment is very important in such cases. This has been confirmed, too, by research.[329]

In India, the situation is grim. According to a study on persons above the age of 30 in India, it was found that within urban population the prevalence of the disease amongst males was 65.4 per 1000 males and amongst the rural population it was 22.8. Amongst urban females 47.8 per 1000 were affected and 17.3 per 1000 rural women were also affected.[330] What is more alarming is that the patients are on an average younger by a decade[331] in comparison to patients from developed countries.

The scope of measurements in epidemiology[332] is very broad and unlimited and includes, measurement of mortality, morbidity, healthcare facilities and utilisation of health services amongst many others.

5.2.9 Thrombolytic Therapy

Thrombolytic therapy is in most cases a life-saving procedure in cardiac strokes and helps to reduce mortality and morbidity immensely. The benefit of thrombolytic therapy is well known in the case of myocardial infraction[333] as well as for elderly patients.[334] A Research conducted on data of rural patients who received thrombolysis by telephone-assisted stroke consultation concluded that this protocol was safe, practical, and effective with treatment times that did not differ significantly from published randomised controlled trials.[335] The process involves insertion of a thrombolytic agent into the blood stream through a catheter-based procedure to dissolve the clot causing the stroke. According to theory, a thrombolytic agent is a drug that is able to dissolve a clot, or thrombus and reopen an artery, or vein. Thrombolytic agents may be used to treat a heart attack, stroke, deep vein thrombosis, which is a clot, in a deep leg vein, pulmonary embolism, and occlusion of a peripheral artery, or indwelling catheter. All thrombolytic agents are *serine proteases* that digest protein and convert *plasminogen to plasmin,* which breaks down the *fibrinogen* and *fibrin* and dissolves the clot. Currently, available thrombolyic agents include *reteplase (r-PA, or Retavase), alteplase (t-PA, or Activase), urokinase (Abbokinase), prourokinase, anisoylated purified streptokinase activator complex (APSAC), and streptokinase.* They are also called clot-buster, clot-dissolving medication, *fibrinolyic* agent. These agents are administered into the patients system through cath-lab procedures,[336] which has been referred to as thrombolytic therapy.

5.3 Internet and Development

5.3.1 Social Development

Social development may be considered an approach to increasing material welfare for most of the citizens through economic development, using different agencies. For many developing countries, including India, this remains partially, or largely unfulfilled inspite of several efforts. In India for instance, the Central as well as the various State governments have introduced several programs that include supplementary nutrition for expectant mothers and children below the age of seven, immunisations, free education with mid-day meals, vocational training for women and adolescents as well as rural community development projects, emergency relief programs for droughts, floods and other disasters as well as some special schemes for tribals, minorities and other backward classes. Despite all these efforts, a huge section of the population continue to remain very poor and illiterate and that shows the inadequacy of these efforts for a wide range of reasons.

However, there are small pockets within the country where small projects have yielded positive results for the resident population, for example, areas where new industries have grown, or new forms of trade like floriculture, or fisheries have come up commercially. When the local population gets an opportunity to opt for an informed decision that will improve their lives in some way rather than be forced into accepting it that is called a participatory activity. Participatory development is necessary in terms of sustainability, relevance and empowerment and is considered better than top-down[337] development approaches. The main endeavour in such processes is to involve economically and socially backward and neglected population[338] in the decisions that affect their lives. Participation, especially in the context of community, is deeply linked to issues of democracy, power, and asymmetries that historically exist within communities.

International organisations like the World Bank and UNICEF have been dealing with community participation through rapid rural appraisal, participative rural appraisal and participative learning for action. Participation is viewed pragmatically and ideologically[339]—something that helps efficiency, satisfaction and progress, but which is also morally right. The role of modern communication technology towards social development in different contexts are being studied closely, but theories and framework can be drawn only in the correct contexts[340] and its improvement is being studied by various researchers.[341]

Brown's[342] information based evaluation methodology is sensitive to context–specificity and seems appropriate in evaluating the success of a participative development project using Internet as a technology. Information-based rather than a knowledge-based approach to evaluate social development projects has two major advantages; relative objectivity and equity. Growth in unbiased flow of information is one of the indicators of social development. This theory measure coverage through volume, source, diversity and range of information, measures linkages through networking processes and feedback mechanisms and measures of direction in terms of diffusion within the target population and origins and access of information flows.

According to Brown:

> "My thesis is that the expansion and consolidation of the information system provides a more meaningful, and altogether less subjective, indicator of social development than either normative change, or progressive empowerment, and that evaluation of social development should proceed by the elaboration of techniques to monitor information flows and not by attempts to ascertain either value shifts, or direct changes in political relationships. I suggest that when one judges any sort of social development activity... a major criterion employed, explicitly, or implicitly, to evaluate effectiveness is the texture of the information system, and that the democratisation of information flows is an important measure of health of any community-based initiatives" (Brown, 1991, p. 262).

Additionally, a project also needs to be measured in terms of its sustainability,[343] scalability and profitability. A project may touch the lives of marginalised persons and add value to them but at the same time it is necessary to ensure that it can be sustained and it is not a temporary intervention. For that a social mission as well as a strong business model is necessary so that the project can be self-sustaining and profit generating. This theory merges with the theory of participative development where there is re-engineering of the business model instead of re-structuring. This enables both scalability and sustainability of a project. Such projects do not do away with middlemen, instead redefine their roles to harness their expertise and reduce operational and transactional costs.

5.4 Internet, the Electorate and Politics

5.4.1 Democracy

A democracy is a creative, beneficial, powerful force that encourages participation, citizenship and political activity in a public environment. Politics is essential to society as it is a means of individuals and communities to pursue their goals and interests. There are different forms of representative democracy; pluralism and corporatism. In India we follow the Parliamentary, or Westminster model following the British model; this is the prime-ministerial indirect democracy based on universal adult suffrage. Such a democracy is known as a popular democracy as people have the ultimate powers and all powers are drawn from the people.

A democratic government as we all know is a government by the people, for the people and of the people.

The two forms of democracy are historically different but are both government by the people operating through organised and competing interest groups, that are different from the government and demand the attention of the government to their concerns.[344] However, these forms do not demand great knowledge and commitment to politics like the direct form but the disadvantage is that the groups that are not adequately organised cannot get their concerns tabled[345] as a bias exists.[346] Another problem that plagues a modern democracy is that large number of the educated population do not participate in the political and civic life, or debates and lack necessary skills and resources like time and money as well as an interest in politics and some people also feel dis-empowered.

When people are associated with political organisation they are more active.[347] When people are habitual consumers of news they tend to be more mobilised, informed and interested than people who only read sensational news.[348] Again, it has been found that youngsters who are normally more inert in terms of political motivation are more likely to engage in information gathering and online political participation than they would if they used traditional methods.[349] With the Internet friendly generation who have all the required information just a click away will find it convenient to collect whatever information they feel is necessary to judge a political party, or a government apart from issues that affect their lives directly.

On the other hand there will remain a huge number of young people who do not have access to this media and are likely to grow disinterested in the political system of the country because they do not experience any positive changes in their lives. Therefore, it is the responsibility of the political parties to convey information to these disenchanted population so that they exercise their political rights. If people start withdrawing from exercising their rights then it is a failure for democracy. People should feel that their opinion matters otherwise they will become cynical about it. It is also thought by some that use of IT will reduce real life interactions of citizens.[350] This is because there are two dimensions of representation of participation[351]—one where citizens, politicians, other organisations are contacted and the second is the protest dimension where petitions, protests and boycotts are done. People can develop their own networks[352] to come closer to politicians. Moreover, often people do not participate, not because they can't but either they did not want to, or because nobody asked them to do.[353] Therefore, if an individual is interested and is a part of an organisation, he is more likely to vote as reported in a study based on Britain's electoral results.[354] Inspite of political information being readily available, society–workplace, family and lifestyle[355] also influence political attitudes and behaviour.

Today, we find that politicians are using the new technologies to engage the citizens. Most political parties have informative websites. Politicains are using short mailing services (SMSs) to send messages to the citizens. Polticians are also using social networking tools like facebook and Twitter to come closer to the new educated, well informed youth of the country. This has been observed all over the world. The electoral campaign for the last US Presidential elections was highly technology-oriented. Even in India, we find almost every political party using the Internet and new communication technologies to establish contact with the citizens. They are also using it as a vehicle to convey messages, campaign and finally, feel the pulse of the electorate.

Political participation can be explained in terms of the effects of three factors. First, those with greater participatory resources like money and time participate more. Resources also include civic skills, such as literacy and verbal skill, organisational and leadership ability, and so on. The next factor is engagement with politics that increases political participation. This includes interest, knowledge and greater psychological attachment to the political system. In addition to personal characteristics; a third factor that plays an important role in promoting participation is recruitment. People do not simply choose to participate on their own. Rather, people are recruited into participation through social networks and connections.

The resources, engagement, and connection with recruitment networks all develop through the life course as; (1) initial characteristics (e.g., race, gender, and parent's education) affect; (2) access to pre-adult experiences (political discussion in the home, education, and high school activities), which affect; (3) institutional involvements (job, religion, and non-political organisations), which affect; (4) participation resources (income, time, civic skills, and political interest and information), which finally affect; (5) participation itself.

This model also suggests that the various stages feed back into each other. Therefore, participation skills and resources (stage 4) feed back to encourage further institutional involvements (stage 3); similarly, actual participation further enhances the skills and involvements that fostered it in the first place. The inter-related effects of skills, institutional connections, and identity help to explain the big differences in participation rates among different people. It may, therefore, be concluded that the various factors that lead to political participation—and to civic engagement more generally—tend to cumulate. That is, people with initial advantages early in life are most likely to be positioned to learn the skills, make the informal and formal connections, be recruited and develop identities that incline them to become and stay engaged in public life.

Because political engagement can translate into material outcomes– both through its effects on the decisions and choices of those in power, and through the positive effects of social capital directly on individuals– this accumulation tends to reinforce other inequalities in society, placing those with initial resources in the best position to improve their position.[356] Therefore, the central story of cumulative disadvantage remains: those individuals who are disadvantaged economically are the very people who are likely to have few resources for civic participation and little access to broad, useful social networks. Thus, if the programs introduced by their government fail to address these issues, the citizens will not see any direct improvement in their lives and that dissatisfaction will get reflected politically.

All these factors[357] have resulted in reduced accountability of the political system, reduction in competition and damage to the integrity of the system, rendering it fragmented, pluralistic and less stable.

5.4.2 Use of Technology in a Government

When citizens are active in government, more and more people start trusting the process, this leads to better policy decisions, allows the existence of diverse and conflicting views, creates accountability and transparency in the government and supports the political system. These ideals and objectives of a normative political theory are central to the democratic government, which promotes the same through the use of information and communication technology.

However, there is an unpredictability of outcome of using modern technology to achieve these political ideals.[358] Studies have been conducted to see the contribution of information and knowledge in solving social problems[359] and the relationship between democracy, social justice and equity with information access and use.[360] Technology can be employed by governments to help citizens in many ways. In India, for instance, most income tax payers upload their income tax returns online. The various forms that are disbursed by various government departments are also available online, thus making it convenient for people to acquire them. It is common practice by the courts in the country to upload the list of matters to be heard by them on the Internet. This has really helped many litigants.

Further, when a person applies for a passport, the passport office constantly updates the status of the application on its website. This helps the applicants immensely and also creates greater transparency in the system. Most exam results held by Universities, or Boards are published online. This technology makes it possible to reach out to a much greater audience at the same time. For example, earlier results would reach district schools of some states a day, or two days later. Now, a student can check his result as soon as it is uploaded provided he has access to Internet, regardless of his location.

Doctor's (1992)[361] broader overview of the role of information technology in social equity in the United States, officially demonstrates that, "existing data provide warning signals about significant disparities in the distribution and use of information resources" (p. 80).

Modern technology in this context means use of Internet technology for websites, digital libraries, databases, e-governance portals, real-time online events and the infrastructure. The difference between this medium and print and electronic mass media is the introduction of interactivity.[362] It is necessary to point out, however, that interactivity was present even earlier, when people had to write to the various departments about their problems and those would be replied to in due course of time. But with the Internet technology most of this has become instantaneous and if not the time of receiving a reply has come down dramatcally.

This creates new opportunities for participation.[363] This medium allows both two-way one-to-one communication as well as many-to-many and one-to-many communication. Use of this technology and feedback mechanism in politics, can enable higher engagement between the participants.[364] This medium differs from print and electronic media in the ease of creation[365] and distribution of content and information which may originate from a wider variety of sources.

The new media can have signinficant effect on the enhancement of citizenship through proper regulations.[366] In this context, it is necessary to remember, that India is a developing country and most of its villages and small town are out of the Internet map. It also needs to be noted that there are other issues with the use of this technology–costs, investments, access, skill, education. So, even though a section of the community will be greatly advantaged when a governement starts using this technology, there will be a significant number who will not be impacted at all. Therefore, because of these differences the advantages are not always visible, integrated,[367] or equally accessible by all in similar settings.

When Internet technology is used in governance, there can be two major predictions in the outcome–highly optimistic, or technological utopianism; or highly pessimistic, or technological *dystopianism,*[368] both these views are significant in creating citizens views and perceptions. Such use of technology is also affected by society and its institutions.[369] This view places technology in a lower rank in comparison to culture, society and political processes. The nature and even existence of technology and its range of usage is determined by the social, political and cultural factors prevalent in a society.[370] These days' governments are trying to connect with the electorate by becoming more service oriented. These are also exercises in rebuilding trust, bringing in transparency and trying to get more people involved in the government processes.[371]

Internet is able to deliver information far easily and at relatively lower costs. Thus, it can be used as a tool to implement public policy.[372] Different government circulars, orders, etc. can be uploaded on websites for easy access by citizens. This will also create greater awareness amongst people. If information related to government tenders, or job employment are made available online, a greater number of people will be able to participate in the process. If people can pay their government dues online, it will be very convenient for atleast a section of the population. However, governmental services also influence power structures.[373] Implementation of e-governance is not an easy task and is not about the technology alone. There will be many powerful people with vested interests who will feel threatened by this technology and will try to stall the implementation; because if governments implement this technology, the governance will become far more transparent which may be detrimental to their interests.

It is seen that the impact of the Internet is, ironically, disproportionately greater than its overall spread. This fits within the general argument that the libertarian culture accorded by ICTs shift the balance of power between states and citizens, especially in developing countries.[374] Again, this medium can also serve as a medium of public participation[375] but citizens should be motivated to judge the information from alternative points of views.[376] By using this medium governments can deliver services as well as information and engage in one-way or two-way communication with its citizens. This will lead to their empowerment.[377] However, there is a view that Internet technology has an amplifying tendency that tends to make politically active people more active and the politically inactive even more detached.[378]

Thus use of such technology may add to the existing economic, social and political disparities in a society, as traditional groups do not adopt such technology in political arenas so easily. Using technology on a greater scale will be possible when the required infrastructure can be made available. Governments cannot insist on accepting only online applications if the facility of forwarding online application is not available uniformly across the country. Therefore in countries like India, where great disparities exist amongst people in terms of economic factors, education, area of residence, etc., using technology to serve people remains a big challenge for governments.

5.4.3 Brief Note on Andhra Pradesh

Andhra Pradesh is the fourth largest state of India situated on the south-east coast. The state capital is Hyderabad. The state is divided into twenty three districts. The official language is Telegu. Other languages spoken are Urdu, English, Tamil, Hindi and Kannada.

After India won her independence in 1947, the Nizam of Hyderabad wanted to retain his independence and refused to accede his kingdom to India. However, in 1948, the Hyderabad state joined India. A commission set up by the government at that time had ruled that no state would be formed on purely linguistic basis. However, this report created a huge repercussion in Andhra as the Andhras had always wanted a province of their own based on language and the government set out to create another commission to look into these problems.

The committee reported that an exception could be made in the case of the province of Andhra if the Madras province could be cut out of it. This was also not acceptable to the Tamils. There were several protests and finally Pt. Jawaharlal Nehru announced in parliament that the State of Andhra Pradesh would come into existence with eleven undisputed districts and three taluks. These were the districts of Srikakulam, Visakhapatnam, East Godavari, West Godavari, Krishna, Guntur, Nellore, Chittoor, Cuddapah, Anantapur and Kurnool, and the taluks of Rayadurg, Adoni and Alur of the Bellary district. On the 1st of October, 1953, Andhra Pradesh State came into existence.

Andhra Pradesh is one of the less developed states of India. The population of the state according to the 2001 census is 76.2 million with a literacy rate of 52.4 per cent that had shown a good rise from the past decade. Almost 73 per cent of the people of Andhra Pradesh work in the agricultural sector as farmers and agricultural labourers. It has historically been described as the 'Rice Bowl of India'. There are many industrial workers as well. The state has a high skilled labour force. The higher educated group prefers the occupation in the non-agricultural sector. The non-agricultural sector earns more than the agricultural sector.

Andhra Pradesh in India, in the early 1990s saw the rise of a new and prolific political leader from the Telegu Desam party–Nara Chandrababu Naidu. He became the Chief Minister of the state in September 1995 by overthrowing N.T. Rama Rao from the same party who was his father-in-law and brought in with him a lot of liberalisation in reforms that changed the track of development in the state. Chandrababu Naidu during his nine-year rule had introduced several market-based reforms as also many time tested populist schemes, which no other chief minister of Andhra Pradesh had ever launched. Information technology and information technology based service sectors boomed during his tenure, giving rise to a separate state level IT policy.

Mr Naidu was a member of the first national task force on Information Technology and software development created by the office of the prime minister–Shri Atal Bihari Vajpaye in May 1998.[379] He focused very heavily in building the IT infrastructure of the state and competed strongly with Bangalore and Karnataka to be the Silicon Valley of India. He was successful in converting Hyderabad into a hi-tech city. He was also instrumental in making use of the Internet for governance, or e-governance. However, in the 2004 national and state polls the TDP under the leadership of Chandrababu Naidu faced a devastating defeat unparallel in the history of Andhra Pradesh. Chandrababu Naidu's over emphasis on IT and ITES was cast as the main reason for this defeat as the rural community felt neglected despite all his development and e-governance projects.

References

1. Hoffman, Joel M., In the Beginning: A Short History of the Hebrew Language, New York University Press, New York, 2004, p. 18.
2. Nadin Mihai, The Civilisation of Illiteracy, Dresden University Press, Dresden, Germany, 1997, p. 106.

3. Hulse Joseph H., Sustainable Development at Risk Ignoring the Past, Inc. NetLibrary, International Development Research Centre, Canada, 2007, p. 316.
4. Simon, L., Type and Type Founding, I.B. Tauris, 2004, p. 8.
5. Hart, Michael, Ts'ai Lun: In 100 A Ranking of the Most Influential Persons in History, New York, Hart Publishing Co., 1978, pp. 36–41.
6. Pathak, A., Public relations manager, Prabhat Prakashan, 2009, p. 44.
7. Basu Jitendra Nath, Romance of Indian Journalism, University of Calcutta, 1979, p. 22.
8. Society for promoting Christian knowledge, The History of printing, W. Clowes and Sons, London, 1855, pp. 10–11.
9. Briggs Asa and Burke Peter, A Social History of the Media, from Gutenberg to the Internet (Second edition), Polity Press, Cambridge, England, 2005, p. 13.
10. Journal of the East India Association, New Series, Vol. 5, 1914, Origin of Newspapers in China by G. Birdwood, p. 279 (Cit. Basu Jitendra Nath, Romance of Indian Journalism, University of Calcutta, 1979, p. 23).
11. Briggs Asa and Burke Peter, A Social History of the Media, from Gutenberg to the Internet (Second edition), Polity Press, Cambridge, England, 2005, p. 13.
12. *Ibid.*, pp. 14–15.
13. Basu Jitendra Nath, Romance of Indian Journalism, University of Calcutta, 1979, p. 21.
14. Briggs Asa and Burke Peter, A Social History of the Media, from Gutenberg to the Internet (Second edition), Polity Press, Cambridge, England, 2005, p. 14.
15. Andrew Alexander, The History of British Journalism, from the foundation of the Newspaper Press in England to the repeal of the Stamp Act in 1855, with Sketches of Press Celebrities, Vol. 2, Richard Bentley, New Burlington Street, London, 1858, pp. 9–10.
16. Basu Jitendra Nath, Romance of Indian Journalism, University of Calcutta, 1979, p. 22.
17. Natarajan S., History of the Press in India, p. 1 (Cit. Basu Jitendra Nath, Romance of Indian Journalism, University of Calcutta, 1979, p. 23).
18. Journal of the East India Association, New Series, Vol. 5, 1914, Origin of Newspapers in China by G. Birdwood, p. 279 (Cit. Basu Jitendra Nath, Romance of Indian Journalism, University of Calcutta, 1979, p. 23).
19. Briggs Asa and Burke Peter, A Social History of the Media, from Gutenberg to the Internet (Second edition), Polity Press, Cambridge, England, 2005, p. 13.

20. *Ibid.*, p. 14.
21. *Ibid.*, p. 15.
22. Andrew Alexander, The History of British Journalism, from the foundation of the Newspaper Press in England to the repeal of the Stamp Act in 1855, with Sketches of Press Celebrities, Vol. 2, Richard Bentley, New Burlington Street, London, 1858, p. 13.
23. Melville, A., 1923, The machine gun of commerce, The Rotarian, Vol. 23(4), p. 18.
24. Vinne, T.L.D., The Practice of Typography, Biblio Bazaar, LLC, 2008, pp. 133–142.
25. Barnhurst, K.G., and Nerone, J., The form of News: A history, Guilford Press, New York, 2002, p. 107.
26. *Ibid.*, p. 133.
27. *Ibid.*, p. 141.
28. Basu Jitendra Nath, Romance of Indian Journalism, University of Calcutta, 1979, p. 21.
29. Pathak, A., Public Relations Manager, Prabhat Prakashan, 2009, p. 45.
30. *Ibid.*
31. Walravens, H., International Newspaper Librarianship for the 21st Century, Vol. 118, Walter de Gruyter, 2006, p. 235.
32. Basu Jitendra Nath, Romance of Indian Journalism, University of Calcutta, 1979, p. 21.
33. Pathak, A., Public Relations Manager, Prabhat Prakashan, 2009, p. 45.
34. *Ibid.*
35. Basu Jitendra Nath, Romance of Indian Journalism, University of Calcutta, 1979, pp. 20–21.
36. Boczkowski Pablo J., Digitising the News, The MIT Press, Cambridge, Massachusetts 02142, USA, 2004, p. 5.
37. Pathak, A., Public Relations Manager, Prabhat Prakashan, 2009, p. 45
38. Basu Jitendra Nath, Romance of Indian Journalism, University of Calcutta, 1979, pp. 20–21.
39. Lievrouw, L.A., and Livingstone, S.A, Handbook of New Media: Social Shaping and Consequences of ICTs, Sage, 2002, p. 270.
40. Thogmartin, C., The national daily press of France, Summa Publications Inc., 1998, pp. 12–14.
41. Craik, G.L., A Manual of English Literature and of the History of the English Language, Oxford University, 1862, pp. 309–310.

42. Basu Jitendra Nath, Romance of Indian Journalism, University of Calcutta, 1979, pp. 20–21.
43. Mott Frank Luther—New Survey of Journalism, pp. 21–23 (Cit. Basu Jitendra Nath, Romance of Indian Journalism, University of Calcutta, 1979, p. 21).
44. Emery E. and Emery M, The Press and America: An Interpretative History of the Mass Media, Fourth edition, Prentice-Hall, 1978, p. 25 (Cit. Boczkowski Pablo J., Digitising the News, The MIT Press, Cambridge, Massachusetts, USA, 2004, p. 6).
45. Mott Frank Luther, American Journalism, A History 1690–1960, MacMillan, New York, 1962, p. 30.
46. American Anti-slavery society, Proceedings of the American Anti-slavery Society: At its third decade, held in the city of Philadelphia, Dec. 3rd and 4th, 1864 [i.e. 1863] Phonographic report by Henry M. Parkhurst, America Anti-slavery Society, 1864, p. 174.
47. Lee, A.M., American journalism, 1690–1940, Vol. 3, Routledge, 2000, p. 102.
48. Briggs, A., and Burke, P., Social History of the Media: From Gutenberg to the Internet, edn. 3, Polity, 2009, p. 106.
49. Smil, V., Creating the twentieth century: technical innovations of 1867–1914 and their lasting impact, Oxford University Press, US, 2005, p. 204.
50. Jones, A., Historical sketch of the electric telegraph: including its rise and progress in the United States, G.P. Putnam, 1852, p. 10.
51. *Ibid.,* p. 11.
52. Raatma, L., Thomas Edison, Compass Point Books, 2003, p. 24.
53. Hudson, F., Lee, A.M. and Mott, F.L., American Journalism, 1690–1940, Vol. 1, Routledge, 2000, p. 628.
54. Sloan, W.D., and Parcell, L.M., American journalism: History, principles, practices, McFarland, 2002, p. 353.
55. Dwyer Joseph D, Russia the Soviet Union and Eastern Europe, Hoover Institution on Was Revolution and Peace, Hoover Institution Press, Stanford University, Stanford, California, 1980, p. 175.
56. Chee Tham Seong (eds), Essays on Literature and Society in Southeast Asia; Political and Sociological Perspectives, Singapore University Press, Singapore, 1981, pp. 83–84.
57. Amrita Bazar Patrika, dated May 13, 1931 (Cit. Basu Jitendra Nath, Romance of Indian Journalism, University of Calcutta, 1979, p. 21).
58. Linkai Nihon Yunesuko Kokunai, Japan its land people and Culture, Printing Bureau, Ministry of Finance Japan, 1964, p. 354.

59. Mehta, J.I., Advanced Study in the History of Medieval India, Vol. 2, Sterling Publishers Pvt. Ltd., 1984, p. 27.

60. Indian text series, Vol. 2, p. 128 (Cit. Basu Jitendra Nath, Romance of Indian Journalism, University of Calcutta, 1979, p. 14).

61. Mehta, J.I., Advanced Study in the History of Medieval India, Vol. 2, Sterling Publishers Pvt. Ltd, 1984, pp. 27–29.

62. Yusuf Ali A., A Cultural History of India During the British Period p. 87 (Cit. Basu Jitendra Nath, Romance of Indian Journalism, University of Calcutta, 1979, p. 13).

63. Basu Jitendra Nath, Romance of Indian Journalism, University of Calcutta, 1979, p. 13.

64. *Ibid.*

65. Pratiyogita darpan, edited by Mahendra Jain, Upkar Prakashan, 2009, p. 25.

66. Basu Jitendra Nath, Romance of Indian Journalism, University of Calcutta, 1979, p. 20.

67. Chaudhuri, A., Indian Advertising: 1780 to 1950 A.D., Tata McGraw-Hill, 2007, pp. 1–8.

68. Basu Jitendra Nath, Romance of Indian Journalism, University of Calcutta, 1979, p. 23.

69. *Ibid.*, pp. 32–36.

70. Chaudhuri, A., Indian Advertising: 1780 to 1950 A.D., Tata McGraw-Hill, 2007, pp. 1–8.

71. Basu Jitendra Nath, Romance of Indian Journalism, University of Calcutta, 1979, p. 36.

72. *Ibid.*

73. *Ibid.*, p. 39.

74. Chaudhuri, A., Indian Advertising: 1780 to 1950 A.D., Tata McGraw-Hill, 2007, p. 4.

75. Rajan, N., 21st century journalism in India, Sage, 2007, p. 61.

76. Chaudhuri, A., Indian advertising: 1780 to 1950 A.D., Tata McGraw-Hill, 2007, pp. 5–6.

77. Basu Jitendra Nath, Romance of Indian Journalism, University of Calcutta, 1979, p. 40.

78. *Ibid.*, p. 43.

79. Laudon, Kenneth C. and Laudon, Jane P, Essentials of Management Information Systems.Upper Saddle River, New Jersey, 2001, p. 266.

80. Tether, T., 2008, DARPA Fifty years of inventing the future 1958–2008, Aerospace America, Vol. 46(2), pp. 30–43.

81. Andrew Pollack, America's answer to Japan's MITI, New York Times, March 5, 1989.

82. Norberg and O'Neill 1996, Cit. by Abbatte J. Inventing the Internet, MIT Press, 1999, p. 36.

83. United States Congress, House Committee on Science and Technology, Task force on Science policy, A history of Science Policy in the United States, 1940–1985. For sale by the Superintendent of documents, US GPO, 1986, p. 54.

84. Abbate Janet, Inventing the Internet, MIT Press, 1999, p. 37.

85. Internet History From ARPANET to Broadband, 2007, Congressional Digest, Vol. 86 (2), pp. 35–64.

86. Hafner, K. and Lyon, M., Where Wizards Stay Up Late: The Origins of the Internet. New York: Simon and Schuster, 1996, p. 10.

87. Leiner Barry M., Cerf Vinton G., Clark David D., Kahn Robert E., Kleinrock Leonard, Lynch Daniel C., Postel Jon, Roberts Larry G., Wolff Stephen, 1997, The past and future history of the Internet, Communications of the ACM, Vol. 40(2), pp. 102–108.

88. *Ibid.*

89. Porter Beth, The net effect, Intellect books, UK, 2001, p. 45.

90. Smith, J. N., 2007, Great moments in World Trade: The making of the Internet, World Trade, Vol. 20(6), p. 62.

91. Leiner Barry M., Cerf Vinton G., Clark David D., Kahn Robert E., Kleinrock Leonard, Lynch Daniel C., Postel Jon, Roberts Larry G., Wolff Stephen, 1997, The past and future history of the Internet, Communications of the ACM, Vol. 40(2), pp. 102–108.

92. Quarterman John, The Matrix: computer networks and conferencing systems worldwide, Bedford M.A, Digital Press, 1990, pp. 141–143.

93. LaQuey Tracey, The user's directory of computer networks, Bedford M.A., Digital Press, 1990, p. 194.

94. Leiner Barry M., Cerf Vinton G., Clark David D., Kahn Robert E., Kleinrock Leonard, Lynch Daniel C., Postel Jon, Roberts Larry G., Wolff Stephen, 1997, The past and future history of the Internet, Communications of the ACM, Vol. 40(2), pp. 102–108.

95. Cavender, S., 1998, Ray Tomlinson, Forbes, Vol. 162(7), pp. 126–127.

96. Mary, B., 1999, Ethernet emerges, Computer World, Vol. 33(25), p. 96.

97. Kaminow Ivan P., and Li Tingye, Optical Fiber Telecommunications IV-B, Academic Press, 2002, p. 31.

98. Gillies James and Cailliau Robert, How the Web was born, Oxford University Press and CERN Accelerator School, 2000, p. 329.

99. Mockapetris, P.V., and Dunlap, K.J., 1995, Development of the domain name system, ACM SIGCOMM Computer Communication Review, Vol. 25(1), pp. 112–122.

100. Hunt, C., TCP-IP network administration, O'Reilly Media, Inc., 2002, 3rd edn., p. 56.

101. Kesmodel, D., The domain game: How people get rich from Internet domain names, ISBN, 2008, p. 18.

102. Leiner Barry M., Cerf Vinton G., Clark David D., Kahn Robert E., Kleinrock Leonard, Lynch Daniel C., Postel Jon, Roberts Larry G., and Wolff Stephen, 1997, The past and future history of the Internet, Communications of the ACM, Vol. 40(2), pp. 102–108.

103. Naughton, J., A brief history of the future: The origins of the Internet, Weidenfeld and Nicolson Ltd., London, 1999, p. 177.

104. Landweber, L., 1979, Theory Net: An electronic mail system, Association for computer machinery, NY, USA, p. 158.

105. Daniel, Stephen, James Ellis, and Tom Truscott, 1980, USENET—A General Access UNIX Network, Durham, NC: Duke University Press. In Quarterman, J. S, The Global Matrix of Minds Global Networks: Computers and International Communications (Eds.) Linda M. Harasim, MIT Press, Cambridge, 1993, pp. 35–56.

106. American Association for the Advancement of Science, Highwire Press and JSTOR, Science, Vol. 231, American Association for the Advancement of Science, 1986, pp. 945–949.

107. Naughton, J., A Brief history of the future: The origins of the Internet, Weidenfeld and Nicolson Ltd., London, 1999, pp. 178–183.

108. Engst, A.C., Internet starter kit for Macintosh, Hayden Books, Michigan, 1993, p. 31.

109. Plankers, S., 1994, Genealogy, A BBS, and You, Ancestry, Vol. 2(2), pp. 14–15.

110. Carlson, D., 2005, Online Timeline, Nieman Reports, Vol. 59(3), pp. 45–83.

111. Cerf, V., 1999, Requiem for the Arpanet, Connexions, Vol. 3(10), p. 27.

112. Grzywa, M., Yurcik, W., and Brumbaugh, L., 2001, Application–level survivality: Resumable FTP, MILCOM, Vol. 1, pp. 107–112.

113. National Research Council, Committee on Internet Navigation and the Domain Name System: Technical Alternatives and Policy Implications, Signposts in Cyberspace: The Domain Name System and Internet Navigation, National Academics, 2005, pp. 290–303.

114. James K.L, The Internet: A user's Guide, Prentice Hall of India, 2004, pp. 253–255.

115. National Research Council, Committee on Internet Navigation and the Domain Name System: Technical Alternatives and Policy Implications, Signposts in Cyberspace: The Domain Name System and Internet Navigation, National Academics, 2005, pp. 290–303.

116. *Ibid.*

117. Naughton, J., A brief history of the future: The origins of the Internet, Weidenfeld and Nicolson Ltd., London, 1999, p. 235.

118. McIver, W.J., and Elmagarmid, A.K., Advances in digital government: technology, human factors, and policy, Springer, USA, 2002, p. 4.

119. Naughton, J., A brief history of the future: The origins of the Internet, Weidenfeld and Nicolson Ltd, London, 1999, p. 235.

120. *Ibid.*, pp. 236–266.

121. Srikantaiah, T.K., and Xiaoying, D., 1998, The Internet and its impact on developing countries: examples from China and India, Asian Libraries, Vol. 7(9), pp. 199–209.

122. *Ibid.*

123. Joseph, P.T., E-Commerce: An Indian Perspective 2nd Ed., PHI Learning Pvt. Ltd., 2006, p. 141.

124. *Ibid.*, pp. 141–142.

125. Srikantaiah, T.K., and Xiaoying, D., 1998, The Internet and its impact on developing countries: examples from China and India, Asian Libraries, Vol. 7(9), pp. 199–209.

126. Singh, S., 1999, India ISP licenses pickup, Infoworld, 23/08/1999, Vol. 21 (34), p. 50A.

127. Indian Internet Subscribers up 215 per cent This. Year, India Telecom, July 15, 2001.

128. Number of Internet users in India reaches 37 million, The Hindu, Saturday, Sep. 23, 2006.

129. Indian users grow to 71 million: IMRB, The Times of India, March 19, 2010.

130. Picard, R.G., 2003, Cash cows or Entercôte: Publishing companies and disruptive technologies, Trends in communication, Vol. 11(2), pp. 127–136.

131. Hendriks, P.C.J., 1998, Newspapers: a lost cause? Strategic management of newspaper firms in the United States and Netherlands, Doctoral thesis, University of Amsterdam.

132. Cowen, N., 2001, The future of British broadsheet newspaper on the world wide web, Aslib Proceedings,Vol. 53(5), pp. 189–200.

133. Mueller, J., and Kamerer, D., 1995, Reader preference for electronic newspapers, Newspaper research journal, Vol. 16(3), pp. 2–13.

134. Mings, S., and White, P.B., Profiting from online news: The search for viable business models. In Kahin, B. and Varain, H.R., (eds) Internet publishing and beyond: The economics of digital information and intellectual property, The MIT press, Cambridge, MA, 2000, pp. 62–96.

135. Peng, F.Y., Tham, N.I., and Xiaoming, H.,1999, Trends in online newspapers: A look at the US web, Newspaper Research Journal, Vol. 20 (2), pp. 52–63.

136. Boczkowski, P.J., The development of online newspapers: What results tell us and what we might want to know. In Lievrouw, L. and Livingstone S., (Eds.): The handbook of new media, Sage Publications, London, 2002, pp. 270–286.

137. Massey, B., and Levy, M., 1999, Interactivity, online journalism, and English-language web newspapers in Asia, Journalism and Mass Communication Quarterly, Vol. 76, pp. 138–51.

138. Gunter, B., News and the Net, 2003, Mahwah, NJ: Lawrence Erlbaum Associates, p. 22.

139. Carlson, D., The history of online journalism, in Kawamoto Kevin's Digital journalism: Emerging media and the changing horizons of journalism, Rowman and Littlefield, USA, 2003, p. 47.

140. Peng, F.Y., Tham, N.I., and Xiaoming, H., 1999, Trends in online newspapers: A look at the US web, Newspaper Research Journal, Vol. 20 (2), pp. 52–63.

141. Chyi, H.I., and Lasorsa, D., 1999, Access, use and preferences for online Newspapers, Newspaper Research Journal, Vol. 20(4), pp. 2–13.

142. Noack, D., 1997, Off-line newspapers: Too small, too busy, or too unsure, some move slowly into cyberspace, Editor and publisher, Vol. 130(6), pp. 321–331.

143. Neuberger, C., Tonnemacher, J., Biebl, M., and Duck, A., 1998, Online—the future of newspapers? Germany's dailies on the World Wide Web, Journal of Computer Mediated Communication, Vol. 4(1), pp. 1–23.

144. Peng, F.Y., Tham, N.I., and Xiaoming, H., 1999, Trends in online newspapers: A look at the US web, Newspaper Research Journal, Vol. 20 (2), pp. 52–63.

145. Kwok, Y., 1998, August 21, Internet campaigns, Asiaweek.

146. Schroth, P.W., Sharma P., 2003, Transnational law and technology as potential forces against corruption in Africa, Management decision, Vol. 41(3), pp. 296–303.

147. McDowell, S.D., and Pashupati, K., 1998, India's Internet Policies: New Media Ownership, Control and Purposes, Media Development, Volume 15(4), pp. 18–24.

148. Chyi, H.I., and Lasorsa, D., 1999, Access, use and preferences for online Newspapers, Newspaper Research Journal, Vol. 20 (4), pp. 2–13.

149. Peng, F.Y., Tham, N.I., and Xiaoming, H., 1999, Trends in online newspapers: A look at the US web, Newspaper Research Journal, Vol. 20 (2), pp. 52–63.

150. Neuberger, C., Tonnemacher, J., Biebl, M., and Duck, A., 1998, Online—the future of newspapers? Germany's dailies on the World Wide Web, Journal of Computer Mediated Communication, Vol. 4(1), pp. 1–23.

151. Carlson, David., 2005, Online timeline, Nieman Reports, Vol. 59(3), pp. 45–83.

152. Shedden, D., 2006, New Media Timeline, Poynter Online. Poynter Institute. Fall 2006.

153. Carlson, David., 2005, Online timeline, Nieman Reports, Vol. 59(3), pp. 45–83.

154. Thalhimer, M., 1994, High-tech news or just "shovelware"?, Media studies journal, Vol. 8, pp. 41–51.

155. Carlson, David., 2005, Online timeline, Nieman Reports, Vol. 59(3), pp. 45–83.

156. *Ibid.*

157. Cochran, W., 1995, Searching for the right mixture, Quill, Vol. 83(4), p. 36.

158. Carlson, David., 2005, Online timeline, Nieman Reports, Vol. 59(3), pp. 45–83.

159. Gunter, B., News and the Net, Lawrence Erlbaum Associates, Mahwah, NJ, 2003, p. 23.

160. Carlson, David, 2005, Online timeline, Nieman Reports, Vol. 59(3), pp. 45–83.

161. Carlson, D., The history of online journalism. In Kawamoto Kevin's Digital journalism: Emerging media and the changing horizons of journalism, Rowman and Littlefield, USA, 2003, p. 50.

162. Carlson, David, 2005, Online timeline, Nieman Reports, Vol. 59(3), pp. 45–83.

163. Carlson, D., The history of online journalism. In Kevin Kawamoto's Digital journalism: Emerging media and the changing horizons of journalism, Rowman and Littlefield, 2003, p. 50.

164. Shedden, D., 2006, New Media Timeline, Poynter Online, Poynter Institute.

165. Gunter, B., News and the Net, Lawrence Erlbaum Associates, Mahwah, NJ, 2003, p. 19.

166. Shedden, D., 2006, New Media Timeline, Poynter Online. Poynter Institute.

167. Carlson, David, 2005, Online timeline, Nieman Reports, Vol. 59(3), pp. 45–83.

168. Shedden, D., 2006, New Media Timeline, Poynter Online, Poynter Institute.

169. Carlson, David., 2005, Online timeline, Nieman Reports, Vol. 59(3), pp. 45–83.

170. Cochran, W., 1995, Searching for the right mixture, Quill, Vol. 83(4), p. 36.

171. Carlson, David., 2005, Online timeline, Nieman Reports, Vol. 59(3), pp. 45–83.

172. David Carlson's virtual world, The Online Timetable. Accessed from http://iml.jou.ufl.edu/carlson/1995s.shtml on 10/4/2007.

173. Beamish, R., The local newspaper in the age of multimedia. In B. Franklin and D. Murphy (Eds), Making Local News: Local Journalism in context. London: Routledge, 1998, pp. 140–53.

174. Carveth, R., Owers, J. and Alexander, A., The Economics of Online Media. In A. Alexander, J. Owers and R. Carveth (Eds). Media Economics—Theory and practice, 1998, pp. 247–273.

175. Garrison, B., 1997, Online services: Internet in 1995 newsrooms, Newspaper research journal, Vol. 18(3), pp. 79–93.

176. Molina, A., 1997, Issues and challenges in the evolution of multimedia: The case of the newspapers, Futures, Vol. 29, pp. 193–212.

177. Greer Jennifer D., and Mensing Donica, The Evolution of online Newspapers: A longitundinal Content Analysis, 1997–2003. In Internet Newspapers—The making of a mainstream medium (Eds) Xigen Li, Lawrence Erlbaum Associates, Publishers, Mahwah, New Jersey, London, 2006, p. 13.

178. David Carlson's virtual world, The Online Timetable. Accessed from http://iml.jou.ufl.edu/carlson/1995s.shtml on 10/4/2007.

179. Shedden, D., 2006, New Media Timeline, Poynter Online, Poynter Institute.

180. Lievrouw, L.A., and Livingstone, S.M., Handbook of new media: Social shaping and consequences of ICTs, Sage, 2002, p. 273.

181. Hashim N.H., and Meloche J.A. 2007, Australian online newspaper: An exploratory study on Internet savvy users using Q-methodology, Research online, University of Wollongong, pp. 1–15.

182. Rainie L., Fox S., and Fallows D., The internet and the Iraq war: How online Americans have used the Internet to learn war news, understand events, and promote their views, Pew Internet and American Life, April 1, 2003, accessed from http://www.pewinternet.org/pdfs/PIP_ Iraq_War_ Report.pdf on 29/07/2008.

183. Website of The Hindu, http://epaper.thehindu.com/ accessed on 02/07/2008.

184. Site Statistics for Telegraphindia.com. Accessed and downloaded from http://www.alexa.com/data/details/main/telegraphindia.com on 23/7/2008.

185. Thakur Kiran, Internet Journalism, Department of Journalism, Pune University, Pune.

186. Website of Indiapress—Indian Newspapers Links and India News, http://www.indiapress.org/, accessed on 22/07/2008.

187. Noack D., 1997, Off-line newspapers: Too small, too busy, or too unsure, some move slowly into cyberspace, Editor and Publisher, p. 323.

188. Outing S., 2003, Hold on (line) tight, Editor and Publisher, p. 41.

189. Katz, E., 1959, Mass communication research and the study of culture, Studies in Public Communication, Vol. 2, pp. 1–6.

190. McQuail, D., 1983, Mass Communication Theory (1st ed.), London, Sage Publication, p. 245.

191. Windahl, S., 1981, Uses and gratifications at the crossroads, Mass Communication Review Yearbook, Vol. 2, pp. 174–185.

192. Ruggiero, T., 2000, Uses and gratifications theory in the 21st century. Mass Communication and Society, Vol. 3(1), pp. 3–37.

193. Katz, E., Blumler, J.G., and Gurevitch, M., Utilisation of mass communication by the individual. In J.G. Blumler, and E. Katz (Eds.), The uses of mass communications: Current perspectives on gratifications research, Beverly Hills: Sage Publication, 1974, pp. 19–34.

194. *Ibid.*

195. LaRose, R., Mastro, D., and Eastin, M.S., 2001, Understanding Internet usage: A social-cognitive approach to uses and gratifications, Social Science Computer Review, Vol. 19(4), pp. 395–413.

196. Dimmick, J., Ecology, economics and gratification utilities. In A. Alexander, J. Owers, and R. Carveth (Eds.), Media economics, Lawrence Erlbaum Associates, Hillsdale, NJ, 1993, pp. 135–136.

197. Becker, L.B., and Shoenbach, K., When media content diversifies: Anticipating audience behaviors. In L.B. Becker and K. Schoenbach (Eds.), Audience responses to media diversification: Coping with plenty, Hillsdale, NJ, Lawrence Erlbaum Associates, 1989, pp. 1–27.

198. Levy, Mark and Windahl, Sven, The concept of audience activity. In K. Rosengren, L.Wenner and P. Palmgreen (Eds.), Media gratifications research: current perspectives, Beverly Hills, CA: Sage Publications, 1989, pp. 109–122.

199. McQuail, D., The rise of media of mass communication. In D. McQuail (Ed.), Mass communication theory: An introduction, London: Sage, 1994, pp. 3–21.

200. Katz, E., Blumler, J., and Gurevitch, M., Utilisation of mass communication by the individual. In J.G. Blumler, and E. Katz (Eds.), The Uses of Mass Communications: Current Perspectives on Gratifications Research, Beverly Hills, Sage Publications, 1974, pp. 19–32.

201. Blumler, J.G., 1979, The role of theory in uses and gratifications studies. Communication Research, Vol. 6, pp. 9–36.

202. Weaver, D.H., 1980, Audience need for orientation and media effects. Communication Research, Vol. 7, pp. 361–376.

203. Rayburn, J.D., II., Uses and gratifications. In M.B. Salwen and D.W. Stacks (Eds.), An integrated approach to communication theory and research, Mahwah NJ: Lawrence Erlbaum Associates, 1996, pp. 15–163.

204. Severin W.J., and Tankard, J. W. (Eds.), Communication Theories: Origins, Methods, and Uses in the Mass Media (3rd ed.), New York: Longman. 1992, pp. 272–275.

205. Wilson, T.D., 1998, Information behaviour: An interdisciplinary perspective, Information processing and management, Vol. 33(4), pp. 551–572.

206. Wilson, T.D., 1999, Models in information behaviour research,Journal of Documentation, Vol. 55(3), pp. 249–270.

207. NiedŸwiedzka, B., 2003, A proposed model of information behaviour, Information Research, Vol. 9. (1), pp. 1–17.

208. Rubin, A.M., and Perse, E.M., 1987, Audience activity and television news gratifications, Communication research, Vol. 14, pp. 58–84.

209. Blumler, J.G., 1979, The role of theory in uses and gratifications studies,Communication Research, Vol. 6, pp. 9–36.

210. Hawkins, R.P., and Pingree, S., 1981, Uniform messages and habitual viewing: Unnecessary assumptions in social reality effects, Human Communication Research, Vol. 7, pp. 291–301.

211. Morris, M., and Ogan, C., 1996, The Internet as mass medium. Journal of communication, Vol. 46(1), pp. 39–50.

212. Perse, E.M., and Courtright, J.A., 1993, Normative images of communication media: Mass and interpersonal channels in the new media environment, Human Communication Research, Vol. 19, pp. 485–503.

213. Mutz, D.C., Roberts, D.F., van Vuuren, D.P., 1993, Reconsidering the displacement hypothesis: Television's influence on children's time use, Communication Reseach, Vol. 20(1), pp. 51–75.

214. Katz, E.M., Gurevitch, M., and Hass, H., 1973, On the uses of mass media for important things, American Sociology Review, Vol. 38(2), pp. 164–181.

215. Kippax, S., and Murray, J.P., 1980, Using the mass media: Need gratification and 'perceived utility', Communication Research, Vol. 7, pp. 335–360.

216. Elliot, W., and Quattlebaum, C.P., 1979, Similarities in patterns of media use: A cluster analysis of media gratifications, The Western Journal of Speech Communication, Vol. 43, pp. 61–72.

217. Weaver, D.H., 1980, Audience need for orientation and media effects, Communication Research, Vol. 7, pp. 361–376.

218. Palmgreen, P., Wenner, L.A., and Rayburn, J.D II., 1980, Relations between gratifications sought and obtained: Study of TV news, Communication Research, Vol. 7, pp. 161–192.

219. Rubin, R.B., Perse, E.M., and Barbato, C.A., 1988, Conceptualisation and measurement of interpersonal communication motives, Human Communication Research, Vol. 14, pp. 602–628.

220. Lichenstein, A., and Rosenfeld, L.B, 1983, Uses and misuses of gratifications research: An explication of media functions, Communications Research, Vol. 10, pp. 97–109.

221. Rubin, A.M., and Perse, E.M., 1987, Audience activity and television news gratifications, Communication research, Vol. 14, pp. 58–84.

222. Lin, C.A., 1999, Online service adoption likelihood, Journal of Advertising Research, Vol. 39(2), pp. 79–89.

223. Diddi, A.. and LaRose, R., 2006, Getting hooked on news: Uses and gratifications and the formation of news habits among college students in an Internet environment, Journal of Broadcasting and Electronic Media, Vol. 50(2), pp. 193–210.

224. Ferguson D.A., and Perse, E.M, 2000, The world wide web as a functional alternative to television, Journal of Broadcasting and Electronic media, Vol. 44(2), pp. 155–174.

225. Kraut, R., Patterson, M., Lundmark, V., Kiesler, S., Mukopadhyay, T., and Scherlis, W., 1998, Internet Paradox: A Social Technology That Reduces Social Involvement and Psychological Well-Being? American Psychologist, Vol. 59(9), pp. 1017–031.

226. Althaus, S.L., and Tewksbury, D., 2000, Patterns of Internet and traditional news media use in a networked community, Political communication, Vol. 17(1), pp. 21–45.

227. Ruggiero, T., 2000, Uses and gratifications theory in the 21st century. Mass Communication and Society, Vol. 3(1), pp. 3–37.

228. Williams, F., Rice, R.E., and Rogers, E.M., Research methods and the New media, New York: Free Press, 1988, p. 10.

229. *Ibid.*, p. 12.

230. Kuehn, S.A., 1994, Computer-mediated communication in instructional settings: A research agenda, Communication Education, Vol. 43, pp. 171–182.

231. Rafaeli, S., Interactivity: From new media to communication. In R. Hawkins et al. (Eds.), Advancing communication science: Merging mass and interpersonal processes, Newbury Park, CA, Sage, 1988, pp. 110–134.

232. Chamberlain, M.A., 1994, New technologies in health communication, American Behavioral Scientist, Vol. 38, pp. 271–284.

233. *Ibid.*, p. 274.

234. Williams, F., Rice, R.E., and Rogers, E.M., Research methods and the new media, Free Press, New York, 1988, p. 10.

235. Tseng, S., and Fogg, B., 1999, Credibility and computing technology, Communications of the ACM, Vol. 42(5), pp. 39–44.

236. Nozato, Y., 2002, Credibility of online newspapers. Paper presented at the Association for Education in Journalism and Mass Communication Annual Convention, Washington, DC, August 2002.

237. Newhagen, J., 1997, The role of feedback in the assessment of news, Information Processing and Management, Vol. 33(5), pp. 583–594.

238. Flanagin, A.J., and Metzger, M.J., 2000, Perceptions of Internet information credibility, Journalism and Mass Communication Quarterly, Vol. 77, pp. 515–540.

239. Flanagin, A.J., and Metzger, M.J., 2001, Internet use in the contemporary media environment, Human Communication Research, Vol. 27(1), pp. 153–181.

240. Schweiger, W., 2000, Media credibility or experience or image: A survey on the credibility of the World Wide Web in Germany in comparison to other media, European Journal of Communication, Vol. 15, pp. 37–59.

241. Johnson, T.J., and Kaye, B.K., 1998, Cruising is believing: Comparing Internet and traditional sources on media credibility measures. Journalism and Mass Communication Quarterly, Vol. 75(2), pp. 325–340.

242. Johnson, T.J., and Kaye, B.K., 2000, Using is believing: The influence of reliance on the credibility of online political information among politically interested Internet users, Journalism and Mass Communication Quarterly, Vol. 77(4), pp. 865–879.

243. Abdulla, R.A., Garrison, B., Salwen, M., Garrison, B., and Driscoll, P., Online news credibility. In M.B Salwen., B. Garrison., and P.D. Driscoll (Eds), Online news and the public, Mahwah, NJ, Lawrence Erlbaum Associates, 2005, pp. 147–163.

244. Kiousis, S., 2001, Public Trust or Mistrust. Perceptions of Media Credibility in the Information Age, Mass Communication and Society, Vol. 4(4), pp. 381–403.

245. Cassidy, W.P., 2007, Online news credibility: An examination of the perceptions of newspaper journalists, Journal of Computer-Mediated Communication, Vol. 12(2), article 7, pp. 1–24.

246. Johnson, T., and Kaye, B., 1998, Cruising is believing? Comparing Internet and traditional sources on media credibility measures, Journalism and mass communication quarterly, Vol. 75(2), pp. 325–40.

247. Pew Research Center for the People and the Press, 1999, The Internet News audience goes ordinary.

248. Mashek, J.W., 1997, Lethargy 1996: How the media covered a listless campaign, Arlington, VA, The Freedom Forum.

249. Abdulla, R.A., Garrison, B., Salwen, M., Garrison, B., and Driscoll, P. Online news and the public, Routledge, 2005, pp. 147–163.

250. Flanagin, A.J., and Metzger, M.J., 2000, Perceptions of Internet information credibility. Journalism and Mass Communication Quarterly, Vol. 77(3), pp. 515–540.

251. Nozato, Y., 2002, Credibility of online newspapers, in Proceedings of the Annual Meeting of the Association for Education in Journalism and Mass Communication (85th, Miami, Florida, August 5–8, 2002. Communication Technology and Policy Division, Collected Works - Proceedings; Reports – Research.

252. Kiousis, S., 2001, Public Trust or Mistrust? Perceptions of Media Credibility in the Information Age, Mass Communication and Society, Vol. 4(4), pp. 381–403.

253. Meyer, P., 1988, Defining and measuring credibility of newspapers: Developing an index. Journalism Quarterly, Vol. 65 (3), pp. 567–574.

254. Rimmer, T., and Weaver, D., 1987, Different questions, different answers? Media use and media credibility. Journalism Quarterly,Vol. 64 (1), pp. 28–36.

255. Jacobson, H.K., 1969, Mass Media Believability,A Study of Receiver Judgements. Journalism Quarterly, Vol. 46 (1), pp. 20–28.

256. Hovland, C.I. and Weiss, W., 1951–52, Winter, The influence of source credibility on communication effectiveness. Public Opinion Quarterly, Vol. 15(4), pp. 635–650.

257. McCombs, M., and Shaw, D.L., 1972, The agenda-setting function of mass media. Public Opinion Quarterly, Vol. 36, pp. 176–187.

258. Infante, D.A., The Construct Validity of Semantic Differential Scales for the Measurement of Source Credibility, Communication Quarterly, 1980, Vol. 28(2), pp. 19–26.

259. Gaziano, C., 1987, News peoples' ideology and the credibility debate. Newspaper Research Journal, Vol. 9(1), pp. 1–18.

260. Rubin, R.B., Palmgren, P., Sypher, H.E., Communication research measures: a sourcebook, Vol. 2, Routledge, 2004, p. 237.

261. Abdulla, R.A., Garrison, B., Salwen, M., Garrison, B., and Driscoll, P. Online news and the public, Routledge, 2005, pp. 147–163.

262. Nozato, Y., 2002, Credibility of online newspapers, in Proceedings of the Annual Meeting of the Association for Education in Journalism and Mass Communication (85th, Miami, Florida, August 5–8, 2002), Communication Technology and Policy Division, Collected Works - Proceedings; Reports – Research.

263. Gaziano, C., and McGrath, K., 1986, Measuring the concept of credibility, Journalism Quarterly, Vol. 63 (3), pp. 451–462.

264. Gaziano, C., 1987, News peoples' ideology and the credibility debate, Newspaper Research Journal, Vol. 9(1), pp. 1–18.

265. Rimmer, T., and Weaver, D., 1987, Different questions, different answers. Media use and media credibility. Journalism Quarterly, Vol. 64 (1), pp. 28–36.

266. Meyer, P., 1988, Defining and measuring credibility of newspapers: Developing an index. Journalism Quarterly, Vol. 65 (3), pp. 567–574.

267. West, M.D., 1994, Validating a scale for the measurement of credibility: A covariance structure modeling approach. Journalism Quarterly, Vol. 71(1), pp. 159–168.

268. Hovland, C., and Weiss, W., 1951, The influence of source credibility on communication effectiveness. Public Opinion Quarterly, Vol. 15, pp. 635–650.

269. Rubin, R.B., Palmgren, P., and Sypher, H.E., Communication research measures: A sourcebook, Volume 2, Routledge, 2004, p. 237.

270. Gaziano, C., and McGrath, K., 1986, Measuring the concept of credibility. Journalism Quarterly, Vol. 63, pp. 451–462.

271. Johnson, T.J., and Kaye, B. K., 1998, Cruising is believing: Comparing Internet and traditional sources on media credibility measures, Journalism and Mass Communication Quarterly, Vol. 75(2), pp. 325–340.

272. Abdulla, R.A., Garrison, B., Salwen, M., Garrison, B., and Driscoll, P. Online news and the public, Routledge, 2005, p. 150.

273. Salwen, M.B., Garrison, B., and Driscoll, P.D., Online news and the public, Routledge, 2005, p. 157.

274. Flanagin, A.J., and Metzger, M.J., 2000, Perceptions of Internet information credibility. Journalism and Mass Communication Quarterly, Vol. 77(3), pp. 515–540.

275. Gaziano, C., 1987, News peoples' ideology and the credibility debate, Newspaper Research Journal, Vol. 9(1), pp. 1–18.

276. Liu, Z., 2003, Perception of credibility of scholarly information on the web. Information processing and management, Vol. 40, pp. 1027–1038.

277. Lazarsfeld, P.F., Radio and the printed page, New York: Dell, Sloan and Pearce, 1940, pp. 94–104.

278. Mendelsohn, H. (Ed.)., Listening to radio, New York: Free Press, 1964.

279. Williams, T.M., The impact of television, New York: Academic Press, 1986.

280. Belson, W.A., 1961, Effects of television on the reading and buying of newspapers and magazines, Public Opinion Quarterly, Vol. 25, pp. 366–381

281. Nie, N., Hillygus, D., and Erbring, L., Internet use, interpersonal relations and sociability: A time diary study. In Barry Wellman and Carolyne Haythorntwaite (Eds.), The Internet in everyday life, Oxford: Blackwell, 2002, pp. 215–243.

282. Kayany, J., and Yelsma, P., 2000, Displacement effects of online media in the socio-technical contexts of households. Journal of Broadcasting and Electronic Media, Vol. 44(2), pp. 215–229.

283. Weiss, W., The impact of mass media. In G. Lindzey and E. Aronson (Eds.), Handbook of Social Psychology Vol. 5, Reading, MA: Addison-Wesley, 1968, pp. 77–195.

284. Robinson, J., 1981, Television and leisure time: A new scenario, Journal of Communication, Vol. 31, pp. 120–130.

285. Kraut, R., Patternson, M., Lundmark, V. Kiesler, S., Mukophadhayay, T., and Scherlis, W., 1998, Internet paradox: A social technology that reduces social involvement and psychological well-being?, The American Psychologist, Vol. 53(9), pp. 1017–1031.

286. Dimmick, J., Chen, Y., and Li, Z., 2004, Competition between the Internet and traditional news media: The gratification–opportunities niche dimension, Journal of Media Economics, Vol. 17 (1), pp. 19–33.

287. James, M.L., Wotring, C.E., and Forrest, E.J., 1995, An exploratory study of the perceived benefits of electronic bulletin board use and their impact on other communication activities, Journal of Broadcasting and Electronic Media, Vol. 39, pp. 30–50.

288. Himmelweit, H.T., Oppenheim, A.N., and Vince, P., Television and the child, London: Oxford University Press, 1958.

289. Grotta, G.L., and Newsom, D., 1982, How does cable television in the home relate to other media use patterns? Journalism Quarterly, Vol. 59, pp. 588–609.

290. Robinson, J.P., Barth, K., and Kohut, A., 1997, Social impact research: Personal computers, mass media and use of time, Social Science Computer Review, Vol. 15 (1), pp. 65–82.

291. Dutta-Bergman, M., 2004, Complementarity in consumption of news types across traditional and new media., Journal of Broadcasting and Electronic Media, Vol. 48(1), pp.41–61.

292. Robinson, J.P., Kestnbaum, M., Neustadtl, A., and Alvarez, A., 2000, Mass Media and Social Life among Internet Users, Social Science Computer Review. Winter, Vol. 18(4), pp. 490–501.

293. Neustadl, A. and Robinson, J.P., 2002, Media use differences between Internet users and nonusers in the general social survey, IT and Society, Vol. 1(2), pp. 100–120.

294. Vyas, R.S., Singh N.P., and Bhabhra S, 2007, Media displacement effect: Investigating the impact of Internet on newspaper reading habits of consumers, Vision: The journal of Business Perspective, Vol. 11(2), pp. 29–40.

295. Kestnbaum, M., Robinson, J.P., Neustadtl, A. and Alvarez, A., 2002, Information Technology and Social Time Displacement, IT and Society, Vol. 1(1), pp. 21–37

296. Stempel, G., Hargrove, T. and Bernt, J., 2000, Relation of growth of use of the Internet to changes in media use from 1995 to 1999, Journalism and Mass Communication Quarterly, Vol. 77(1), pp. 71–79.

297. Franzen, A., 2000, Does the Internet Make Us Lonely? European Sociological Review, Vol. 16(4), pp. 427–438.

298. Stempel, G., Hargrove, T. and Bernt, J., 2000, Relation of growth of use of the Internet to changes in media use from 1995 to 1999, Journalism and Mass Communication Quarterly, Vol. 77(1), pp. 71–79.

299. Robinson, J., Kestnbaum, M., Neustadtl, A. and Aivarez, A., 2000, Mass media use and social life among Internet users, Social Science Computer Review, Vol. 18(4), pp. 490–501.

300. Lee, W., Tan, T.M.K. and Hameed, S.S., 2005, Polychronicity, the Internet, and the mass media: A Singapore study, Journal of Computer-Mediated Communication, Vol. 11(1), pp. 1–18.

301. Hawley, A.H., Human ecology. In D. L. Sills (Ed.) International Encyclopedia of the Social Sciences, New York: Macmillan, 1968, pp. 328–337.

302. Dimmick, J., and E. Rothenbuhler, 1984, The theory of the niche: Quantifying competition among media industries, Journal of Communication, Vol. 34, pp. 103–119.

303. *Ibid.*, p. 106.

304. McLeod, J.M., and Reeves, B., On the nature of mass media effects. In Withey, S.B. and. Abeles, R.P., (Eds), Television and social behaviour: Beyond violence and children, Hillsdale, NJ: Lawrence Erlbaum Associates,1980, pp. 17–54.

305. Brown N., 1995, A brief history of telemedicine, Telemedicine Information Exchange, Vol. 105, pp. 833–835.

306. Puskin, D.H., Brink, L.H., Mintzer, C.L., and Waseem, C.J., 1995, Joint Federal Initiative for Creating a Telemedicine Evaluation Framework. Letter to the Editor, Telemedicine Journal, Vol. 1(4), p. 394.

307. Grigsby, J., Barton, P.L., Kaehny, M.M., Schlenker, R.E., Shaughnessy, P.W., and Beale, S.K., 1993, Analysis of Expansion of Access to Care Through Use of Telemedicine and Mobile Health Services. Report 1, Literature Review and Analytic Framework, Denver: Center for Health Policy Research, p. 13.

308. Bashshur, R., Sanders, J., and Shannon, G., Telemedicine Theory and Practice, Springfield, IL: Charles C. Thomas, 1997. In Darkins, A.W., Cary, M.A., Telemedicine and telehealth: Principles, policies, performance and pitfalls, Springer Publishing Company, New York, 2000, p. 2.

309. Grigsby, J., and Sanders J.H., 1998, Telemedicine: Where it is and here it's going, Annals of Internal Medicine, Vol. 129(2), pp. 123–127.

310. Benger, J., 2000, A review of telemedicine in accident and emergency: The story so far, Journal of accident and emergency medicine, Vol. 17 (3), pp. 157–64.

311. Navein, J., Fisher, A., Geiling, J., Richards, D. Roller, J., and Hagmann, J., 1998, Portable satellite telemedicine in practice, Journal of Telemedicine and Telecare, Vol. 4 (l), pp. 25–28.

312. Cunningham, T., and Bartlett, K., 1996, Integrated telematic support for paediatrics: a practical model, Journal of Telemedicine and Telecare, Vol. 2 (l), pp. 50–54.

313. Healthcare in India, Emerging market report 2007, 2007, Pricewater House Coopers, pp. 1–26.

314. Otto, C., and Pipe, A., 1997, Remote, mobile telemedicine: the satellite transmission of medical data from Mount Logan, Journal of Telemedicine and Telecare, Vol. 3 (1), pp. 84–85.

315. Press Information Bureau, Government of India, Press Release, August 20, 2007.

316. Press Information Bureau, Government of India, Press Release, May 12, 2007.
317. Frommel, D., May, 2002, Exporting health: Global market in medical workers, Le Monde diplomatique, p. 28.
318. Census – 1981: Census of India 1981 - Five Per cent Sample Report, GOI, New Delhi, 1984.
319. Ohinmaa, A., Hailey, D., and Roine, R., 2001, Assessing telemedicine: A systematic review of the literature. Canadian Medical Association Journal, Vol. 165(6), pp. 765–771.
320. Schwamm, L.H., Rosenthal, E.S., Hirshberg, A., Schaaefer, P.W., Little, E.A., Kvedar, J.C., Petkovska, I., Koroshetz, W.J., and Levine, S., 2004, Virtual telestroke support for the emergency department evaluation of acute stroke, Academic Emergency Medicine, Vol. 11(11), pp. 1193–97.
321. Olver, I., and Selva-Nayagam, S., 2000, Evaluation of a telemedicine link between Darwin and Adelaide to facilitate cancer management, Telemedicine Journal, Vol. 6(2), pp. 213–218.
322. Ellis, I., 2004, Is telehealth the right tool for remote communities? Improving health status in rural Australia, Contemporary nurse, Vol. 16 (3), pp. 163–168.
323. Bedi, B.S., 2008, Tele-medicine: Indian perspective and DIT initiatives, paper presented at United Nations/India Regional Workshop on using Space Technology for Tele-Epidemiology to Benefit Asia and the Pacific Region, October 21st, 2008, at School of Telemedicine and Biomedical Informatics, Sanjay Gandhi Postgraduate Institute of Medical Sciences, Lucknow, U.P., India.
324. Ghosh, K.K., 2008, Telelmedicine initiative by DIT', paper presented at United Nations/India Regional Workshop on Using Space Technology for Tele-Epidemiology to Benefit Asia and the Pacific Region, October 21st, 2008, at School of Telemedicine and Biomedical Informatics, Sanjay Gandhi Postgraduate Institute of Medical Sciences, Lucknow, U.P., India.
325. Park, K., Park's textbook of preventive and social medicine, Banarsidas Bhanot, Jabalpur, 2005, p. 286.
326. *Ibid.*
327. *Ibid.*, 287.
328. *Ibid.*, 288.
329. Giovas, P., Papadoyannis, D., Thomakos, D., Papazachos, G., Rallidis, M., Soulis, D., Stamatopoulos, C., Mavrogeni, S., and Katsilambros, N., 1998, Transmission of electrocardiograms from a moving ambulance, Journal of Telemedicine and Telecare, Vol. 4 (l), pp. 5–7.
330. Dewan, B.D., Malhotra, K.C., Gupta, S.P., 1974, Epidemiology study of coronary heart diseases in a rural community in Haryana, Indian Heart Journal, Vol. 26, pp. 26–68.
331. Sinha B.C., 1970, Ischaemic heart diseases in India, Journal of Indian Medical Association, Vol. 55, p. 171.

332. Park, K., Park's textbook of preventive and social medicine, Banarsidas Bhanot, Jabalpur, 2005, p. 49.
333. Woo, K.S., Tse, K.K., Mak, Y.K., Chung, H.K., 1992, The impact of thrombolytic therapy on hospital mortality from acute myocardial infarction in the Chinese in Hong Kong, International journal of cardiology, Vol. 37(2), pp. 169–175.
334. Sakai, M., Imai, T., Kuboki, K., Maeda, S., Ueda, S., Kuwajima, I., Ohkawa, S., and Matshushita, S., 1999, Usefulness and safety of intravenous thrombolytic therapy for elderly patients with acute myocardial infarction: relationship with cardiac rupture, Journal of cardiology, Vol. 33(3), pp. 153–61.
335. Vaishnav A.G., Pettigrew L.C., Ryan S., 2008, Telephonic guidance of systemic thrombolysis in acute ischemic stroke: safety outcome in rural hospitals, Clinical Neurology and Neurosurgery, Vol. 110(5), pp. 451–454.
336. Adair, O.V., 2001, Cardiology secrets, Elsevier health sciences, ed. 2., pp. 289–293.
337. Cooke, B., and Kothari, U., The case for participation as tyranny. In B. Cooke and U. Kothari (Eds.), Participation: The new tyranny, New York, Zed Books, 2002, pp. 1–15.
338. Guijt, I., 1999, Participatory monitoring and evaluation for natural resource management and research, Socio-economic Methodologies for Natural Resources Research. Chatham, UK, Natural Resources Institute, pp. 1–22.
339. Mumford, E., Participation—from Aristotle to today, in T. Bemelmans (Eds.), Beyond productivity: Information Systems Development for Organisational Effectiveness, Amsterdam, the Netherlands, North-Holland Press, 1984, pp. 95–104.
340. Sahay, S., and Avgerou, C., 2002, Introducing the special issue on information and communication technologies in developing countries, The Information Society, Vol. 18, pp. 73–76.
341. Madon, S., and Sahay, S., 2002, An information-based model of NGO mediation for the empowerment of slum dwellers in Bangalore, The Information Society, Vol. 18 (1), pp. 13–19.
342. Brown, D., 1991, Methodological considerations in the evaluation of social development programmes—an alternative approach, Community Development Journal, Vol. 26(4), pp. 259–265.
343. Sunden, S., and Wicander, G., 2006, Information and communication technology applied for developing countries in a rural context :Towards a framework for analysing factors influencing sustainable use, Karlstad University Studies 2006, Vol. 69, pp. 18–34.
344. Janda, K., Berry, J. M., and Goldman, J., The challenge of democracy: Government in America (4th ed.), Houghton Mifflin, Boston, 1995, p. 42.
345. *Ibid.*, p. 47.

346. Berry, J.M., The Internet group society (3rd ed.), Longman, New York, 1997, p. 218.
347. Hibbing, J.R., and Theiss-Morse, E., Stealth democracy: Americans' beliefs about how government should work. Cambridge, UK: Cambridge University Press, 2002.
348. Norris, P., (Eds), Critical citizens: Global support for democratic government, New York, Oxford University Press, 1999.
349. Norris, P., Who surfs? New technology, old voters and virtual democracy. In E. Kamarck and J. Nye (Eds), democracy.com? Governance in a networked world, Hollis, NH: Hollis Publishing, 1999, pp. 71–98.
350. Putnam R.D., 1995a, Bowling alone, America's declining social capital, Journal of democracy, Vol. 6(1), pp. 65–78.
351. Uslaner, E.M., 2004, Trust, civic engagement, and the Internet, Political communication,Vol. 21, pp. 223–242.
352. Verba, S., Schlozman, K.L., Brady, H., and Nie, N. H., 1993, Race, ethnicity, and political resources: Participation in the United States, British Journal of Political Science, Vol. 23(4), pp. 453–497.
353. Verba, S., Schlozman, K.L., and Brady, H. E., Voice and equality: Civic voluntarism in American politics, Harvard University Press, Cambridge, MA, 1995, p. 640.
354. Clarke, H.D., Sanders, D., Stewart, M.C., and Whiteley, P.F., 2003, Britain (not) at the polls 2001, Political Science and Politics, Vol. 36(1), pp. 59–64.
355. Webster, F., Democracy and information in a network society. In S. Criddle, L. Dempsey, and R. Heseltine (Eds.), Information landscapes for a learning society: Networking and the future of libraries, Library Association,, London, 1999, pp. 235–254.
356. Verba, S., Schlozman, K.L., and Brady, H.E., 1995, Voice and equality: Civic voluntarism in American politics, Harvard University Press, Cambridge, MA, p. 640.
357. Bimber, B., 1998, The Internet and political transformation: Populism, community, and accelerated pluralism, Polity, Vol. 31(1), pp. 133–160.
358. Sawyer, S., and Eschenfelder, K.R., 2002, Social informatics: Perspectives, examples, and trends, Annual Review of Information Science and Technology, Vol. 36, pp. 427–467.
359. Kling, R., and Callahan, E., 2003, Electronic journals, the Internet, and scholarly communication, Annual Review of Information Science and Technology, Vol. 37, pp. 127–177.
360. Kochen, M., 1983, Information and society, Annual Review of Information Science and Technology, Vol. 18, pp. 277–304.
361. Doctor, R.D., 1992, Social equity and information technologies: Moving toward information democracy, Annual Review of Information Science and Technology, Vol. 27, pp. 43–96.
362. Lievrouw, L., and Farb, S., 2003, Information and equity, Annual Review of Information Science and Technology, Vol. 37, pp. 499–540.

363. Berman, J., and Witzner, D.J., 1997, Technology and democracy, Social Research, Vol. 64(3), pp. 1313–1320.
364. Stromer-Galley, J., 2000b, On-line interaction and why candidates avoid it, Journal of Communication, Vol. 50 (4), pp. 111–132.
365. London, S., 1995, Teledemocracy vs. deliberative democracy: A comparative look at two models of public talk, Journal of Interpersonal Computing and Technology, Vol. 3(2), pp. 33–55.
366. Tambini, D., 1999, New media and democracy: The civic networking movement. New Media and Society, Vol. 1 (3), pp. 305–329.
367. Carveth, R., and Metz, J., 1996, Frederick Jackson Turner and the democratisation of the electronic frontier, American Sociologist, Vol. 27 (1), pp. 72–100.
368. Dijk, J.V., Widening Information Gaps and Policies of Prevention. In K. Hacker and J. van Dijk (Eds.) Digital Democracy, Issues of theory and practice, London, Thousand Oaks, New Delhi: Sage Publications, 2000, pp. 166–183.
369. Bellamy, C., and Taylor, J.A., Governing in the information age, Buckingham, UK, Open University Press,1998, pp. 15–20.
370. Mackenzie, D., and Wajcman, J., (Eds), The social shaping of technology (2nd edn), Buckingham, UK, Open University Press, 1999.
371. Bellamy, C., and Taylor, J.A., Governing in the information age, Buckingham, UK, Open University Press, 1998, pp. 18–19.
372. Kettl, D.F., 2000, Public Administration at the Millennium: The State of the Field, Journal of Public Administration Research and Theory, Vol. 10(1), pp. 7–34.
373. La porte, T.M., Demchak, C.C., and De Jong, M., 2002, Democracy and bureaucracy in the age of the web: Empirical findings and theoretical speculations, Administration and society, Vol. 34(4), pp. 411–446.
374. Ott, D., 1998, Power to the people: The role of electronic media in promoting democracy in Africa, First Monday, Vol. 3(4). Retrieved January 20, 2008, from http://www.firstmonday.dk/issues/issue3_4/ott/index.html.
375. Zhang, J., 2002, Will the government serve the people? The development of Chinese e-government. New Media and Society, Vol. 4(2), pp. 163–184.
376. Becker, T., 2001, Rating the impact of new technology on democracy, Communication of the ACM, Vol. 44(1), pp. 39–43.
377. Klein, Hans, 1999, Tocqueville in Cyberspace: Using the Internet for Citizen Associations, The Information Society, Vol. 15, pp. 1–4.
378. La porte, T.M., Demchak, C.C., and De Jong, M., 2002, Democracy and bureaucracy in the age of the web: Empirical findings and theoretical speculations, Administration and Society, Vol. 34(4), pp. 411–446.
379. Special website on National task force on IT and Software development. Available at http://it-taskforce.nic.in/ accessed on 26/12/2008.

6

Methods of Analysis

This chapter presents in detail the methods used and hypotheses tested for the four studies as each study is unique and therefore methods of analysis applied are different.

This chapter is divided into four sections. The first presents the methods of analysis used for the study on 'Internet as a medium of news'. The second presents the same for the study on 'Internet in healthcare services'. The third section similarly states the study design for the study on 'Internet in agriculture and rural development' and the fourth explains 'Internet and politics'.

6.1 Internet as a Medium of News

The objective of this research is to ascertain the status and impact of the Internet as a medium of news in India in comparison to the print and electronic news media like the Print newspapers and TV news and find answers to the research questions R1-R7 in the Indian context. Presented below are the methods used and hypotheses posited for this research.

6.1.1 Empirical Model, Statistical Tests and Tools

ANOVA has been considered for research question R1 and *t*-test for research questions R2, R3 and R4. Paired *t*-tests were considered for the research question R7.

The logistic regression model was considered for the research question R5 and multiple regression models in the case of research question R6.

All of these models and tests have been presented below:

6.1.1.1 Test for Research Question 1: ANOVA

ANOVA is a univariate procedure as it is used to assess group differences on a single metric dependent variable. It is used to determine the probability that differences in means across groups are solely due to sampling error. Two independent estimates of the variance for the dependent variable are compared. The first reflects the general variability of respondents within the groups and the second represents the differences between groups attributable to the treatment effects.

The ratio of the mean square between groups to the mean square within groups gives us the F statistic, which has been used for hypothesis testing. The basic reason for selecting this test is that it was necessary to collect data from a normally distributed population. This data will represent the number of days that a person acquires news from the three media sources namely Print newspapers, TV and Internet in a typical week. Finally, a hypothesis will be tested based on the data.

6.1.1.2 Further Test for Research Question 1: Tukey's HSD Multiple Comparative Test

Tukey's multiple comparison test is one of several tests that can be used to determine which means amongst a set of means differ from the rest. Tukey's multiple comparison test is also called Tukey's Honestly Signifcant Difference test, or Tukey's HSD. With only two groups of observations we could compare the two group means using a *t*-test. When we have more than two groups, it is inappropriate to simply compare each pair using a *t*-test because of the problem of multiple testing. The correct way to do the analysis is to use a one-way analysis of variance (ANOVA) to evaluate whether there is any evidence that the means of the populations differ. If the ANOVA leads to a conclusion that there is evidence that the group means differ, we might then be interested in investigating which of the means are different. This is where the Tukey multiple comparison test is used. The test compares the difference between each pair of means with appropriate adjustment for the multiple testing. The results are presented as a matrix showing the result for each pair, either as a *P*-value or as a confidence interval. The Tukey multiple comparison test, like both the *t*-test and ANOVA, assumes that the data from the different groups come from populations where the observations have a normal distribution and the standard deviation is the same for each group. Hence, if results of ANOVA indicate that there is difference between groups with respect to newsgathering habit from print newspapers, TV news and Internet news, this test will be used to identify where these differences lie.

6.1.1.3 Test for Research Questions 2, 3 and 4: *t*-test

The *t*-test assesses the statistical significance of the difference between two independent sample means for a single dependent variable. The *t*-test is widely used because it works well with small group sizes and is easy to apply and interpret. This test will be used for hypothesis testing.

Two groups will be created based on whether the respondent reads Internet news. *t*-tests of weekly Print newspaper readership and TV news viewership between readers and non-readers of Internet news will be performed and the hypotheses tested.

6.1.1.4 Test for Research Question 7: Paired *t*-test

Paired *t*-tests are used to compare two sets of quantitative data when data in each sample set are related in a special way: the number of points in each data set must be the same, and they must be organised in pairs, in which there is a definite relationship between each pair of data points. Based on these criteria, it is felt to be the most appropriate test in the case of comparing the perceived and observed utility ratings of Internet news by each respondent.

6.1.1.5 Model for Research Question 5

Logistic regression analysis (LRA) extends the technique of multiple regression analysis to research situations in which the outcome variable is categorical. In practice, situations involving categorical outcome are quite common.

The simplified form of the logistic regression model (Equation 6.1) has been derived and presented as:

Equation 6.1: $$\ln\left[\frac{P}{1-P}\right] = \alpha + \beta X_i + \varepsilon$$

where,

$$p = \frac{\exp(\alpha + \beta Xi + \varepsilon)}{1 + \exp(\alpha + \beta Xi + \varepsilon)},\ 1 - p$$

$$= 1/(1 + exp\ (\alpha + \beta Xi + \varepsilon)),\ p/1{-}p = exp\ (\alpha + \beta Xi + \varepsilon)$$

X_i = Average number of days of ith individual gathering news from TV and print newspapers and ε = Standard error.

This formula has been taken into consideration since our dependent variable 'read Internet news' is categorical as the response can be 'yes', or 'no'.

The basic tenet of choosing the logistic regression equation is that the researcher wants to classify the respondents into two groups (yes, or no) on the basis of their habit of reading Internet news. Further, this form has been chosen, since it is widely used in the field of marketing for categorical dependent variable.

However, in the case of categorical dependent variable, the discriminant analysis can also be applied instead of logistic regression model.[1] Perhaps, the former claims stricter assumptions than demanded by the latter with respect to predictor variables.[2] Moreover, the interpretations of the results with respect to logistic regression analysis are much easier than discriminant one on the basis of these reasons, the logistic regression with maximum likelihood estimators (MLE) algorithm has been preferred to discriminant analysis in this study.

6.1.1.6 Model for Research Question 6

An additive form of multiple regression model (equation 6.2) has been considered for the research question R6 as mentioned earlier and the dependent variable is assumed to be normally distributed and postulated as:

Equation 6.2: $$Y = b_0 + \sum_{i=1}^{n} b_i X_i + x_i$$

where,

Y = News gathering habit from TV and print newspaper (in days)

b_0 = Constant

b_i = Regression coefficient of the ith variable

X_i = Value of the ith independent variable. All the variables have been defined in the table 6.1 below.

x_i = Random error of ith observation.

To fully understand how the growing use of Internet news might be related to the trend in print and electronic news media consumption, namely reading print newspapers and TV new viewing, it is necessary to control the demographic variables of gender, age, education, profession, socio-economic variables like annual income, Internet connectivity at home and also Internet usage patterns. As previous studies have shown, all of these exogenous variables strongly affect Internet news consumption. Also, important will be the credibility perception of Internet news and the credibility perceptions of print newspapers and TV news and the perceived change in dependence on Internet. Table 6.1 shows the variables to be used in the multiple regression analysis model for this study.

Table 6.1: Variables to be Used in the Multiple Regression Analysis Model

Demographic Variables	*Measurement*
Gender	Male = 0, Female = 1
Age	18–28 years = 1, 29 – 38 years = 2 (base group), > 38 years = 3
Socio-economic Variables	
Education	Graduate = 1, Postgraduate = 2, Others = 3 (base group)
Annual income	Less than or equal to 4 lakhs = 0, Greater than 4 lakhs = 1
Profession	Students = 1, Self employed = 2, Unemployed = 3, Teachers = 4, Others (base group) = 5
Internet connectivity at home	Yes = 1, No = 0
Cognitive Variables	
Internet dependence	Has increased = 1, Not increased = 0
Credibility perception of Internet news	Has been measured by the following equation: $X_{i(I)} = \sum_{j=1}^{n} CJ/n$, (j = 1, 2, 3, 4, 5, 6, 7) where, $X_{i(I)}$ is average perception of the ith individual towards all items (j = 7) for Internet news construct.

Demographic Variables	*Measurement*
Credibility perception of TV news and Print newspapers	Has been measured by the following equation: $X_{i(TP)} = (X_{i(TV)} + X_{i(PN)})/2$ Where $X_{i(TV)} = \sum_{j=1}^{n} Tj/n$ and $X_{i(PN)} = \sum_{j=1}^{n} Pj/n$, (j = 1, 2, 3, 4, 5, 6, 7) $X_{i(TV)}$ is average perception of the ith individual towards all items (j = 7) for TV news construct and $X_{i(PN)}$ is the average perception of the ith individual towards all items (j = 7) for Print newspapers construct.
Ratio Variables	
Weekly Internet news consumption in days	As measured in days for each respondent
Time spent on the Internet in a day in hours	As measured in days for each respondent

6.1.1.7 Model for Research Question 7

Three independent regression equations using ordinary least square algorithm have been considered and the purpose was to test the impact of the perceived utility constructs (Interpersonal communication, Entertainment, Information skimming and Information scanning) of print newspapers and TV news (print and electronic media) on the gaps observed between the perceived and observed values of the three different utility constructs of Internet namely information skimming and scanning, entertainment and interpersonal communication.

An additive form of multiple regression models have been considered for each of the three regression equations as:

$$\sum_{i=1}^{3} Y_i = b_0 + \sum_{j=1}^{4} b_j X_j + \sum_{k=1}^{4} b_K X_K + x_I$$

where, Y_i = observed gaps between the perceived and observed values of the utility construct of Internet; b_0 = Constant; X_j = value of the jth construct of print newspaper; X_k = value of the kth construct of TV news; b_j = Regression coefficient of jth constraint for print newspapers;

b_k = Regression coefficient of kth constraint for TV news; I = Random error of ith observation of that utility.

6.1.2 Research Hypotheses

The contemporary view about media uses and needs is an audiencecentered view that assumes that media behaviour is purposive, goal-directed and motivated, people select media content to satisfy their needs or desire, social and psychological dispositions mediate that behavior and the media compete with other forms of communication — or functional alternatives – such as interpersonal interaction for selection, attention and use. Audiences are not the same and they seek and consume media based on their choices. Media on the other hand comes in different formats and provides different uses to its users. Within the audience who have access to print newspapers, TV news and Internet news in India it is necessary to know whether there is a difference in the newsgathering habit from different media and that will answer the first research question through the following hypothesis H1.1:

H1.1: There is a difference between groups of audience with respect to newsgathering habit from Print newspapers, TV news and Internet news.

Mathematically,

H_0: $\mu p = \mu t = \mu i$ against H_a: $\mu p \neq \mu t \neq \mu i$

Further, amongst this audience, some read Internet news and some don't. Between readers and non-readers of Internet news and also within the groups of readers and non-readers of Internet news, it is necessary to see whether there is a difference in the newsgathering habits from print newspapers and TV news which leads to the research questions R2, R3 and R4. This will provide a better understanding about the preferences of these groups and for that hypotheses H2.1, H2.2, H3.1 and H4.1 have been positied.

Hypotheses H2.1 and H2.2 answers the second research question, hypothesis H3.1 answers the third research question and hypothesis H4.1 answers the fourth.

H2.1: There is difference in the news gathering habit from Print newspaper between the groups of Internet news readers (A) and non-readers (B).

Mathematically,

H_0: XPN(A) = X PN(B) against H_a: XPN(A) $\neq$ XPN(B)

H2.2: There is difference in the news gathering habit from TV news between the groups of Internet news readers (A) and non-readers (B).

Mathematically,

H_0: XTV(A) = X TV(B) against H_a: XTV(A) ≠ XTV(B)

H3.1: There is difference in the news gathering habit from Print newspapers and TV news within the group of non readers of Internet news (B).

Mathematically,

H_0: XPN(B) = X TV(B) against H_a: XPN(B) ≠ XTV(B)

H4.1: There is difference in the news gathering habit from Print newspapers and TV news within the group of Internet newsreaders (A).

Mathematically,

H_0: XPN(A) = X TV(A) against H_a: XPN(A) ≠ XTV(A)

Existing theory suggests a change in the media use patterns following introduction of a new communication technology. It has been also observed that media choice depends on the users past experience with the media and how well his different communication needs have been satisfied by it. Further, if time is a zero-sum phenomeon then the time spent on a new activity would be at the cost of some other activity. It would be justified to hypothesize then, that in terms of time spent there is a negative impact of print and electronic media habits too on newsgathering habits from the Internet. Hence to answer the fifth research question the following hypothesis has been framed. This will add to the research literature by studying the impact of print and electronic media habits on the news gathering habit from Internet in the Indian context.

H5.1: There is a negative impact of the combined (reading print newspapers and watching TV news) print and electronic media habits on the news gathering habit from Internet.

Mathematically,

H_0: $\beta i = 0$ against H_a: $\beta i < 0$

To answer the sixth research question, it is necessary to test the impact of different factors on newsgathering habits (in days) from print newspapers and TV news. Education and age are the most important factors that seem to affect Internet usage and the longer their association with the medium the more variety of use is reported[3]. In Italy for instance, it was found[4] that Internet use amongst children who lived with better-educated parents was significantly higher than the ones whose parents were less educated. Additionally, gender, generation and other social factors also affect the usage of media amongst users[5]. The female newspaper readership in India for instance is growing faster than the male readership as per a recent study.[6]

Research on deprivation and dependency have shown that in some individuals high levels of attachment and dependence on media arise from conditions like confinement at home,low income and some forms of stress. These media could be both television[7] and print newspapers.[8] There is also a significant relationship between perception of credibility of Internet and getting news from the Internet.[9] Finally, expectations from the media also guide user's behaviour.[10]

Thus we see that various demographic,socio economic and cognitive variables affect media use. Based on these variables, to answer the sixth research question it can thus be predicted that:

H6.1: Female Internet users collate news more in days from TV news and print newspapers than male Internet users.

That is, mathematically H_0: $\beta_1 = 0$ against H_a: $\beta_1 > 0$

H6.2: Internet users in the age group of 18-28 years collate news less from print newspapers and TV news in days than Internet users in the age group of 29–38 years.

That is, mathematically H_0: $\beta_2 = 0$ against H_a: $\beta_2 < 0$

H6.3: Internet users in the age group of > 38 years collate news from TV news and print newspapers in days less than Internet users in the age group of 29–38 years.

That is, mathematically H_0: $\beta_3 = 0$ against H_a: $\beta_3 < 0$

H6.4: Post graduate Internet users collate news from TV news and print newspapers in days more than Internet users in the others group.

That is, mathematically H_0: $\beta_4 = 0$ against H_a: $\beta_4 > 0$

H6.5: Graduate Internet users collate news from TV news and print newspapers in days more than Internet users in the others group.

That is, mathematically H_0: $\beta_5 = 0$ against H_a: $\beta_5 > 0$

H6.6: Internet users earning more than Rs. 4 lakhs collate news less from TV news and print newspapers in days than Internet users earning less than Rs. 4 lakhs.

That is, mathematically H_0: $\beta_6 = 0$ against H_a: $\beta_6 < 0$

H6.7: Internet users having Internet connectivity at home collate news less from TV news and print newspapers in days than Internet users who do not have Internet connectivity at home.

That is, mathematically H_0: $\beta_7 = 0$ against H_a: $\beta_7 < 0$

H6.8: Internet users, who are students collate news more from TV news and print newspapers in days than Internet users in the others group.

That is, mathematically H_0: $\beta_8 = 0$ against H_a: $\beta_8 > 0$

H6.9: Internet users, who are self employed collate news more from TV news and print newspapers in days than Internet users in the others group.

That is, mathematically H_0: $\beta_9 = 0$ against H_a: $\beta_9 > 0$

H6.10: Internet users, who are unemployed collate news more from TV news and print newspapers in days than Internet users in the others group.

That is, mathematically H_0: $\beta_{10} = 0$ against H_a: $\beta_{10} > 0$

H6.11: Internet users, who are teachers collate news more from TV news and print newspapers in days than Internet users in the others group.

That is, mathematically H_0: $\beta_{11} = 0$ against H_a: $\beta_{11} > 0$

Studies of media credibility show that as usage of a particular medium increases, its credibility ratings also increases. A study[11] discussed the crossover in credibility ratings between newspapers and television as television gained popularity. The positive association between usage of or reliance on a medium and perceptions of its credibility were found by other studies[12] as well. In a study by the Pew Research Center[13], it was found that higher consumption of Internet news by Internet users resulted in higher accuracy ratings of Internet news outlets. This suggests that there should be some relationship between the users credibility perception of a media and its usage and hence the expectations of this study are that:

H6.12: Credibility perception of Internet has a negative impact on collating news from TV news and print newspapers in days.

That is, mathematically H_0: $\beta_{12} = 0$ against H_a: $\beta_{12} < 0$

H6.13: Credibility perception of Print newspapersand TV news have a positive impact on collating news from TV news and print newspapers in days.

That is, mathematically H_0: $\beta_{13} = 0$ against H_a: $\beta_{13} > 0$

Findings of earlier displacement research suggest that the introduction of Internet media into a user's schedule of activities will result in reduction of time spent in other activities. Assuming a zero sum relationship among the various activities, we expect time displacement effects on the use of television and newspaper.

Therefore posit that,

H6.14: No of days of weekly Internet news consumption has a negative impact on collating news from TV news and print newspapers in days.

That is, mathematically H_0: $\beta_{14} = 0$ against H_a: $\beta_{14} < 0$

H6.15: Daily Internet usage in hours has a negative impact on collating news from TV news and print newspapers in days.

That is, mathematically H_0: $\beta_{16} = 0$ against H_a: $\beta_{16} < 0$

Pew Research Center also found[14] that Internet users associate Internet news to have greater accuracy than other news media and this result was significantly different from non-users of Inernet.This suggests that experience with a medium should have an influence on its usage. Moreover, Internet users have been found to be more active in their need for news and as such:

H6.16: Internet users whose Internet dependence has increased collate news more from TV news and print newspapers in days than Internet users whose dependence has remain unchanged.

That is, mathematically H_0: $\beta_{15} = 0$ against H_a: $\beta_{15} > 0$.

The following hypothesis has been framed to answer the research question R7a (Is there any difference between the perceived and observed utilities of Internet news?)

H7: There is a difference between respondent's perceived and observed utilities for Internet news (information scanning and skimming utiltiy, entertainment utiltiy and interpersonal communication utility respectively)

$H_0 \, d\bar{i} = 0; : H_1: d\bar{i} \neq 0$

To answer the research question R7b, the following hypotheses H7b, H7c, H7d.

(as i = 1, 2, 3) have been postulated:

There would be impact of jth and k^{th} construct of print newspapers and TV news on the gap between the perceived and observed values with respect to i^{th} construct of Internet news.

6.1.3 Research Instrument

6.1.3.1 For the purpose of measurement of credibility perception of a news medium, the survey instrument used is a self-designed questionnaire.

Extensive literature review has been done.[15] All the questionnaire reported in the literature is confined to the western countries. No questionnaire could be found for this particular set of respondents in India. Moreover, the few studies that were explored in the Indian context were investigating research questions other than the ones required in this research. A modest attempt has been made to frame a suitable questionnaire to gauge the perception of the respondents. In the early stage, that is concept development phase (what is to be measured and what can be measured), an extensive review of literature on the subject and an analysis of possible components to be measured have been done. Some were established measures, while others were modified or developed for this study based on intuition, knowledge and experience.

After identifying a set of possible items an intensive discussion with a group of target respondents (individuals having access to Internet, print newspapers and TV news) has been done to assess the proposed concepts, definition, terminology and final selection of the relevant items. In the next stage, face-to-face in-depth interviews with three managers (one from the print newspaper industry, one from the TV news industry and one from an Internet news portal) have been conducted to divide all the items into three constructs (print newspapers, TV news and Internet news).

After having consultation with two academicians, these items have been confirmed and questions framed on them on a 5-point Likert scale (1 = strongly disagree to 5 = strongly agree). The Likert scale has been used as it is a reliable and commonly used scale that can be easily interpreted. All the items are framed in closed-end form.

For the purpose of pre testing the questionnaire a pilot survey has been performed on 83 respondents. This helps to get ideas on respondent's comprehension of instruction and definition, problems with records retrieval including reasons for item non-response, records availability and time burden. Further, this procedure helps to redesign the layout of the questionnaire and flow of items in respective constructs.

Moreover, the data from this pilot survey have been used to measure the reliability and validity of the questionnaire as discussed in the sub-section 6.1.3.1.1.

The measurement of media credibility has been debated for long and it has been shown that the credibility ratings are dependent on the the concept of credibility.[16] The most consistent dimensions of media credibility are trustworthiness, fairness, believability, balance and accuracy. Further, two other dimensions of credibiliy namely currency of reporting and timeliness have also been used by researchers engaged in research on online news. Therefore, in this study media credibility was operationalised as a multidimensional concept consisting of trustworthiness, fairness, believability, balance, accuracy, currency of reporting and timeliness of reporting.

Three scales were designed for the three constructs namely–print newspapers, TV news and Internet news to measure individually, one dependent variable–the credibility perception of the media. Each of the three scales had seven identical items, namely, Trustworthiness, Currency of reporting, Fairness, Believability, Balance, Accuracy and Timeliness.

The dependent variable perception of credibility was measured through a self-report questionnaire using a standard 5 point Likert scale to rate the items. The subjects rated each of the three media-print newspapers, TV news and Internet news according to their experience of use. Perception was computed using the values obtained on all seven items.

Additionally, information regarding the demographic profile, the socio-economic profile, perception about increased dependence on Internet were also collected.

6.1.3.1.1 Evaluation of Valididty and Reliability of the Questionnaire

A pilot survey was conducted on 83 respondents to see the reliability and validity of the questionnaire discussed below; the number of respondents in the initial survey was within acceptable limit.[17]

***Reliability*:** There are various methods, which can be used to measure the reliability of a research instrument; they are test-retest reliability, internal-consistency reliability (Cronbach's alpha),[18] alternative form reliability, intra-observer reliability and inter-observer reliability. However, all of these methods vary in different aspects such as characteristics as well as measurement procedures. Thus, choosing the appropriate one from various methods is a little arbitrary. It also depends on the amount of time, money and energy devoted by the researcher.

In this study, the news credibility perception scale consists of 7 items. The reliability of each of the constructs is tested using Cronbach's coefficient alpha.[19]

A reliability test of the seven items for print newspapers using Cronbach's alpha yielded a standard item alpha 0.83. A reliability test of the seven items for TV news using Cronbach's alpha yielded a standard item alpha 0.87. A reliability test of the seven items for Internet news using Cronbach's alpha yielded a standard item alpha 0.86.

Further, Nunnally (1978) also suggests that the value of reliability coefficient over 0.5 is adequate for basic research, but under apparent reconsideration. That is, the reliability coefficients of all constructs in this study have passed the cut-off value (0.5). Hence it has been confirmed that the research instrument is reliable in this context.

Validity: Besides reliability, it is also necessary to measure the validity of the research instrument. There are various ways that can be used to measure the validity of the questionnaire. They are construct validity, convergent validity, discriminant validity, face validity, criterion-concurrent validity, criterion-predictive validity and internal validity.[20] All of these methods vary in different aspects such as characteristics as well as measurement procedures. That is, choosing an appropriate one from the above-mentioned methods is again a little arbitrary. In this study, an attempt has been made to measure the construct validity of the scale as discussed below.

To identify the construct validity[21] of research instrument, many scholars in the field of marketing have suggested a multivariate technique factor analysis.[22] The same has been followed here and a factor analysis (PCA) was done for each of the three constructs to assess the construct validity of the instrument in question. A single factor was extracted in each case, and the first factor was particularly dominant for every construct. Further, after orthogonal rotation using varimax method for each construct, most of the items were found to load heavily on first factor, which explain 49–56 per cent of total variance for different constructs. A validity test using Principal component analysis for print newspapers yielded one factor, eigenvalue 3.48 with 49.75 per cent variance explained. All items loaded higher than 0.62 on one factor as shown in Table 6.2 below and thus all tne items were retained for the print newspaper scale.

A validity test of the seven items for TV news Principal component analysis yielded one factor, eigenvalue 3.91 with 55.81 per cent variance explained. All items loaded higher than 0.65 on one factor as shown in Table 6.3 below and thus all the items were retained for the TV news scale.

Finally, the validity test of the seven items for Internet news using Principal component analysis yielded one factor, eigenvalue 3.9 with 55.65 per cent variance explained. All items loaded higher than 0.69 except fairness (0.5), on one factor as shown in Table 6.4 below and thus all the items were retained for the Internet news scale.

This lends support to the unidimensionality of each construct and thereby confirms the construct validity of the scale. The results are indicated in Tables 6.2, 6.3 and 6.4 respectively.

Table 6.2: Principal component analysis of seven items measuring perception of print newspapers

Items	*Factor loading*
Trustworthiness	0.78
Currency of reporting	0.63
Fairness	0.71
Believability	0.76
Balance	0.67
Accuracy	0.73
Timeliness	0.64
Eigenvalue	3.48
Variance explained	49.75
Cronbach's alpha	0.83

Table 6.3: Principal component analysis of seven items measuring perception of TV news

Items	*Factor loading*
Trustworthiness	0.76
Currency of reporting	0.71
Fairness	0.79
Believability	0.82
Balance	0.66
Accuracy	0.80
Timeliness	0.67
Eigenvalue	3.91
Variance explained	55.81
Cronbach's alpha	0.87

Table 6.4: Principal component analysis of seven items measuring perception of Internet news

Items	*Factor loading*
Trustworthiness	0.82
Currency of reporting	0.70
Fairness	0.50
Believability	0.86
Balance	0.73
Accuracy	0.80
Timeliness	0.78
Eigenvalue	3.9
Variance explained	55.65
Cronbach's alpha	0.86

6.1.1.3.2 To answer the research question R7, the research instrument used was a questionnaire designed by Lin and Salwen (2006),[23] who had grouped fourteen items or reasons for use for Internet news and Print newspapers into four factors or utilities, namely, Entertainment utility the first factor (having items: fun to read, amusing news, entertaining news, enjoyable news), Interpersonal communication utility; second factor (to use in conversations, stories to share, learning about things), Information scanning utility; third factor (keeping up with the news, getting an overall picture of world events, learning the major news of the day, following the major news of the day) and Information skimming utility; fourth factor (going directly to important news, skipping the unimportant news, seeking important news) based on factor analysis procedure through Principal component analysis with Varimax rotation. This questionnaire could not be used directly in the Indian context without testing the reliability, validity and making necessary modifications, since the questionnaire had been tested previously in a different country. Further, Lin and Salwen (2006) had undertaken this PCA on fourteen items for Internet news and Print newspapers only. In addition, the researcher has used the same fourteen items for TV news and so the PCA undertaken by the researcher differs from the original study with respect to TV news construct, respondents (Indian context), location and time.

Varimax rotation via the Kaiser normalisation procedure will be used to calculate the rotated factor matrix. The rotation makes the factors easier to interpret by maximising the differences between the variable. The rotation takes place in such a way that all the components of the factors are closer to +1, 0, or –1, representing the importance of each variable. A loading close to ±1 indicates a strong correlation between a variable and the factor, while a loadıng close to 0 indicates a weak correlation. Factor loadings have substantially large standard errors than typical correlations. Thus factor loadings should be evaluated at considerably stricter levels.

Therefore, in the present case a higher rotated factor loading of 0.5 and above will be considered significant.[24] Each of the PC-axis or factors, (with high loadings on one or more variables) may be representing an independent source of variation in the data matrix and these may give some clues to genetic processes.[25] The results obtained, its analysis and the subsequent modifications based on the same are presented in the next section.

6.1.1.3.2.1 Modifications of the questionnaire based on results obtained at the design stage

The results of this analysis based on the final data obtained from the 481 respondents have been presented below. No qualitative difference was observed between the pilot and the final surveys in terms of the factors, or groupings of the items for each of the three constructs and hence only the final results have been reported.

The sample size in this case is 481, and there is a 43 to 1 ratio of observations to variables, which falls within acceptable limits. Also, the sample size of 481 provides and adequate basis for the calculation of the correlations between variables.

In the present work, PCA has been applied using SPSS v. 10 software.

The results of the Principal component analysis of TV news, Print newspapers and Internet news using 481 samples are shown below in Tables 6.5, 6.6 and 6.7 respectively. The principal components are the eigenvectors of a variance-covariance matrix. Factor 1 is related to the largest eigenvalue and explains the greatest amount of variance in the data set. Factor 2 (orthogonal to and unrelated to the first) explains the greatest of the remaining variance and so forth.

Table 6.5: Results of the Principal component analysis of questionnaire on TV news

Utility Measures/ items	*Loading on PC axes*			
TV news	*Entertainment*	*Interpersonal communication*	*Information scanning*	*Information skimming*
Fun to read	**0.761**	0.324	0.387	0.237
Amusing news	**0.736**	0.380	0.372	0.308
Entertaining news	**0.804**	0.306	0.248	0.293
Enjoyable stories	**0.816**	0.325	0.238	0.269
To use in conversations	0.439	**0.759**	0.316	0.263
Stories to share	0.370	**0.788**	0.276	0.340
Learning about things	0.308	**0.792**	0.360	0.305
Keeping up with the news	0.428	0.511	**0.576**	0.341
Getting an overall picture of world events	0.435	0.468	**0.644**	0.331
Learning the major news of the day	0.405	0.480	**0.640**	0.360
Following the major news of the day	0.431	0.483	**0.601**	0.336
Going directly to important news	0.492	0.276	**0.550**	0.473
Skipping unimportant news	0.362	0.353	0.259	**0.793**
Seeking important news	0.340	0.386	0.418	**0.681**
% Eigenvalue	29.06	25.47	19.80	16.94
Cum %	29.06	54.54	74.34	91.29

Table 6.6: Results of the Principal component analysis of questionnaire on Print newspapers

Utility Measures/items	*Loading on PC axes*			
Print news-papers	*Interpersonal communication*	*Entertainment*	*Information scanning*	*Information skimming*
Fun to read	0.292	0.815	0.121	0.055
Amusing news	0.285	0.847	0.148	0.055
Entertaining news	0.174	0.886	0.106	0.126
Enjoyable stories	0.209	0.801	0.075	0.234
To use in conversations	0.828	0.270	0.092	0.109
Stories to share	0.819	0.293	0.104	0.030
Learning about things	0.872	0.184	0.150	0.059
Keeping up with the news	0.256	0.145	0.928	0.39
Getting an overall picture of world events	0.731	0.185	0.240	0.279
Learning the major news of the day	0.675	0.277	0.276	0.284
Following the major news of the day	0.186	0.151	0.942	0.111
Going directly to important news	0.530	0.298	0.204	0.536
Skipping unimportant news	0.081	0.119	0.051	0.877
Seeking important news	0.499	0.136	0.199	0.524
% Eigenvalue	28.490	23.413	14.708	11.404
Cum %	28.490	51.904	66.611	78.015

Table 6.7: Results of the Principal component analysis of questionnaire on Internet news

Utility Measures/items	*Loading on PC axes*		
Internet news	*Information scanning and skimming*	*Entertainment*	*Interpersonal communication*
Fun to read	0.313	0.891	0.069
Amusing news	0.323	0.852	0.170
Entertaining news	0.295	0.867	0.280
Enjoyable stories	0.356	0.838	0.224
To use in conversations	0.264	0.231	0.851
Stories to share	0.402	0.307	0.556
Learning about things	0.425	0.146	0.838
Keeping up with the news	0.771	0.339	0.319
Getting an overall picture of world events	0.707	0.287	0.490
Learning the major news of the day	0.822	0.333	0.197
Following the major news of the day	0.804	0.383	0.218
Going directly to important news	0.797	0.387	0.268
Skipping unimportant news	0.771	0.259	0.298
Seeking important news	0.757	0.319	0.367
% Eigenvalue	36.05	27.95	18.73
Cum %	36.05	64.01	82.74

The original authors did not measure TV news and therefore the output of the principal component analysis will be compared with the scales for online news and print newspapers of the original authors.

The output of the PCA (Table 6.5) for TV news reveals that the first four eigen values together account for 91.29 per cent of the total variability of the combined population or variable. Further, it is observed that in the case of TV news, the first factor, has four items: fun to read, amusing news, entertaining news and enjoyable news that have been loaded highly on it and accounts for more than 29 per cent of the total variance. These 4 items comprised the entertainment scale of the original authors and thus the first factor in this case will also be called the Entertainment scale.

The second factor, has three items, namely: to use in conversations, stories to share and keeping up with the news that have been loaded highly on it and accounts for 25.47 per cent of the rest of the variance. These 3 items belong to the Interpersonal communication factor of the original authors, and therefore, in this case too the same name will be retained for the construct.

On the third factor, four items—keeping up with the news, getting an overall picture of world events, learning the major news of the day, following the major news of the day and going directly to important news have been highly loaded and that accounts for 19.8 per cent of the remaining variance. The first 4 items mentioned belong to the Information scanning utility of the original authors and the last belongs to the information skimming utility.

In this case, the researcher shall continue to call this construct–information scanning utility of TV news. Two items: skipping unimportant news and seeking important news have been highly loaded on the fourth factor and it accounts for 16.94 per cent of the remaining variability. These are the remaining items of the Information skimming construct of the original authors and thus this factor will also be called so.

The output of the PCA (Table 6.1.6) reveals that the first four eigen values together account for over 78 per cent of the total variability of the combined population /variable in the case of print newspapers. Five items: to use in conversations, stories to share, learning about things, getting an overall picture of world events and learning the major news of the day, getting an overall picture of world events and learning the major news of the day, have been loaded highly on the first factor that accounts for 28.47 per cent of the total variability.

The first 3 of these items belong to the Interpersonal communication construct for print newspapers of Lin and Salwen (2006) and the last two belong to the Information scanning construct. Here the first factor will be called Interpersonal communication construct for print newspapers. Hence the Interpersonal communication scale for print newspapers in this case will differ from that of the original authors.

The second principal component, has been loaded highly on four items–fun to read, amusing news, entertaining news and enjoyable news which accounts for 23.41 per cent of the remaining variance and as this loading pattern agrees with the original entertainment construct for print newspapers by the original authors, it shall be called the same. Similar results have been observed on the fourth factor that accounts for 11.40 per cent of the remaining variability. The loadings match the information skimming construct for print newspapers of the original authors and will therefore be called the same by the researcher.

The third factor has been loaded highly on keeping up with the news and following the major news of the day, accounts for 14.71 per cent of the variability. These are the remaining two items of Information scanning of the original authors. Hence the information-skimming construct for print newspapers in this case will be different from the original authors and will have just these two items.

In the case of Internet news, the output of the PCA (Table 6.7) reveals that the first three eigen values together account for 82.74 per cent of the total variability of the combined population/variable. The first factor has been loaded highly on 7 items: keeping up with the news, getting an overall picture of world events, learning the major news of the day, following the major news of the day and going directly to important news, skipping unimportant news, seeking important news and accounts for over 36 per cent of the total variability.

The first four items mentioned above comprise the complete Information scanning scale of the original authors and the last three items the Information skimming scale for online news. Thus it appears that in the Indian context these two utilities have become one and so will be called Information scanning and skimming utility for Internet news in the present study. This is radically different from the findings of the original authors.

The second factor has been highly loaded on 4 items: fun to read, amusing news, entertaining news and enjoyable news and accounts for 27.95 per cent of the remaining variability. These four items match the items in the Entertainment construct for online news of the original authors, and therefore, will be called the same. Three items, namely: to use in conversations, stories to share and keeping up with the news have been highly loaded on the third factor that accounts for 18.73 per cent of the remaining variability. These three items comprise the complete Interpersonal communication construct of the original authors and therefore will also be called the same.

It is observed that all the fourteen items have loaded on three factors only that have explained almost 83 per cent of the total variability, whereas the original authors had 4 factors for online news. Thus the utility constructs of Internet news in this case are different from that of the original authors.

It is thus found that there is difference in the loading pattern as well as the items in some of the utility constructs of the three media in comparison with the original authors.

In order to measure the reliability coefficient to assess the consistency of the scales, Cronbach's alpha[26] measures have been chosen and reported below in Tables 6.8, 6.9 and 6.10 for Print newspapers, TV news and Internet news respectively. This is an appropriate measure according to Nunnally[27].

Table 6.8: Results of the Cronbach's alpha measures of the four constructs for Print newspapers

Name and items of construct for print newspapers	*Cronbach's alpha values*
Interpersonal communication	0.9075
To use in conversations	
Stories to share	
Learning about things	
Getting a overall picture of world events	
Learning the major news of the day	
Entertainment	0.9089
Fun to read	
Amusing news	
Entertaining news	
Enjoyable stories	
Information scanning	0.9596
Keeping up with the news	
Following the major news of the day	
Information skimming	0.6284
Going directly to important news	
Skipping unimportant news	
Seeking important news	

Table 6.9: Results of the Cronbach's alpha measures of the four constructs for TV news

Name and items of construct for TV news	*Cronbach's alpha values*
Entertainment	0.9601
Fun to read	
Amusing news	
Entertaining news	
Enjoyable stories	
Interpersonal communication	
To use in conversations	
Stories to share	0.9688
Learning about things	
Information scanning	
Keeping up with the news	0.9690
Getting an overall picture of world events	
Learning the major news of the day	
Following the major news of the day	
Information skimming	
Going directly to important news	0.9197
Skipping unimportant news	
Seeking important news	

Table 6.10: Results of the Cronbach's alpha measures of the three constructs for Internet news

Name and items of construct for Internet news	*Cronbach's alpha values*
Information scanning and skimming	0.9606
Keeping up with the news	
Getting an overall picture of world events	
Learning the major news of the day	
Following the major news of the day	
Going directly to important news	
Skipping unimportant news	
Seeking important news	

Name and items of construct for Internet news	*Cronbach's alpha values*
Entertainment	0.9568
Fun to read	
Amusing news	
Entertaining news	
Enjoyable stories	
Interpersonal communication	0.8827
To use in conversations	
Stories to share	
Learning about things	

Table 6.10 shows that all the values are above the minimum lower limit[28] and therefore, the scales are valid and perfectly suitable for this purpose. Similar interpretation may be made in the cases of TV news as well as Internet news.

Overall, the diagnostic with respect to validity and reliability indicate that the questionnaires after the modifications from their original forms by the researcher can now be used for larger survey of print newspapers, TV news and Internet news with the respective modifications and changes. Based on these changes they are now found to be suitable for use in the Indian context.

Respondents were asked to rate their perceived utilities based on the above changes, on a Likert style table in a self-report questionnaire on items discussed above with values between 1 and 7 of agreement, where 1 was lowest and 7 highest about Print newspapers, TV news and Internet news. The respondents also used identical scales in the case of Internet construct to rate the observed Internet utilities alongside their perceived utilities. This is a further deviation from the original study since the authors had only measured the perceived utilities of Print newspapers and "Online" news.

6.1.4 Sampling Technique for the Survey

The target popuation for the study were Indian adult consumers of news media, having access to Internet, who have a greater exposure to media sources and a cosmopolitan lifestyle as they are expected to have more activation needs[29] than the others. Moreover, according to the National Readership Study (2006)[30] there has been a dip in the number of readers of print newspapers in the metro cities. In this case, the samples were drawn from four metropolitan cities of India, namely, Kolkata, Mumbai, Delhi and Chennai. Sample frame was not available. The samples were drawn from people who have access to Internet and as such there was no databank of mailing addresses available and neither was the data bank for telephone numbers available. Hence by compulsion, the researcher conducted the sample survey through an interview method using the above detailed questionnaire. A pilot survey was conducted on 83 respondents to see the reliability and validity of the questionnaires.

6.1.5 Sample Size

The sample comprised of Indian adult males and females who gathered news by reading print newspapers, TV news and had access to Internet. Data was collected from residents of four metro cities of India– Kolkata, Delhi, Chennai and Mumbai. The population is represented by students, self-employeds, unemployed, teachers, retired persons and others who did not fit into the above category and had atleast some formal education.

The survey was done based on a questionnaire. One hundred and twenty five (125) questionnaires were assigned to each metropolitan city making a total of five hundred (500) questionnaires. Data was collected from four hundred and eighty four (484) respondents across the four cities. Three cases had to be rejected for incomplete information and the research was conducted on four hundred and eighty one (481) samples.

6.1.6 Method of Interview

The Interview with the questionnaire was conducted during the period 14th February, 2009 and June 20th, 2009 by the researcher in the four cities. The survey was used for speed, economy and control of respondent type. Further, the presence of the researcher as the interviewer ensured a higher response rate and eliminated differences in recording the response.

The context and the reason for the survey were explained to the respondent at the beginning of the survey and all questions were clarified before the survey was conducted. The complete process took around 20 minutes on an average. The respondents were knowledgeable and hence did not require much assistance during filling up the forms. The respondents responded voluntarily and no remuneration was paid to anyone.

6.1.7 Summary of Methods of Analysis

To test the first hypothesis H1.1, method of analysis used was ANOVA and the test statistic was F, since there are three groups in the present study–namely print newspapers, TV news and Internet news and as such *t*-test or z-test could not be performed in this case. Data have been collected from 481 respondents, which has been assumed as normally distributed. This data represent the number of days that a person acquires news from the three media sources namely Print newspapers, TV and Internet in a typical week.

A one-way ANOVA has been performed on the data to test the hypothesis as mentioned above and the results are presented in Table 7.1 of Chapter 7. Further, to identify, where the difference lies between the news acquiring habits from the three media, Tukey's HSG multiple comparative test has been performed. Results of this test have been presented in Table 7.2 of Chapter 7.

To test the hypotheses H2.1 and H2.2, two groups have been created based on whether the respondent reads Internet news. *t*-tests of weekly Print newspaper readership and TV news viewership between readers and non-readers of Internet news has been performed and results have been presented in Table 7.3 in Chapter 7.

To test the hypotheses H3.1 and H4.1 as stated above, *t*-test was conducted within two groups, namely– non-readers of Internet news and readers of Internet news with respect to their newspaper reading habits and news watching on TV habits and the results are presented in Table 7.4 of Chapter 7.

To test the hypothesis H5.1, logistic regression using the maximum likelihood estimation method has been used on the data. The sample size required for logistic regression is adequate.[31] The dependent variable is News gathering from Internet, with the reference category 'yes' coded 1 and the 'do not read Internet news' category coded 0.The independent variable is Avg, which is the average number of days that print newspaper is read and/or TV news is viewed. The results of the analysis are presented in the Tables 7.5 and 7.6 of Chapter 7.

The additive form of multiple regression models will be used and ordinary least square algorithm has been considered to estimate the regression coefficients and test of hypotheses H6.1 – H6.16 as mentioned earlier. The impact of the variables on the dependent variable will also be measured. One dependent variable, News gathering from TV and print newspaper (in days), will be measured with sixteen items (gender, age, annual income, Internet connectivity at home, Internet dependence, perception towards Internet news, perception towards print-newspapers and TV news, weekly Internet usage in days and daily Internet usage in hours), through a self-report questionnaire.

The items: perception towards Internet news and perception towards print newspapers and TV news comprises of seven items on perception of Internet news, Print newspapers, TV news and will be measured using a five point Likert scale. The respondents will rate the three media –print newspapers, TV news and Internet news according to their perception of its trustworthiness, currency of reporting, fairness, believability, balance, accuracy, timeliness. A reliability test of the seven items using Cronbach's alpha yielded a standard item alpha. 87 for Internet news,. 83 for TV news and. 78 for Print newspapers.

Table 7.7 in Chapter 7, shows the result of the multiple regression analysis, which tests the impact of perception and Internet usage on the combined usage of print newspapers and TV news. It also shows the beta values, which indicate the variables explanatory power.

Three paired *t*-tests need to be performed to test whether there is any difference between the perceived and observed utilities of the ith construct of Internet news by formulating the following hypotheses:

H7: There is a difference between respondent's perceived and observed utilities for Internet news (information scanning and skimming utiltiy, entertainment utiltiy and interpersonal communication utility respectively)

$$H_0: d\bar{i} = 0 \; ; \; H_1: d\bar{i} \neq 0$$

Then three regressions using ordinary least square method have to be carried out to estimate the impact of various utilities with respect to the identified gaps as well as to test the relevant hypotheses (as mentioned in section 6.1.2). The results have been presented in Tables 7.9–7.12.

6.2 Internet in Healthcare Services

Healthcare is of critical importance in reducing poverty and bringing in development. Internet technology is being used to facilitate remote consultation, diagnosis and treatment. Use of Internet in delivery of healthcare enables healthcare self-employed individuals and institutions to render critical medical services to rural communities especially those in remote locations and those that lack qualified medical personnel and services.

The case study method will be applied to carry out a qualitative analysis[32] by observation, interviews through focused and non-directive methods and data collection with an intention to study the impact of Internet on health, especially in critical cardiac health problems amongst population which are located in areas without proper medical facilities in India and thus answer the research question R8.

To understand how the growing use of Internet technology is impacting the performance of cardiac care units and thus the health of critical patients at the local hospitals in stabilising critical cardiac patients, the discharge of patients from the cardiac care unit of the local hospitals will be chosen as the response, while the variables of expiry, patients thrombolysed and patients referred to the referral centre for further treatment will be controlled. The following Table 6.11 shows the variables and their description to be used in the multiple regression analysis model Equation 6.3 as shown below.

6.2.1 Empirical Model

The additive form of multiple regression model (equation 6.3) has been considered for the research question R8 as mentioned earlier and the dependent variable is assumed to be normally distributed and postulated as:

$$\text{Equation 6.3: } Y = b_0 + \sum_{i=1}^{n} b_i X_i + x_i$$

where,

Y = Discharge from the cardiac care unit

b_0 = Constant

b_i = Regression coefficient of the ith variable

X_i = Value of the ith independent variable

x_i = Random error of ith observation

Table 6.12: Description of independent variables to be used in the multiple regression analysis model

Ratio variables	*Measurement*
Expired (X1)	If yes, X1 = 1, else = 2
Referred to referral hospital (X2)	If yes, X2 = 1, else = 2
Thrombolysed (X3)	If yes, X3 = 1, else = 2

6.2.2 Research Hypotheses

The admitted patients are normally in a very critical and damaged state and the disease may be complex. Hence it may not always be possible to save the life inspite of intervention by local doctors and specialists from the referral centre using Internet technologies. As expiry in the cardiac care unit is a negative outcome of treatment it should, therefore, affect the discharge rate negatively. Improvement in management of patients is associated with reduction in death rates.[33]

H8.1: Discharge of patients receiving medical care using the Internet technologies available in the local cardiac care unit is negatively related to the expiry in the cardiac care unit.

That is, mathematically H_0: $\beta_1 = 0$ against H_a: $\beta_1 < 0$

Hospital discharge referral decision-making is a complex, multi-disciplinary process with many obstacles, challenges, and shortfalls. Shortened lengths of hospital stay,[34] inability to stabilise patients, inconsistent assessment criteria, and varying levels of expertise and risk tolerance in clinical decision making are among the barriers that impede the ability to make accurate referral decisions.[35] These can result in very adverse situations for the patient and the family.

Being able to anticipate post-acute needs and making referrals for follow-up care are crucial for quality discharge planning. Research[36] has confirmed the existence of serious gaps in quality for these common and important processes. Taking such important decisions from a referral hospital using Internet technology makes the process even more critical. Based on the above studies, it is necessary to test the following hypothesis.

H8.2: Referral of patients to the referral centre based on tele-consultation has a positive impact on discharge of patients.

That is, mathematically H_0: $\beta_2 = 0$ against H_a: $\beta_2 > 0$

The thrombolytic procedure that is used to dissolve the clots that cause strokes is often a life saving measure. The process involves insertion of a thrombolytic agent into the blood stream through a catheter-based procedure to dissolve the clot causing the stroke. At the local cardiac care units, this critical procedure is conducted on patients based on the assessment of the doctor from the referral hospital. The process is relayed through video-conference and monitored by the referral doctor while it is performed locally. The present study will assess whether telemedicine (real-time, two-way audio and video, and digital imaging and communications in medicine) was effective for decision-making in acute telemedicine consultations. The primary outcome measure is whether the decision to give thrombolytic treatment was correct. Based on this the third hypothesis is.

H8.3: Thrombolytic therapy using Internet is effective in increasing the stability of patients in cardiac care units of telemedicine centres.

That is, mathematically H_0: $\beta_3 = 0$ against H_a: $\beta_3 > 0$

The above hypotheses will provide answers to the research question R8–whether the use of Internet technology positively impacted the stabilisation of acutely unwell patients in the telemedicine cardiac care units at the three active telemedicine centers connected to the Rabindranath Tagore International Institute of Cardiac Sciences (RTIICS), Kolkata.

6.2.3 Study Design

The data were collected by the present author from Rabindranath Tagore International Institute of Cardiac Sciences (RTIICS), Kolkata, and the three active telemedicine units connected to it, namely, Siliguri and Bankura in West Bengal and Udaipur in Tripura between 30/11/2008 and 10/02/2009 through field visits. The data were collected month-wise for the period July 2001 to December 2008 in the cases of Siliguri and Bankura and for the period August 2001 to December 2008 in the case of Udaipur.

The period was based on complete data available at these centers. The data indicate death while in the cardiac care unit, number of patients that underwent Thrombolysis, number of patients discharged from cardiac care unit (to home or to a general ward in the hospital), or referred to RTIICS, or institutional care[37] upon increase in stability of health.

Detailed interviews were conducted with the doctors incharge of the three cardiac care units: Dr Tapas Dutta of Udaipur center, Dr Tapas Roy of the Bankura centre and Dr Goutam Dasgupta of the Siliguri centre. Personal interviews were also conducted with the head of the telemedicine unit at RTIICS—Dr Madhav Chakraborty, the remote CCU Incharge and consultant of telemedicine cardiology at RTIICS–Dr V.K. Gupta who is deeply involved in this project.

Live sessions of teleconsultation through video-conferencing and trans-telephonic ECG procedures were observed and studied. A videoconference based interview was provided by Dr Devi Shetty, renowned cardiac surgeon and Chairman, Narayan Hrudalaya Pvt Ltd.

6.2.4 Data

One dependent variable (y)—discharge was measured using three items using data from the three-telemedicine units and the referral hospital to assess the performance of the cardiac care unit.[38]

Discharge has been computed as discharge from the cardiac care unit to either home or a general ward in the hospital once the condition of the patient has improved to the necessary level.

The variable Expiry (X1) indicates the number of patients who expired in spite of intervention by local doctors and specialists from the referral centre through telemedicine while being lodged in the cardiac care unit.

Referral cases (X2) indicate the critical patients who after stabilisation are sent to RTIICS for further treatment, in most cases for surgery. Only the specialist doctor takes this decision from the referral hospital. This is a very important decision in delivering quality care. This variable also indicates that the patient's life at that critical hour could be saved and his/her condition improved to an ambulatory state. It, therefore, indicates reduction in mortality.

Thrombolysed (X3) indicates the number of critical patients who have undergone thrombolytic therapy at the telemedicine centre.

6.2.5 Summary of Methods of Analysis

Ordinary least square algorithm has been considered and the purpose was to estimate the regression coefficients and test of hypotheses H8.1–H8.3 as mentioned earlier. Multiple regression analysis will be used to test the impact of the telemedicine application on clinical care. The results have been presented in Tables 7.1–7.2 in Chapter 7.

6.3 Internet in Agriculture and Rural Development

Internet can be utilised as an extensive source of information to aid farmers and traders to make educated business decisions and reduce the business risks. Market information can benefit farmers, traders, consumers and policymakers.

In this context, to answer the research question R9, on whether Internet has been able to bridge the gap in opportunities and bring global resources as well as best farming practices to the Indian farmers and thereby contribute to the alleviation of their poverty and marginalisation the researcher will be using the case of ITC's *e-choupal.*

6.3.1 Study Design

This will be an exploratory study based on a background and research approach. In this exploratory study Internet and participation will be the basic components, by selecting five experts in the field. This will be a scientific research work based on different information gathered from various authentic sources. The researcher will conduct interviews personally with these experts, to gain a better understanding of the linkages among Internet, participatory development and social development. The interviews will be conducted to obtain necessary information on scalability, profitability and sustainability of the project, along with the range covered, new linkages formed and communication channels established.

Information systems are not just about the end product, but also about the process by which they come into being and are redefined over time. Participation by both designers and users is obligatory in the process of designing and using any such system. A social developmental approach stresses the importance of process as a goal in itself. For example, the way in which we collect data must embrace developmental principles. In the context of rural development, which is the focus of this study, information on existing systems can be used to explain, more generally, the developmental context of a society.

6.4 Internet in Politics

E-governance is the application of electronic means in the interaction between government and citizens and government and businesses and internal government operations to simplify and improve democratic, government and business aspects[39] of governance. The strategic objective of e-governance is to support and simplify governance of all parties: government, citizens and businesses. Internet technology can connect these three parties and support processes and activities that they engage in.

E-governance involves new styles of leadership, new ways of listening to citizens, new ways of educating the public and the service providers and new ways of delivering information and services.

In a country like India that is plagued by poor infrastructure, high rural population, problems of electricity and water, illiteracy, lack of IT training and language barriers,[40] there are many reasons for the poor implementation of e-governance projects. People rely more on hand written documents and are not satisfied with computerised copies. Further, our existing systems are not adequate. Good systems require good manpower, appropriate technologies and efficient processes. IT and Internet are only enablers. It is important to reengineer processes and systems before computerisation.

E-governance cannot transform a country immediately, or forever. It is a process, most often a struggle that presents costs and risks–both financial and political. Achieving success requires a change management process to create awareness, understanding, trust, common reason and willingness from all quarters to move it from an idea to reality. The challenges are enormous and ironically more cultural than technical.

In this context, the outcome of the 2004 State Elections in Andhra Pradesh will be considered the case and basis of the study to answer the final research question R10—What was the political outcome of Internet in a democratic process?

6.4.1 Study Design

An exploratory study based on focus group interviews was conducted by the researcher to study the impact of Internet on the political outcome of the Andhra Pradesh state elections held in 2004.

A focus group was chosen, as it is a form of qualitative research developed after the rise of statistical survey methods in which a group of people is asked about their perceptions, opinions, beliefs and attitudes towards a product, service, concept, idea, or event. Focus groups are a powerful means to evaluate services or test new ideas. Focus groups are interviews, but of 6–10 people at the same time in the same group. Focus groups allow interviewers to study people in a more natural setting than a one-to-one interview and it can be used for gaining access to various cultural and social groups, selecting questions to study and raising unexpected issues for exploration. It is similar to survey methodology in terms of commitment to rigorousness.

Focus group method differs from survey methods since individuals who participate in focus group sessions are not restricted in their answers by the choices made available by the researcher. Thus the reactions and answers are considered to be more natural.[41] Since the researcher is able to also observe the emotions, contradictions and tensions along with the group discussion it provides the researcher with a deeper insight.

Questions are asked in an interactive group setting where participants are free to talk with other group members. Group discussion produces data and insights that would be less accessible without interaction found in a group setting—listening to others' verbalised experiences stimulates memories, ideas, and experiences in participants. This is also known as the group effect where group members engage in "a kind of 'chaining', or 'cascading' effect; talk links to, or tumbles out of, the topics and expressions preceding it" as members discover a common language to describe similar experiences.[42]

This enables the capture of a common thought to understand the situation. Thus a great deal of information can be gathered during a focus group session. However, even though focus groups can provide trustworthy naturalistic data and important insights about human behaviors, they are not designed to provide generalisation[43] as is obtained in a survey method.

Ernest Dichter, the psychologist and marketing expert used it in the social sciences. Focus groups have a high apparent validity—since the idea is easy to understand and the results are believable as qualitative research reports actual statements from real peole. Also, they are low in cost, one can get results relatively quickly, and they can increase the sample size of a report by talking with several people at once. Focus groups also provide an opportunity for disclosure among similar others in a setting where participants are validated. In the analysis stage, while survey research required transformation of numbers with statisitcal tests, focus groups rely upon words spoken by participants and thus is qualitative in nature.[44] It is necessary to prepare for the session by identifying the major objective of the meeting, followed by developing five to six relevant questions. A focus group interview normally lasts for an hour and a half.

The present study centers on the objective of finding an answer to the principal question of what was the impact of over emphasis on Internet on the political outcome in a democratic process. A focus group interview method with the group comprising of educated individuals who had voted against Chandrababu Naidu in the state elections, in 2004, was felt to be the best method to address the following specific questions:

1. Economic development under Chandrababu Naidu;
2. Contributions of the Naidu government towards development of IT facilities and IT industry in the state;
3. Did over emphasis on Internet have an impact on the way the electorate voted;
4. Did the electorate benefit because of the introduction of Internet based services;

5. Did this new technology bring in opportunities for employment; and
6. A summary for the reasons of failure.

The expert focus groups will comprise of journalists, renowned academicians, software professionals, government officials and some residents of Andhra Pradesh from different parts of Andhra Pradesh who had voted in the state elections. The role of the researcher will be of a moderator, to make the discussion one-dimensional. The group discussion will not exceed the permitted limit and a consensus building approach will been taken to identify relevant dimensions in questions.

References

1. Hair, J.F., Anderson, R.E., Tatham, R.L., and Black, W.C., Multivariate data analysis (5th edn), Pearson education, Delhi, 2005, p. 276.
2. Hosmer, D.W., and Lemeshow, S., Applied Logistic Regression, Wiley, New York, 2000, pp. 1–259.
3. Atkin, D., 1993, Adoption of cable amidst a multimedia environment, Telematics and Informatics, Vol. 10, pp. 51–58.
4. Morrone, A., and Zannella, L., 2004, IT and Mass media use among Italian youth, IT and Society, Vol. 1(6), pp. 59–67.
5. Grant, A.E., Guthrie, K.K., and Ball-Rokeach, S., 1991, Television shopping: A media dependency perspective, Communication Research, Vol. 18, pp. 773–798.
6. FICCI–PWC, 2006, Indian Entertainment and Media Industry–Unravelling the potential, Frames-2006.
7. Grant, A.E., Guthrie, K.K., and Ball-Rokeach, S., 1991, Television shopping: A media dependency perspective, Communication Research, Vol. 18, pp. 773–798.
8. Loges, W.E., and Ball-Rokeach, S., 1993, Dependency relations and newspaper readership, Journalism Quarterly, Vol. 70, pp. 601–614.
9. Lu, H., and Andrews, J.E., 2006, College students' perception of the absolute media credibility about SARS-related news during the SARS outbreak in Taiwan, China, Media Research, Vol. 2(2), pp. 85–93.
10. Mehrabi, D., Hassan, M.A., and Ali, M.S.S, 2009, News Media Credibility of the Internet and Television, European Journal of Social Sciences, Vol. 11(1), pp. 136–148.
11. Ball-Rokeah, S., and DeFleur, M., 1989, A dependency model of mass communication effects, Communication Research, Vol. 3, pp. 3–21.

12. Flanagin, A.J., and Metzger, M.J., 2000, Perceptions of Internet information credibility, Journalism and Mass Communication Quarterly, Vol. 77(3), pp. 515–540.
13. Pew Research Center for the People and the Press, 1999, The Internet News audience goes ordinary.
14. *Ibid.*
15. Bearden, W.O., and Netemeyer, R.G., Handbook of Marketing scales, Sage Publications (2nd ed), England, 1999, p. 552.
16. Gaziao, C., and McGrath, K., 1986, Measuring the concept of credibility, Journalism quarterly, Vol. 63, pp. 451–462.
17. Hair, J.F., Anderson, R.E., Tatham, R.L., and Black, W.C., Multivariate data analysis (5th edn), Pearson education, Delhi, 2005, pp. 164–166.
18. Churchill, G.A., 1979, A Paradigm for developing better measures for marketing constructs, Journal of Marketing Research, Vol. 16, pp. 64–73.
19. Nunnaly, J.L., and Bernstein, I.H., Psychometric theory, 3rd ed., McGraw-Hill, New York, 1994, pp. 83–112.
20. Malhotra, N.K., Marketing research and applied orientation, Pearson Education Limited, England, 2007, pp. 369–473.
21. *Ibid.*
22. Gaski, R.M., and Etzel, M.J., 1986, The index of consumer sentiment towards marketing, Journal of marketing, Vol. 50(3), pp. 71–81.
23. Lin, C.A., and Salwen, M.B., Utilities of online and offline news use. In Li, Xigen, (eds), Internet newspapers, Lawrence Erlbaum Associates, Mahwah, NJ, 2006, pp. 209–226.
24. Hair, J.F., Anderson, R.E., Tatham, R.L., and Black, W.C., Multivariate data analysis (5th edn.), Pearson education, Delhi, 2005, pp. 126–127.
25. Harman, H.H., Modern Factor Analysis, 2nd edition. University Chicago Press: Chicago, 1976, pp. 1–362.
26. Cronbach, L.J., 1951, Coefficient alpha and the internal structure of the tests, Psychometrika, Vol. 16, pp. 297–334.
27. Nunnaly, J.L., and Bernstein, I.H., Psychometric theory, 3rd ed., McGraw-Hill, New York, 1994, pp. 83–112.
28. Hair, J.F., Anderson, R.E., Tatham, R.L., and Black, W.C., Multivariate data analysis (5th edn), Pearson education, Delhi, 2005, p. 118.
29. Donohew, L., Palmgreen P., and Rayburn, J.D., II., 1987, Social and psychological origins of media use: A lifestyle analysis, Journal of Broadcasting and Electronic Media, Vol. 31, pp. 255–278.
30. National Readership Study 2006 (NRS 2006).

31. Hair, J.F., Anderson, R.E., Tatham, R.L., and Black, W.C., Multivariate data analysis (5th edn), Pearson education, Delhi, 2005, pp. 258–314.
32. Whitten, P.S. and Allen, A., 1995, Analysis of Telemedicine from an Organisational Perspective, Telemedicine Journal, Vol. 1(3), pp. 203–14.
33. Fox, K.A., Steg, A., Eagle, P.G., Goodman, K.A., Anderson, S.G., Granger, C.B., Flather, M.D., Budaj, A., Quill, A., and Gore, J.M, 2007, Decline in rates of death and heart failure in acute coronary syndromes, 1999–2006, Journal of the American Medical Association, Vol. 297(17), pp. 1892–1900.
34. Clemens, E.L., and Hayes, H.E., 1997, Assessing and balancing elder risk, safety and autonomy: Decision-making practices of healthcare professionals, Home Healthcare Services Quarterly, Vol. 16 (3), pp. 3–21.
35. Bowles, K.H., Naylor, M.D., and Foust, J.B., 2000, Patient characteristics at hospital discharge and a comparison of discharge referral decisions, Journal of the American Geriatric Society, Vol. 50, pp. 336–42.
36. Bowles, K.H, Ratcliffe, S.J., Holmes, J.H., Liberatore, M, Nydick, and R., Naylor, 2008, Post-acute referral decisions made by multidisciplinary experts compared to hospital clinicians and the patients' 12-week outcomes, Medical Care, Vol. 46(2), pp. 158–66.
37. Audebert, H.J., Schultes, K., Tietz V., Heuschmann, P.U., Bogdahn, U., Haberl, R.L., and Schenkel, J., 2009, Long-term effects of specialised stroke care with telemedicine support in community hospitals on behalf of the Telemedical Project for Integrative Stroke Care (TEMPiS), Stroke, Vol. 40, pp. 902–908.
38. Fiser, D.H., 2000, Relationship of pediatric overall performance category and pediatric cerebral performance category scores at pediatric intensive care unit discharge with outcome measures collected at hospital discharge and 1 and 6 month follow-up assessments, Critical Care Medicine, Vol. 28(7), pp. 2616–20.
39. Backus, M., 2001, E-governance in developing countries, International Institute for Communication and Development Research report, pp. 1–4.
40. Dasgupta, D., 2006, E-governance in India: Global CEO, November, pp. 26–28.
41. Kreuger, R.A., and M.A. Casey, Focus groups: A practical guide for applied research, 3rd edition, Thousand Oaks, Sage, California, 2000, pp. 1–18.
42. Lindlof, T.R., and Taylor, B.C., Qualitative Communication Research Methods, 2nd Edition, Thousand Oaks, Sage, California, 2002, p. 182.
43. Fern, E.F., 1982, The use of focus groups for idea generation: the effects of group size, acquaintanceship, and moderator on response quantity and quality, Journal of Marketing Research, Vol. 26 (February), pp. 1–13.
44. Cresswell, J.W., Qualitative Inquiry and Research Design: Choosing among five traditions, Thousand Oaks, Sage, California, 1998, pp. 27–28.

7

Results and Discussions

The purpose of this chapter has been to present the results obtained from the four independent studies, in an organised and objective way followed by a discussion of the results, together with their analysis. This chapter also explores the social relevance of the findings and discusses them in terms of theoretical knowledge of communication technologies.

The studies considered are the following:

- Internet as a medium of news
- Internet in healthcare services
- Internet in agriculture and rural development
- Internet and politics

The goal of this study was to explore the potentially growing effect of Internet news consumption on print and electronic news usage and vice versa. Unlike previous analyses, this study has tracked the effect of Internet as medium of news. It has assesed the use of print and electronic mass media such as print newspapers and TV news by identifying the relationship between them and new media in terms of the newsgathering habits of people in metropolitan cities of India who have access to print newspapers, TV news and Internet news. A one way ANOVA confirmed that there is a significant difference amongst people in terms of their newsgathering habits from the three media.

Results of the Tukey's HSD multiple comparative test between Print newspaper, TV news and Internet news confirmed that there is significant difference in the news acquiring habits of people between Print newspapers and TV news, Print newspapers and Internet news and also between Internet news and TV news. It has thus been inferred that all these media are perceived to be distinct and people use them differently for different needs. However, no significant difference was found when t-tests were done between the news gathering habits of readers and non-readers of Internet news with respect to newsgathering nabit from print newspapers, or TV news, and therefore, it can be concluded that there is no significant difference between the groups with respect to newsgathering habits from print newspapers and TV news. In order to test whether there is any significant difference between the groups of Internet news readers and non-readers in the way they acquire news from print newspapers and TV news, t-tests were again performed on the sample means, and it has been found that, even though there is no significant difference in the way non readers of Internet news gather news from print newspapers or TV news, there is a significant difference in the way the readers of Internet news treat these two media and hence print newspapers and TV news are competitors in the case of readers of Internet news.

To examine the relationship further, a logistic regression was performed to see whether acquiring news from print newspapers and TV news has a negative impact on reading Internet news and the result confirmed the negative impact. The results have further indicated that if the newsgathering habit from print newspapers and TV news sources can be increased then the habit of reading news from the Internet will further reduce.

The study then investigates the impact of the demographic variables of gender, age, education, profession and socio-economic variables like annual income, Internet connectivity at home, Internet usage patterns, credibility perception of Internet news, the credibility perceptions of print newspapers and TV news combined as well as the perceived change in dependence on Internet on the trend in print and electronic news media consumption. Regression analysis has confirmed that age has a negative impact, while higher education and profession both have positive impact. Further, when the credibility perception of Internet increases then that negatively affects newsgathering habits from print and electronic sources and when the credibility perceptions of print and electronic news media increase then it has a positive impact on the trend. It has also been found that number of days of Internet news weekly consumption and daily Internet usage in hours have a negative impact on collating news from TV news and print newspapers.

The study has been extended further to test whether there is any difference between respondents' perceived and observed utility perceptions with respect to Internet news (as detailed in Sections 6.4.1.7 and 6.4.1.3.2.1). The three utility constructs for Internet news were Information scanning and skimming utility construct, Entertainment utility construct and Interpersonal communication construct. Results of the paired *t*-tests between observed and perceived values of Internet news utilities confirm that that there is significant difference between the observed and perceived values in all the three utilities of Internet news and in all cases it was found that the observed values are less than the perceived values of all the utilities thus indicating that the Internet users are not fully satisfied.

Therefore, it has been assumed that there is an impact of the perceived Interpersonal communication, Entertainment, Information scanning and Information skimming utilities of print newspapers and TV news on these identifiable gaps. For that reason, a regression equation, using ordinary least square method has been performed on the data. The results show that there are significant impacts on these gaps. This study has tried to analyse the displacement and complementary relationship of media in greater detail based on the above and has found that displacement relationship exists between the Internet news and print newspapers and also TV news in some utilities but a complementary relationship exists between the media in some other utilities.

The study has touched two other directions–healthcare and rural development. In the former it has tried to assess the effect of using Internet in delivery of healthcare to critical cardiac patients amongst population, which are located in areas without proper medical facilities in India. For that the telemedicine project at the Rabindranath Tagore International Institute of Cardiac Sciences was chosen, for carrying out a case study based on qualitative analysis by observation, interviews through focused and non-directive methods as well as data collection. Three local centers at Bankura, Udaipur and Siliguri have been considered along with the referral centre at Kolkata. These centers are equipped to provide teleconsultation, transtelephonic electrocardiograph, consultation on medical reports and virtual rounds by doctors.

The study has tried to estimate the success of providing thrombolytic therapy and referrals to the referral hospital in Kolkata based on video-consultation with specialists from the referral centers on the discharge of patients from the critical cardiac care units of the local telemedicine center to examine the impact of Internet technology on critical cardiac care by using a ordinary least square algorithm on the collected data.

Results confirm the success of using thrombolytic therapy and video-consultation based on Internet technology on the patients of regions never exposed to such sophisticated treatment before. The study also shows how telementoring can be used as a tool for training healthcare professionals.

The next study, which intends to study the effect of Internet in agriculture, is exploratory in nature based on a case study method with a background and research approach as detailed earlier. This is a scientific research work based on different information gathered from various authentic sources. This study is analytical in nature since by using analytical rather than statistical logic, case studies help understand complex phenomena better. This exploratory study on ITC's *e-choupal* has been conducted by selecting five experts in this field and through field visits. The researcher conducted personal interviews with these experts, to gain a better understanding of the linkages among Internet, participatory development and social development. The interviews were conducted to obtain necessary information on existing systems, scalability, profitability and sustainability of the project, along with the range covered, new linkages formed and communication channels established. The study has analysed the *e-choupal* model on the basis of Brown's information based evaluation methodology. Based on Brown's theory of evaluation of social development programmes, it is seen that this Internet based model has in every way been successful in providing social development and empowerment to the rural population in a quick and easy way by ensuring a very wide coverage, providing a scientific medium of trade, setting up linkages between the rural community and the rest of the country and world and setting up a bi-directional communication channel.

In the end, the study has tried to analyse through an exploratory case study on Andhra Pradesh the principal question of what can be the impact of over emphasis on Internet on the political outcome in a democratic process. The scientific research is based on ten focus group interviews, each with 10 knowledgeable members who had voted in the 2004 elections. The interviews focused on the economic development under Chandrababu Naidu, contributions of the Naidu government towards development of IT facilities and IT industry in the state, whether over emphasis on Internet had an impact on the way the electorate voted, did the electorate benefit because of the introduction of Internet based services, did this new technology bring in opportunities for employment and a summary for the reasons of the democratic defeat of the government. The study concludes that inspite of all the utilities that the e-governance projects in Andhra Pradesh provided as well as the various popular projects that the government undertook; the focus on Internet technology had a very negative impact on the fate of the ruling party. The people were not comfortable using the medium. The reach was not adequate and the infrastructure requirements were also beyond the common man's means. Most of the electorate could not find any direct benefit and felt that the huge spending on the infrastructure was a huge waste and the government had neglected the cause of the common man in its pursuit of bringing in Internet.

This chapter consists of 4 major sections based on the four studies conducted to examine Internet as a medium of news (Section 7.1), Internet in healthcare services (Section 7.2), Internet in agriculture and rural development (Section 7.3) and Internet and politics (Section 7.4). Each of these sections is subdivided into subsections that present among other details the results, discussions and a brief summary of findings.

7.1 Internet as a Medium of News

This study attempts to identify the difference if any in the newsgathering habit of the Indian audience exposed to print newspapers, TV news and the Internet from the three media—print newspapers, TV news and Internet news.This is followed by group-wise (readers and non-readers of Internet news) test for the same purpose. Regression analysis has then been considered to study the impact of different demographic, socio-economic, cognitive (perception of Internet, perception of TV news and print newspapers, change in dependence on Internet) and ratio variables (use of Internet) on the newsgathering habit of this audience from print and electronic sources. Next, it has tried to see the impact of audience's newsgathering habits from print and electronic sources on reading Internet news. Tests have been performed to assess the gap between the observed and perceived utilities of Internet news followed by regression analysis to assess the impact of utility perceptions of the print and electronic media on these identified gaps.

A survey was conducted on Indian adult consumers of news media, having access to Internet, who has a greater exposure to media sources and a cosmopolitan lifestyle from four-metropolitan cities in India–Kolkata, Delhi, Mumbai and Chennai on 484 randomly selected respondents. The population is represented by students, professionals, unemployed individuals, teachers, retired persons and also others who did not fit into the above category and had atleast some formal education as described in section 6.4.1.3-6.4.1.7 of Chapter 6.

The results obtained are presented in the following four subsections: the first section presents the descriptive statistics of the sample, the second presents the inferential statistics, the third presents the causal relationships and the last section provides a brief conclusion of the findings.

7.1.1 Descriptive Statistics

7.1.1.1 Respondent profile

There were 481 completed questionnaires (as explained in section 4.4.1.5), yielding a response rate of 96.2 per cent. There were an almost equal proportion of male (50.3 per cent) and female (49.7 per cent) respondents. The respondents were aged 19–62 years and the mean age was 35.7 years. There was also an almost equal proportion of representation from respondents earning below Rs. 4 lakhs a year (47.4 per cent) and earning above Rs. 4 lakhs (52.6 per cent).

7.1.1.2 Respondents' response

In response to the question on online activities engaged in, it was observed that most people use the Internet for reading news (67.36 per cent), followed by using it for e-mailing (65.28 per cent, as a tool for communication), a large number use it for recreational activities like—music, films, video and games (45.11 per cent). This also indicates the use of Internet as a resource for these activities. Social networking is catching up very fast, with more than 42 per cent engaged in it. In response to the question: Do you think print newspapers will be eventually replaced by Internet news, 53 per cent said 'no', where as 47 per cent said 'yes'.

58 per cent of the respondents said they prefer to read news from a print newspaper compared to 42 per cent who preferred reading from an online source. 52 per cent of respondents said that they used the Internet– websites, search engines, social networking sites, or blogs to learn about new products and services, compared to 19 per cent who chose print newspapers and 28 per cent who chose TV. Radio hardly came into reckoning at 1 per cent.

7.1.2 Inferential Statistics

Amongst the audience who have access to print newspapers, TV news and Internet news in India, it is necessary to learn more about their newsgathering habits and for that one must first know whether there is any significant difference in the way they gather news from these three media and thus the first hypothesis H1.1 as stated in Chapter 6, section 6.4.1.2 and referred below has been posited.

H1.1: There is a difference between groups with respect to newsgathering habit from Print newspapers, TV news and Internet news.

A one-way ANOVA has been performed to assess the differences in the number of days that a person acquires news from the three media and the results have been presented below in Table 7.1.

Table 7.1: Results of ANOVA performed on the data

Source	*SS*	*df*	*MS*	*F*	*P*
Between groups	1639.01	2	819.51	172.86	<0.001*
Within groups	6637.12	1400	54.74		
Total	8276.13	1402			

Note: *P< 0.001, SS = sums of squares, df = degrees of freedom, M.S = SS/df.

The *F* value, which has been presented in the table, is highly significant for the sample data. Thus the hypothesis (H1.1) mentioned earlier has been confirmed.

Now it is necessary to identify, where these differences lie. For this purpose, Tukey's HSD multiple comparative test has been performed. Results of this test have been presented below in Table 7.2.

Table 7.2: Results of the Tukey's HSD multiple comparative test

		t	*P*
Print newspapers	Internet news	17.45	<0.001*
	TV news	3.41	0.001*
TV news	Print newspapers	3.41	0.001*
	Internet news	13.65	<0.001*
Internet news	Print newspapers	17.45	<0.001*
	TV news	13.65	<0.001*

Note: *P < 0.001.

Findings in Table 7.2 confirm that there is significant difference in the news acquiring habits of people between Print newspapers and TV news, Print newspapers and Internet news and also between Internet news and TV news. It can thus be inferred that all these media are perceived to be distinct and people use them differently for different needs.

Analytical interpretation of the tests for Hypothesis H1: When more than two groups are involved, then ANOVA is used to test the difference amongst the mean values of these groups. In this case, we had three groups—Print newspapers, TV news and Internet news. Significant difference was found (Table 7.1) indicating that there is a difference between groups with respect to newsgathering habit from Print newspapers, TV news and Internet news. Since significant difference was found, it was necessary to investigate further, to find where the differences were situated. For that the Tukey's HSD multiple comparative test was performed. This test helps us to identify the difference between two groups instead of all the groups simultaneously. The results (Table 7.2) show that there is significant difference in the news acquiring habits of people between Print newspapers and TV news, Print newspapers and Internet news and also between Internet news and TV news. It has thus been inferred that all these media are perceived to be distinct and people use them differently for different needs.

Amongst this audience, some read Internet news and some don't. To obtain a better understanding of the audience, it is necessary to see whether there is any significant difference in the way the two groups gather news from print newspapers and TV news. For this reason the following two hypotheses H2.1 and H2.2 as stated in Chapter 6 will be tested:

H2.1: There is difference in the news gathering habit from Print newspaper between the groups of Internet news readers (A) and non-readers (B).

H2.2: There is difference in the news gathering habit from TV news between the groups of Internet news readers (A) and non-readers (B).

To test the above hypotheses, the sample has been divided into two groups based on whether they read Internet news. *t*-test has been performed to test whether there is any significant difference in the sample means of newsgathering habit from Print newspapers and TV news between the two groups. The results are presented in Table 7.3 below.

Table 7.3: *t*–statistics for weekly Print newspaper readership and TV news viewership between readers and non-readers of Internet news

Media	*t*	*P*
Print newspapers	–0.87	0.386
TV news	0.43	0.669

Note: $*p < 0.05$.

From the results presented in Table 7.3 we find that neither the hypothesis H2.1 nor the hypothesis H2.2 is confirmed in this work. Hence there is no significant difference between the news gathering habits of readers and non-readers of Internet news with respect to print newspapers or TV news.

To further explore the difference amongst the group who read Internet news and those who do not, it is necessary to test whether there is any significant difference within the groups in the way they gather news from print newspapers and TV news. This will provide a better understanding about the preferences of these groups and we can compare the results between the groups and for that hypotheses H3.1 and H4.1 as stated in Chapter 6 and given below have been framed:

H3.1: There is difference in the news gathering habit from Print newspapers and TV news within the group of non-readers of Internet news (B).

H4.1: There is difference in the news gathering habit from Print newspapers and TV news within the group of Internet newsreaders (A).

The sample has once again been divided into two groups based on whether they read news on the Internet or not. To test the hypothesis H3.1, *t*-test has been performed within the group of non-Internet newsreaders to test whether there is any significant difference in the way they gather news from Print newspapers and TV news. Similar procedure has been followed on the group of Internet newsreaders to test the hypothesis H4.1 and the results are presented in Table 7.4 below.

Table 7.4: *t*-statistics for weekly print newspaper readership and TV news viewing within the groups of non-readers of Internet news and readers of Internet news

Group	*t*	*P*
Readers of Internet news	2.59	0.010*
Non-readers of Internet news	–0.41	0.683

Note: $^*p < 0.05$.

Results suggest that hypothesis H3.1 is not confirmed in this work. However, a significant difference in the news gathering habit from Print newspapers and TV news is observed within the group of Internet newsreaders and hence the hypothesis H4.1, as mentioned earlier has been confirmed in this work. This shows that readers of Internet news treat print newspapers and TV news differently and so for this group there is a competition between print newspapers and TV news.

Analytical interpretation of the tests for Hypotheses: H2.1, H2.2, H3.1, H4.1

In the above case (for hypotheses H2.1 and H2.2), the standard deviation of the three groups are people who read print newspapers, watch TV news and read Internet news as shown in Table 7.3 and for hypotheses H3.1 and H4.1 are the two groups—Readers of Internet news and Non-readers of Internet news, as shown in Table 7.4) are unknown, t-test is being used instead of the *z*-test. A *t*-test is a statistical hypothesis test. Standard deviation has been calculated for these groups from the sample data and then t-tests have been performed.

7.1.3 Causal Relationships

Reading news on the Internet is a relatively new activity. Uses and gratification theory suggests a change in the media use patterns following introduction of a new communication technology. Previous research has shown that time is a zero sum game. Therefore, there should be a mutual displacement tendency in terms of time spent between the print and electronic media and Internet news. It would be justified to hypothesize then, that there is a negative impact of print and electronic media habits on newsgathering habits from the Internet. This relationship between media habits of reading print newspapers and viewing TV news and reading Internet news has been explored by the researcher through the hypothesis H5.1 stated in Chapter 6 and quoted below.

H5.1: There is a negative impact of the combined (reading print newspapers and watching TV news) print and electronic media habits on the news gathering habit from Internet.

The logistic regression method has been used to test this hypothesis. The basic tenet of choosing the logistic regression equation is that the researcher wants to classify the respondents into two groups (yes or no) on the basis of their habit of reading Internet news. Logistic regression models the probability of an outcome bounded by 0 and 1. The basic assumption is that each one unit increase in the habit of newsgathering from Print newspapers and TV news will multiply the odd of news gathering habit from Internet by a certain factor.

The independent variable is Avg, which is the average number of days that print newspaper is read or TV news is viewed. The dependent variable, which measures whether a person reads Internet news, or not is equal to 1 if the respondent says yes and 0 otherwise. The logistic regression model is used to estimate the factors, which influence this behavior. The results of the analysis are presented in the Tables 7.5 and 7.6.

Table 7.5: Validation statistics of Logistic Regression

−2 LL	*P*	*HL*	*P*	*Hit ratio*
438.59	0.079	5.905	0.316	82.7

Note: LL: Log Likelihood, HL: Hosmer-Lemeshow goodness of fit.

Table 7.6: Variables in the equation

	B	*S.E*	*Wald*	*df*	*Sig*	*Exp (B)*
AVG	–0.130	0.077	2.883	1	0.045*	0.878
Constant	2.301	0.461	24.969	1	0.000*	9.988

Note: *p < 0.05.

It is observed from the results presented in Table 7.5, that the Log likelihood value (–219.295) is insignificant (0.079).

Further, the result of the Hosmer-Lemeshow Goodness-of-fit test result is also insignificant (c2 = 5.905, df = 5, p = 0.316). Hence the null hypothesis of the logistic regression, that, there is no difference between the observed and predicted values of the dependent; is not rejected in this case.

It is observed from Table 7.6 that the Wald statistic is significant and hence the parameter – average number of days that print newspaper is read, or TV news is viewed is significant in the model. Here the Exp (B), or the odds ratio for the parameter is less than 1 (0.878) indicating that there is a decreasing or negative impact on the dependent variable. Based on the above, the hypothesis H5.1 is confirmed in this study. It is also concluded from the study that if the habit of newsgathering from Print newspapers and TV news can be increased, then the news gathering habit from Internet will decrease.

Analytical interpretation of the test for Hypothesis: H5.1: Logistic regression identifies the impact of some variables on a categorical variable (yes/no, true/false, 0/1, etc.). In this instance, the independent variable is Avg, which is the average number of days that print newspaper is read, or TV news is viewed that was considered for its impact on the categorical dependent variable—whether a person reads Internet news, or not and is equal to 1 if the respondent says, yes, and 0 otherwise. The results show that the independent variable (reading print newspapers and watching TV news) has a negative impact on shifting reading habits towards reading Internet news.

To have a better understanding of how the growing use of Internet might be related to the trend in print and electronic news media consumption, namely, reading print newspapers and TV news viewing, the demographic variables of gender, age, education, profession, socio-economic variables like annual income, Internet connectivity at home and also Internet usage patterns were controlled. The credibility perception of Internet news, the credibility perceptions of print newspapers and TV news combined and the perceived change in dependence on Internet were also controlled.

To measure the impact on newsgathering from print newspapers and TV news, of different variables (as detailed in Chapter 6, section 6.4.1.1.6), ordinary least square algorithm has been considered and the purpose was to estimate the regression coefficients and test of hypotheses H6.1-H6.16 as mentioned in Chapter 6. One dependent variable, news gathering from print newspapers and TV news (in days), was measured with sixteen items, through a self-report questionnaire. The items X12 and X13 comprised of seven items on perception (trustworthiness, currency of reporting, fairness, believability, balance, accuracy and timeliness) of Print newspapers, TV news and Internet news and were measured using a five point Likert scale.

Table 7.7 shows the result of the multiple regression analysis. It also shows the beta values, which indicate the variables' explanatory power. The model cannot be interpreted before checking the multicollinearity of the independent variables. This is because, when high level of correlation exists between two or more independent variables used in the regression, then it is difficult to determine the contribution of each independent variable, because their effects are confounded[1]. For this the variance inflation factor (VIF) has been assessed. The values are within the common cutoff threshold of 10[2].

Table 7.7: Results of the regression analysis between average number of days of reading print newspapers and TV news viewing and other variables

The regression equation is:

$$y = 3.64 - 0.401\,x1 - 1.02\,x2 - 0.423\,x3 + 0.308\,x4 + 0.304\,x5 - 0.174\,x6 - 0.129\,x7 + 0.425\,x8 + 0.521\,x9 + 1.91\,x10 + 1.11\,x11 - 0.323\,x12 + 1.13\,x13 - 0.0989\,x14 + 0.280\,x15 - 0.114\,x16$$

Predictor	*Coefficient*	*SE*	*T*	*Beta*	*VIF*
Constant	3.6368	0.7764	4.684*		
X1 Gender	–0.4014	0.1342	–2.991**	–0.121	1.1
X2 Age between 18–28 years	–1.0227	0.1977	–5.172*	–0.311	2.4
X3 Age above 38 years	–0.4228	0.2013	–2.100**	–0.119	2.1
X4 Post graduate	0.3076	0.1627	1.891	0.090	1.5
X5 Graduate	0.3039	0.1660	1.831**	0.088	1.5
X6 Annual family income > Rs 4 lakhs	–0.1736	0.1493	–1.163	–0.053	1.4
X7 Have Internet connectivity at home	–0.1285	0.1619	–0.794	–0.035	1.3
X8 Student	0.4246	0.2859	1.485***	0.121	4.3
X9 Self employed	0.5206	0.2500	2.083**	0.156	3.7
X10 Unemployed	1.9150	0.3313	5.780*	0.342	2.3
X11 Teacher	1.1112	0.3298	3.370*	0.174	1.8
X12 Mean perception of credibility of Internet news	–0.3230	0.1228	–2.631*	–0.111	1.2
X13 Mean perception of credibility of TV news and Print newspaper	1.1316	0.1542	7.337*	0.298	1.1

Predictor	*Coefficient*	*SE*	*T*	*Beta*	*VIF*
X14 No of days of Internet news consumption in a week	–0.0989	0.0436	–2.269**	–0.102	1.3
X15 Internet dependence has increased	0.2800	0.1994	1.404***	0.058	1.1
X16 No of hours spent on the Internet on an average in a day	–0.1142	0.0312	–3.661*	–0.168	1.4

Notes: *P < 0.001, ** P< 0.05, *** P.< 0.1, R^2 = 32.7 per cent (F = 13.48, P = 0.000), y = newsgathering from print newspapers and TV news.

From the results presented in Table 7.7, it can be observed that the regression coefficient is negative in the case of gender, age, annual family income, Internet connectivity at home, credibility perception of Internet news, number of days of Internet news consumption in a week and number of hours spent on the Internet on an average. This indicates that these variables have a negative relationship with the dependent variable — average number of days of reading print newspapers and TV news viewing. On the other hand, educational qualification, professions, credibility perception of print newspapers and TV news and increase in Internet dependence, all have a positive relationship with the dependent variable. The R^2 value, or variance explained is significant at 32.7 per cent (F = 13.48, P = 0.000) as expected[3] shown in Table 7.8 below.

Table 7.8: Validation statistics

R^2	*F*	*P*
32.7%	13.48	0.000

From the Table 7.7, it can be seen, in the cases of both of X2 (Age between 18–28 years) and X3 (Age above 38 years), the t values are significant at desired level, and the direction of regression coefficients are as was expected, and hence both the hypotheses H6.2 and H6.3 as mentioned earlier have been confirmed in this work. Further, the results in Table 7.7 indicate that hypotheses H6.5, H6.8–H6.13 have also been confirmed since the *t* values of the respective variables are significant and the direction of the regression coefficient is as expected.

Thus, amongst others findings, credibility perception of Internet has a negative impact on reading newspapers and TV news but the impact of gender, annual income, or having Internet connectivity at home could not be confirmed. Similarly, the hypotheses H6.14 and H6.15 are also confirmed, supporting previous research findings that number of days of Internet news weekly consumption and daily Internet usage in hours have a negative impact on collating news from TV news and print newspapers. Thus news on the Internet will have a displacement effect on print medium[4]. Similar results were obtained in a study in Texas[5] where business people and users of an Internet service reported spending less hours on print newspapers. In another study[6] it was observed that time spent on television viewing and newspaper reading were affected by greater Internet usage.

Finally, in case of increased dependence on Internet, the *t*-value was found to be significant at the desired level and the direction was also priori. Hence, the hypothesis H6.16 as stated earlier has also been confirmed in this work. This finding agrees with previous research, that frequent Internet news and information users use print and electronic sources more frequently than non-frequent users.[7]

From the results presented in Table 7.7, the standardised beta coefficients indicate the impact that each independent variable has on the dependent variable. The maximum impact is of X10 (unemployed, 0.342), followed by the age group 18–28 years (X2) who have an impact of 0.311. The third highest impact is of the mean perception of TV news and print newspaper (X13) at 0.298, followed by the profession, Teacher (X11) at 0.174.

The fifth highest impact is that of number of hours spent on the Internet on an average (X16) at 0.168. The self employed (X9) has the next highest impact at 0.156, followed by gender (X1) at 0.121 and Age above 38 years (X3) at 0.119.

The credibility perception of Internet news (X12) ranks ninth in terms of impact, followed by number of days of Internet news weekly consumption (X14) and then the educational qualification variables Post graduate (X4) followed by Graduate (X5). Thus profession, age, credibility perception of print newspapers and TV news are very strong predictors of newsgathering from print newspapers and TV news.

Analytical interpretation of the tests for Hypotheses: H6.1–H.6.16: In summary, the regression analysis is basically applied to identify the impact of one variable on another. In the above paragraphs the impact of the variables gender, age, qualification, annual family income, profession, credibility perception of print newspapers and TV news, credibility perception of Internet news, number of days of Internet consumption and time spent on the Internet were considered on news-gathering from print newspapers and TV news.

The regression coefficients in the regression equation indicate the positive or negative impact of the variable on the news-gathering habit from the print and electronic media. So if a negative sign precedes the coefficient then it indicates a negative impact and if a positive sign precedes it then it indicates a positive impact of that variable (refer regression equation in Table 7.7).

The parameters (beta values) indicate the extent of impact of the variables and can thus be used for ranking the variables in terms of impact. Here we do not consider the sign; we only consider which variable has the highest impact and so on. The R^2 statistic indicates the variance explained in the data and can be reported only if it is significant otherwise the regression equation has to be rejected. In this case the R^2 value has been found to be 32 per cent and significant. This is sufficient for social science studies and hence based on the above it was possible to test the hypotheses and present the results as above.

To test the hypotheses H7 (There is a difference between respondent's perceived and observed utilities for Internet news (information scanning and skimming utility, entertainment utility and interpersonal communication utility respectively), three paired *t*-tests one each for Information scanning and skimming utility construct, Entertainment utility construct and Interpersonal communication utility construct have been performed for Internet news on the data of the 481 respondents, based on their perceived and observed utility ratings on a Likert style table in a self-report questionnaire on items discussed earlier (Section 6.4.1.3.2) with values between 1 and 7 of agreement, where 1 was lowest and 7 highest. These paired *t*-tests have been used to compare the means of the observed and perceived utilities of the media. The respondents also used the relevant scales in the case of print newspapers and TV news constructs to rate their respective observed utilities in a similar manner. The results have been presented in Table 7.9.

Table 7.9: Results of the paired *t*-tests between perceived and observed values of Internet news utilities

News medium	*Utility construct*		*Mean*	*Std Dev*	*T*	*P*
Internet news	Information scanning and skimming	Perceived	4.023	0.7485	-6.81^*	<0.001
		Observed	3.963	1.9732		
	Entertai-nment	Perceived	3.976	0.9557	-2.26^{**}	0.024
		Observed	3.394	2.1409		
	Interpersonal communi-cation	Perceived	3.931	1.1462	-3.54^*	<0.001
		Observed	3.716	1.8230		

Note: $^*P < 0.001$, $^{**}P < 0.05$.

It is observed from Table 7.9 that there is significant difference between the observed and perceived values in all the three utilities of Internet news. Hence all the three null hypotheses related to Internet news as mentioned above are rejected and the alternate hypotheses have been accepted.

Analytical interpretation of the tests for Hypothesis: H7: The paired *t*-test provides a hypothesis test of the difference between population means for a pair of random samples whose differences are approximately normally distributed. It is used in situations that have a before and after scenario. In the present case, the three different utility constructs of Internet news, namely, Information scanning and skimming, Entertainment and Interpersonal communication were measured as perceived (before) and observed (after) situations.

So the respondent initially had a perception of the three different utilities of the medium initially (perceived) and then after using it he has a perception (observed). Therefore the hypothesis could be tested using this test (Table 7.9). Significant gaps have been found between the perceived and observed perceptions. It is necessary to reduce these gaps or else the users will stop using the medium, as they will increasingly grow dissatisfied with it.

In the next few paragraphs, regression equations have been used (Tables 7.10–7.11) to measure the negative or positive impact (based on the coefficients) and the strength of the impacts (based on the significant t-values) of various utilities of the print and electronic media on these identified gaps to be able to focus better on reducing these gaps. Moreover the hypotheses related to their impact (H7b, H7c, H7d) have also been tested here as regression equations enable us to measure and predict the impact of a variable on another.

Since significant gaps have been identified in the cases of all the utilities and further since the observed values are less than the perceived values in the cases of all the utilities; this is an indication that the Internet news portals could not satisfy the respondents' Information scanning and skimming, Entertainment or Interpersonal communication needs. To minimise this gap it is necessary to examine the impact of the perceived Interpersonal communication, Entertainment, Information scanning and Information skimming utilities of print newspapers and TV news on these identifiable gaps.

Three regression equations using ordinary least square algorithm have been considered and performed on the data and the purpose was to test the impact of the perceived Interpersonal communication, Entertainment, Information skimming and Information scanning utility constructs of print newspapers and TV news (print and electronic media) on the gaps observed between the perceived and observed values of the three different utility constructs of Internet, namely, Information skimming and scanning, Entertainment and Interpersonal communication and to also test the hypotheses H7b, H7c, H7d (*There would be impact of jth and k^{th} construct of print newspapers and TV news on the gap between the perceived and observed values with respect to i^{th} construct of Internet news*) as detailed earlier (Chapter 6).

Each of the three dependent variables, difference in the perceived and observed values of (1) Information scanning and skimming utility, (2) Entertainment utility and (3) Interpersonal communication utility were measured with the eight items (the four utility constructs each of print newspapers and TV news), respectively through three independent regression equations. The items comprised of all the utility constructs of Print newspapers and TV news. Tables 7.10–7.12 show the results of the multiple regression analyses.

Table 7.10: Results of the regression analysis between the difference in the perceived and observed values of Information scanning and skimming utility of Internet news and other variables

The regression equation is:

idiff1 = – 0.190 + 0.0137 pf1 + 0.490 pf2 – 0.109 pf3 – 0.173 pf4 – 0.0974 tf1+ 0.176 tf2 + 0.0770 tf3 – 0.155 tf4

Predictor	*Coefficient*	*SE*	*T*	*Rank*
Constant	–0.1897	0.02274	–0.83	
Interpersonal communication utility of print newspapers (pf1)	0.01367	0.06384	0.21	
Entertainment utility of print newspapers (pf2)	0.49048	0.09568	5.13**	1
Information scanning utility of print newspapers (pf3)	–0.10878	0.08571	–1.27	
Information skimming utility of print newspapers (pf4)	–0.17252	0.06622	–2.61*	2
Entertainment utility of TV news (tf1)	–0.09741	0.07388	–1.32	
Interpersonal communication utility of TV news (tf2)	0.17627	0.08192	2.15*	3
Information scanning utility of TV news (tf3)	0.07699	0.09184	0.84	
Information skimming utility of TV news (tf4)	–0.15523	0.07584	–2.05*	4

Notes: idiff1 = difference between the observed and perceived Information scanning and skimming utility of Internet news *$P < 0.001$, **$P < 0.05$, R^2 = 15.8 per cent (F = 7.70, P = 0.000).

Table 7.11: Results of the regression analysis between the differences in the perceived and observed values of Entertainment utility of Internet news and other variables

The regression equation is:

idiff2 = – 2.11 + 0.496 pf1 + 0.380 pf2 – 0.192 pf3 – 0.0521 pf4 – 0.0964 tf1 + 0.225 tf2 + 0.032 tf3 – 0.139 tf4

Predictor	*Coefficient*	*SE*	*T*	*Rank*
Constant	–2.1106	0.2992	–7.05**	
Interpersonal communication utility of print newspapers (pf1)	0.49636	0.08334	5.96**	1
Entertainment utility of print newspapers (pf2)	0.3798	0.1265	3.00*	2
Information scanning utility of print newspapers (pf3)	–0.1924	0.1138	–1.69	
Information skimming utility of print newspapers (pf4)	–0.05214	0.08720	–0.60	
Entertainment utility of TV news (tf1)	–0.09641	0.09802	–0.98	
Interpersonal communication utility of TV news (tf2)	0.2253	0.1098	2.05*	3
Information scanning utility of TV news (tf3)	0.0317	0.1205	0.26	
Information skimming utility of TV news (tf4)	–0.13899	0.09892	–1.40	

Notes: idiff2 = difference between the observed and perceived Entertainment utility of Internet news *P < 0.001, ** P< 0.05, R^2 = 20.7 per cent (F = 14.02, P = 0.000).

Table 7.12: Results of the regression analysis between the differences in the perceived and observed values of Interpersonal communication utility of Internet news and other variables

The regression equation is:

Idiff3 = – 0.130 + 0.126 pf1 – 0.635 pf2 + 0.318 pf3 + 0.0744 pf4 + 0.0036 tf1 – 0.262 tf2 + 0.0610 tf3 + 0.274 tf4

Predictor	*Coefficient*	*SE*	*T*	*Rank*
Constant	–0.1302	0. 2386	–0.55	
Interpersonal communication utility of print newspapers (pf1)	0.12613	0.07004	1.80	

Predictor	*Coefficient*	*SE*	*T*	*Rank*
Constant	–0.1302	0. 2386	–0.55	
Entertainment utility of print newspapers (pf2)	–0.6352	0.1012	–6.28**	1
Information scanning utility of print newspapers (pf3)	0.31788	0.09309	3.41*	2
Information skimming utility of print newspapers (pf4)	0.07441	0.06998	1.06	
Entertainment utility of TV news (tf1)	0.00364	0.08187	0.04	
Interpersonal communication utility of TV news (tf2)	–0.26197	0.08865	–2.96*	4
Information scanning utility of TV news (tf3)	0.06098	0.09851	0.62	
Information skimming utility of TV news (tf4)	0.27432	0.08257	3.32*	3

Notes: Idiff3 = difference between the observed and perceived Interpersonal communication utility of Internet news, *P <0.001, **P< 0.05, R^2 = 20.2 per cent (F = 12.38, P = 0.000).

The R^2 value or variance explained is significant at R^2 = 15.8 per cent (F = 7.70, P = 0.000), in the first regression equation (Table 7.1.10). Similar results have been obtained in the next two regression equations too: R^2 = 20.7 per cent (F = 14.02, P = 0.000) (Table 7.11) and R^2 = 20.2 per cent (F =12.38, P = 0.000) (Table 7.12) respectively.

From the results shown in Table 7.1.10, it is observed that the dependent variable–difference in the perceived and observed values of Information skimming and scanning construct of Internet news has a positive relationship with the entertainment construct of Print newspapers and Interpersonal communication utility construct of TV news. However, in the cases of information scanning constructs of print newspapers and TV news, the regression coefficient has an inverse relationship and indicates that as the respective perceptions of these constructs increase, the gap between the perceived and observed utility of the Internet utilities reduce. In the case of the Entertainment utility of Internet news, it is observed (Table 7.11) that the regression coefficient is positive in the cases of Interpersonal communication and entertainment utility constructs of Print newspapers as well as Interpersonal communication utility of TV news. Finally in the case of the Interpersonal communication utility of Internet news, its is observed from the results in Table 7.12 that information scanning utility of print newspapers and information skimming utility of TV news have a positive relationship with the dependent variable. However, the entertainment utility of print newspapers and interpersonal communication utility construct of TV news have a negative relationship with Interpersonal communication utility construct of Internet news. Thus the hypotheses as mentioned above are accepted.

These regression coefficients do not indicate the relative impact of the different variables on the respective dependent variables. So to identify the relative importance, the researcher has used T values to rank the variables in question[8]. These T values indicate the rank of the independent variables in terms of their impact on the dependent variable.

From the results presented in Table 7.10, it is observed that the maximum impact on the Information skimming and scanning utility of Internet is of the entertainment utility construct of print newspapers, followed by the information scanning utility construct of print newspapers, interpersonal communication utility construct of TV news and the information skimming utility construct of TV news.

In the case of the entertainment utility of Internet news (Table 7.11), it is observed that the highest impact on it is of the interpersonal communication utility construct of print newspapers followed by the entertainment utility construct of print newspapers and interpersonal communication utility construct of TV news.

Finally, entertainment utility construct of print newspapers has the maximum impact on the Interpersonal communication utility of Internet (Table 7.1.12), followed by the information scanning utility construct of print newspapers, utility information skimming utility and interpersonal communication utility constructs of TV news.

The results that have been presented a few paragraphs earlier may be interpreted differently. The researcher has considered two aspects of interpretation-displacement and complementary relationship.

Displacement may be defined as per unit increase in a certain utility of print newspapers or TV news which will result in unit increase in gap between observed and perceived utility of Internet news and complementary relationship may be defined as per unit decrease in a utility of print newspapers or TV news that will result in unit decrease in gap between observed and perceived utility of Internet news.

It is thus observed from the results shown in Table 7.10, that interpersonal communication and entertainment utilities of print newspapers along with entertainment and information scanning utility of TV news have a displacement effect on the Information scanning and skimming utility of Internet news and information scanning and information skimming utilities of print newspapers and interpersonal communication and information skimming utility of TV news have a complementary relationship.

Similar results have been observed in the case of Entertainment utility of Internet news (Table 7.11). However, it is observed from the results in Table 7.12 that interpersonal communication, information scanning and information skimming utilities of both print newspapers and TV news have a displacement effect on the interpersonal communication utility of Internet news, whereas the entertainment utility of both have a complementary relationship.

7.1.4 Summary of the Findings

It has been confirmed in this study that there is a difference in the way the Indian audience consume news from the three different media and all the media are distinct. No significant difference was found between the groups of Internet newsreaders and non-readers with respect to the news gathering habits from print newspapers or TV news. However, amongst Internet newsreaders a distinct difference was confirmed in the newsgathering habits from print newspapers and TV news in this study, whereas, no such difference was confirmed in the population that did not read Internet news.

A negative impact of print and electronic media-print newspapers and TV news on the news gathering habit from Internet is confirmed in this study. It is also concluded that if the habit of newsgathering from Print newspapers and TV news can be increased, then the news gathering habit from Internet will decrease. This confirms the competition between print and electronic news media and the Internet news in terms of time spent. Moreover, this also confirms the time displacement hypotheses, that people experience a certain reduction in the amount of time they spend on other media, when a new media activity is introduced, adding to the theory of time being a zero-sum phenomenon.

Factors such as education, profession are predictors of newsgathering habits from Print newspapers and TV news. Credibility perception of print and electronic news media, positively impacts the amount of time spent on it. This finding is consistent with earlier work conducted by Gunther (1992)[9]. Credibility perception of Internet negatively impacts the amount of time spent on print and electronic media. Internet connectivity at home, number of days of Internet weekly use and number of hours spent on the Internet on an average also have a negative relationship with average number of days of TV news viewing and reading print newspapers. However, education, profession and increase in Internet dependence have a positive relationship with increased print and electronic media usage. People whose Internet dependence for news has increased show greater affinity to gathering news from print and electronic sources, too. The unemployed audience has maximum impact on average number of days of TV news viewing and reading print newspapers, followed by people in the age group of 18–28 years. The next highest impact is that of the mean credibility perception of TV news and print newspaper, followed by audiences who are teachers followed by the impact of average number of hours spent on the Internet. Mean credibility perception of Internet news and number of days of Internet weekly use have much lower impact.

It may be thus concluded that media choice and usage is based on user's experience with the medium, the individuals' perceptions and how well the different needs have been satisfied. This agrees with previous research.[10]

The study confirms the presence of a competition too between the print newspaper, TV News and Internet news. The novelty associated with a new medium may be partially responsible for this. The functional niche of the new medium occurs only over time and hence it might still be premature to observe functional displacement in the Indian context. However, there are indications of a displacement process in progress, as Internet usage does seem to be affecting print and electronic media usage.

It has been seen that there are significant gaps between the perceived and observed utilitics of Internet news. This implies that Internet news portal have not been able to satisfy their users and therefore need to focus on reducing these gaps. We have seen that the entertainment utility of print newspapers, information scanning utility construct of print newspapers, interpersonal communication utility construct of TV news and the information skimming utility construct of TV news all have significant impact on the Information skimming and scanning utility of Internet news. Again, interpersonal communication utility construct of print newspapers, entertainment utility construct of print newspapers and interpersonal communication utility construct of TV news have significant impact on the entertainment utility of Internet news. Finally, entertainment utility construct of print newspapers, information scanning utility construct of print newspapers, information skimming utility and interpersonal communication utility constructs of TV news all have significant impact on the Interpersonal communication utility of Internet news.

This study has tried to analyse the displacement and complementary relationship of media in greater detail based on the utility perceptions and has found that, that interpersonal communication and entertainment utilities of print newspapers along with entertainment and information scanning utility of TV news have a displacement effect on the Information scanning and skimming utility of Internet news and information scanning and information skimming utilities of print newspapers and interpersonal communication and information skimming utility of TV news have a complementary relationship. Similar results have been observed in the case of Entertainment utility of Internet news. However it is observed that interpersonal communication, information scanning and information skimming utilities of both print newspapers and TV news have a displacement effect on the interpersonal communication utility of Internet news, whereas the entertainment utility of both have a complementary relationship. A telephone-based survey had concluded that the Internet has a displacement effect on print and electronic sources (e.g. TV and newspapers) in daily news[11]. Similar trends were also observed in Taiwan.[12] Similarity in utility and gratification between the traditional and new media can be a cause for displacement. The concept of complementarity arises when, people with a strong need for news and information adopt the Internet for this purpose without reducing their use of traditional sources. The chance for this scenario of increasing budget is quite high because media time spending is not necessarily constant. The time increase in total news and information usage might come from a number of sources such as time previously spent on entertainment on television or radio as also seen through research.[13] It was inferred from the findings of a research[14] that Internet users might be information seekers, who either could listen to radio when surfing the net; or might turn to newspapers for more in-depth news than what was read on the net (or *vice versa*); or might see both the Internet and newspapers as useful information sources.

It may in brief thus be concluded that print newspapers, TV news and Internet news serve different purposes for the public. There are clear indications of displacement as well as a complementary relationship between Internet news and print and electronic news media-which are all, dependent on the different utilities that these media offer. Thus there is a subtle substitutability between the media for viewers, however since there is not just one news and information market but multiple markets no effective competition between media types has been observed.

7.2 Internet in Healthcare Services

Internet technology is being used to facilitate remote consultation, diagnosis and treatment of patients. Use of Internet in delivery of healthcare enables healthcare professionals and institutions to render critical medical services to rural communities especially those in remote locations and those that lack qualified medical personnel and services. To study the impact of Internet in critical cardiac health problems amongst population which are located in areas without proper medical facilities in India the telemedicine project at the Rabindranath Tagore International Institute of Cardiac Sciences was chosen, for carrying out a qualitative analysis by observation, interviews through focused and non-directive methods and data collection. Three local centers at Bankura, Udaipur and Siliguri have been considered along with the referral centre at Kolkata. Section 7.2.1 states the case in detail, section 7.2.2 presents the results of the statistical tests and hypotheses tested, the section 7.2.3 presents relevant discussions and finally section 7.2.4 provides a brief summary of the findings. Regression equation using ordinary least square algorithm has been considered to estimate the regression coefficients, test the hypotheses H8.1-H8.3 and compute the impact of death, referral and thrombolysis on the discharge of the critical patients.

7.2.1 The Case

The Integrated Telemedicine Tele-health Project is a first-of-its-kind initiative jointly sponsored by the Indian Space Research Organisation (ISRO), Hewlett Packard (HP), the Asia Heart Foundation at the Rabindranath Tagore International Institute of Cardiac Sciences (RTIICS), Kolkata and Narayana Hrudayalaya in Bangalore and was initiated in 2001 along with the state governments of seven north-eastern states of India. The Rabindranath Institute at Kolkata and Narayana Hrudayalaya at Bangalore are the main Telemedicine linking hub for the seven states. The specialists at both the institutions offer their services for this project entirely free of cost. Asia Heart Foundation and Narayana Hrudayalaya have initiated telemedicine activities with the help of high speed telephone connectivity, or Integrated Services Digital Network (ISDN) connectivity to connect remote Intensive Care Units to provide critical care to cardiac patients admitted in government district level or sub-divisional hospitals to their hospitals in Kolkata and Bangalore over and above ISRO's telemedicine network association.

The project tried to identify a 100-bedded hospital in each of these participating states and the hospitals were to be selected based on distance from the state capital and the lack of a coronary care unit. The first three centers along with the adjoining Coronary Care units (CCU's) were set up in Siliguri and Bankura in West Bengal and Udaipur in Tripura with the first Coronary Care Unit inaugurated in Siliguri District Hospital, Siliguri, West Bengal on 24th June, 2001. The next coronary cardiac care unit was inaugurated at Bankura Sammilani Medical College and Hospital, Bankura, West Bengal on 21st July, 2001.The Udaipur center in Tripura was started on 22nd August, 2001. RTIICS was the referral hospital for all these centers.

This project based on Fisher's[15] hub-and-spoke model of telemedicine-delivered cardiac care designed to enhance the administration of acute stroke therapies was unique since all previous telemedicine projects in India were based on Outpatient basis, where patients came for consultation through Internet technology and then left, as in other outpatient departments. Dr Devi Shetty, a renowned cardiac surgeon and Chairman, Asia Heart Foundation and Narayana Hrudayalaya, felt that this kind of treatment of patients was inadequate in cases of cardiology where, if someone came after a heart attack, by merely-confirming the same through a teleconsultation would be inadequate to save the life and so he started a six bedded fully equipped CCU in each of these centers for patients who required immediate admission, thrombolytic therapy, or some other super specialty treatment in addition to the tele-consultation. It was intended to provide patients with acute stroke a timely, adequate assessment and emergency stroke treatments.

The respective governments in their local hospitals provided these spaces for the Critical Coronary Care units and the manpower was initially provided by the RTIICS. This manpower comprised trained staff—doctors, nurses and CCU technicians who could take the special Electro Cardiogram (ECG), perform catheter-lab procedures, use defibrillators and administer life saving drugs in the critical hour of a heart attack. They were also trained in IT technology to manage and run the services independently. After the initial handholding, at the Siliguri center, the nurses were provided by the government hospitals. In Udaipur, the doctors and the nurses were provided by the hospital and the technicians were provided by RTIICS. In Bankura, all the three types of staff were provided by RTIICS. The life-saving drug Streptokinase was also provided free of cost to the patients from that center by RTIICS. In the other two centers the respective governments provided the drug free of cost to its patients.

Apart from government collaboration, certain centers were also started with private partners in 2002. These were at Tinsukia in Assam and at Purulia, Jamshedpur and Chittaranjan in West Bengal. All these seven centers were connected to RTIICS in Kolkata.

The center at Purulia did not perform satisfactorily and therefore was eventually closed down. The centre at Jamshedpur, which was being run by a doctor and the one in Tinsukia were closed down too when the group inaugurated the Brahmananda Narayan Hrudalaya hospital in Jamshedpur and another hospital in Tinsukia.

In West Bengal, there are presently 13 centres with Transtelephonic ECG facilities within this network. In south India, the centers are at Sargur, Hulkoti, Kundapur, Bidar and Chamranrajnagar. These were set up by Narayana Hrudalaya at Bangalore and remain connected to it.

The project implementers have devised pioneering ways and means to reduce the cost of installation of telemedicine without compromising on the quality of care. They have used ISDN and telephone line connectivity that are easily available from BSNL even in very remote areas today. This technology also supports easy data transfers and video calls to very long distances. Secondly, good video-conferencing cameras are available in the market from various manufacturers with lot of options at affordable prices. The basic infrastructure requires a computer (PIV or higher) and an EECG device unit, which costs around Rs 12,500. Apart from this an Internet support, which can be even through a normal telephone line for EECG and broadband, VSAT or ISDN, web cameras and a TV screen for video-conferencing.

Expensive Telemedicine Software or high end gadgets like digital cameras, online microscopes, medical scanners that transfer and store medical data like X-rays, CT Scans and MRIs have not been used in the local centers so far as there is no trained manpower available to use these gadgets and provide high-tech examinations to patients at those remote locations.

Dr Devi Shetty in his interview pointed out that the beauty of telemedicine was that it could make ordinary people do extra-ordinary things. He supported his argument by citing an example from his personal experience where he has seen ordinary MBBS doctors and para-medics in district hospitals of Bankura and Siliguri in West Bengal, Chamrajnagar in Karnataka, Udaipur in Agartala treat patients suffering with Myocardial Infarction, Ischemia, Unstable Anginas successfully, with assistance from senior cardiologists in the hub hospitals in RTIICS, Kolkata and Narayana Hrudalaya, Bangalore. Without the use of Internet technology this would not have been possible.

Therefore, this is a wonderful and easy way of training doctors as well as reaching quality healthcare to under developed areas. Further, he mentioned that he along with his colleagues conduct outpatient consultations to over 100 patients via Internet from various remote centres, every day, free of cost.

These centers provide round the clock services every day of the year. There is extensive use of Internet technology in all these centers. The services provided may be listed as follows:

Tele-consultation in Outpatient department by using video-conferencing facilities for emergency, non-emergency and follow-up cases: For the patients who do not require immediate hospitalisation, they can avail of tele-consultation. In these cases all vital reports related to the patient are sent in advance to the referral hospital in a digital format (X-ray reports, Scan report, Tele-ECG and others) either as an e-mail or through net-meeting. At the appointed time the specialist sits in the studio of the referral hospital while the patient along with a local doctor sits in the studio of the local hospital and the consultation takes place. There are certain doctors interested in tele-medicine who take special interest in this project and provide maximum consultations, however, the patient may also choose a doctor, who then gives an appointment. Incase of follow up of patients, the same process as OPD consultation is repeated. The other advantage of such a system is the reduction in waiting time of a patient. In most cases there is no waiting time unless there is another Video-conference going on, because the center has only one Video Conference unit at the moment.

At the Kolkata center, many patients come specifically to be treated and checked by Dr Devi Shetty–the head of the institution and a renowned cardiologist, who is presently based in Bangalore. For that, they are provided with tele-consultation through video-conference facility. The patients' reports like–angiogram film, ECG report, previous observations by other doctors are sent in advance through Internet and are kept ready at the Bangalore console of Dr Shetty. At the appointed time, Dr Shetty arrives at the studio, the patient, his kin and a resident doctor are ready at the Kolkata studio.

The tele-consultation begins like any normal consultation in real-time–with Dr Shetty asking questions to the patient. He simultaneously reads the reports and plays the films on his monitor and provides consultation. The local doctor provides necessary clarification to both Dr Shetty and the patient.

All this is done at RTIICS through a VSAT link provided free of cost by ISRO, using Internet technology. RTIICS provides both the tele-consultation and ECG services free of cost.

Exhibit 7: Picture taken of a live teleconsultation with Dr Shetty.

Transtelephonic ECG (Electrocardiograph)—A general physician cannot confirm a heart attack without performing an ECG and in most remote locations ECG clinics are not available. To counter this problem, each of these telemedicine units have a special six lead ECG machine developed by S.N. Informatics in Bangalore, to conduct a transtelephonic electrocardiograph using special software. The ECG can be taken for 10–20 seconds or as desired. Once an ECG is taken, the local centre connects to the referral hospital through special software and a telephone line using Internet technology to transfer the data. At the referral hospital's monitor there is an alert every time a fresh ECG arrives, almost like an e-mail. A specialist looks at the same and fills in an online format with his opinion and observation. Once completed, it is sent back to the local hospital through the Internet connection in the same way. This report is printed locally on arrival and the residing local doctor, gets the opinion, observation and advice of his senior colleague from the referral centre along with the report and is able to treat the patient accordingly. This entire process takes a maximum of 15–20 minutes—when in any normal case the complete activity requires atleast six hours. Further, no clinic works round the clock for these kinds of tests and consultations in the regions where these facilities have been made available.

Consultation on medical reports—Other medical reports like radiology reports, CT Scans, Ultra sound reports, are scanned locally and sent to the referral hospital. Very soon new machines are going to be installed where the reports will be created digitally and sent automatically to the referral hospital.

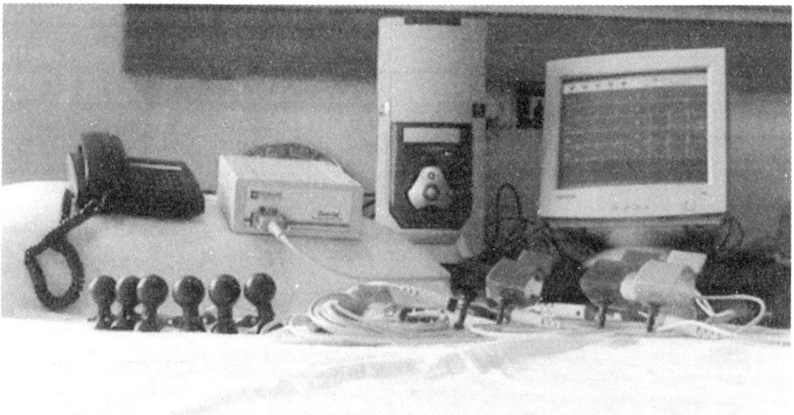

Exhibit 7.2: Equipments used for the transtelephonic electrocardiograph at the local hospital.

Emergency admissions and In-patients department—When a patient arrives with a serious cardiac condition, the doctor on call can admit the patient and consult the specialist at the referral centre using the videoconference facility with the referral hospital in addition to performing the trans telephonic ECG and sending other basic test reports. The specialist then assesses the condition of the patient and decides on the line of treatment which is then administered locally–like use of defibrillators or performing catheter-lab procedures like thrombolysis.

This facility is of tremendous help to patients and increases their chances of survival incase of severe blockages causing the attack if they receive this medical attention within an hour of the heart attack, known as golden hour. It also provides the patient with a specialist who is far more experienced in handling such cases than the local doctor without having to go through either the trauma or the delay in travel to a specialty hospital.

Virtual rounds—A specialist from the referral center goes on virtual rounds through video-conferencing to check the condition and progress of admitted patients on a regular basis. He can in one session monitor the condition of patients in all the centers, while sitting at his own desk since every bed has its own monitor and camera unit.

This specialist consultant from the referral center virtually takes charge of the disease management of these patients and instructs doctors, technicians and staff to administer the treatment locally through a two-way Internet based video-conference. This continues until the patient is discharged from the CCU. In most cases, these doctors at the local hospitals are not as experienced or qualified as the doctor from the referral hospital.

These centers are thus able to provide best quality treatment to their patients using lower level manpower in backward, underdeveloped and far-flung areas because of Internet technology through a virtual experience very close to the real practice. In the process, they are also being able to bridge the distance gap and reduce the traveling agony of their critical patients by bringing the service closer home. It may also be noted that the cost of bridging the distance through this technology is quite minimal, at times the cost of a local phone-call only.

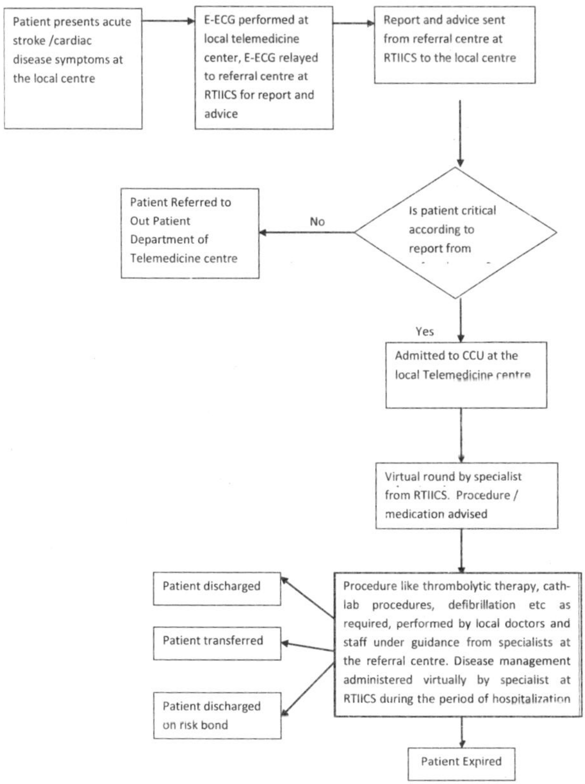

Diagram 7.1: Flow chart showing the patient flow.

7.2.2 Causal Relationships

To understand how the growing use of Internet technology in this project is impacting the performance of cardiac care units at the local and referral hospitals, the discharge of patients from the cardiac care unit of the local hospitals will be chosen as the response, while the variables of expiry, patients thrombolysed and patients referred to the referral centre for further treatment will be controlled. Death, or expiry in the cardiac care unit may be due to several other reasons like extent, complexity of disease and sudden or existing damage and this may occur in some cases in spite of intervention by local doctors and specialists from the referral centre through telemedicine.

Patient referrals indicate that the conditions of the patients have improved and they have been stabilised during their stay at the cardiac care unit to an ambulatory state. They may either be shifted immediately or later since many cases require surgical intervention, which the local centers are not equipped to provide. Thrombolytic therapy is a life saving procedure in certain cases of strokes. It requires sophisticated skills and its application has to be carefully monitored.

Ordinary least square algorithm has been considered and the purpose was to estimate the regression coefficients and test the hypotheses H8.1–H8.3. The impact of each of the independent variables on the discharge of the critical patient have also been computed using the standardised beta coefficients.

The hypotheses being tested are:

H8.1: Discharge of patients receiving medical care using the Internet technologies available in the local cardiac care unit is negatively related to the expiry in the cardiac care unit.

H8.2: Referral of patients to the referral centre based on tele-consultation has a positive impact on discharge of patients.

H8.3: Thrombolytic therapy using Internet is effective in increasing the stability of patients in cardiac care units of telemedicine centres.

Table 7.13 shows the result of the multiple regression analysis, which estimates the regression coefficients and tests the impact of the telemedicine application on clinical care.

Table 7.13: Results of the regression analysis between discharge from the cardiac care unit and other variables

The regression equation is : y = –3.8 + 4.38 X1 + 1.32 X2 + 2.84 X3					
Predictor	*Coefficient*	*SE*	*T*	*Beta*	*VIF*
Constant	-3.76	22.49	-0.17		
X1 Patient Expired	4.378	0.444	9.86*	0.754	1.6
X2 Patient referred to referral hospital	1.316	0.711	1.85**	0.137	1.5
X3 Patient undergone thrombolytic therapy	2.842	0.563	5.05*	0.321	1.1

Notes: *P < 0.001, **P<.05, R^2 = 92.9 per cent (F = 82.91, P = 0.000), DW Statistic = 2.26 y = discharge of patients from the cardiac care unit.

From Table 7.13, it can be observed that the regression coefficient is positive in the case of expiry (X1), referred to referral hospital (X2) and Thrombolysed (X3). This indicates that these variables have a positive relationship with the dependent variable-discharge from cardiac care unit.

Table 7.14: Validation statistics

R^2	*F*	*P*
92.9 %	82.91	0.000

Since, this is a cross sectional analysis, it was necessary to check the VI factor for possible multi-collinearity. The VI factor in all cases was found to be less than 10[16] and hence there is no multi-collinearity in the data.

The results in Table 7.13 indicate that hypotheses H8.2 and H8.3 have been both confirmed since the t-values of the respective variables are significant and the direction of the respective regression coefficients are as expected.

The standardised beta coefficients as shown in Table 7.13, indicate the impact that each independent variable has on the dependent variable. The maximum impact is Expiry (0.321). This result is obvious, since, if patients die while in the cardiac care unit it directly reduces the chances of discharges.

This signifies the need to reduce the number of deaths in the cardiac care unit to increase chances of discharge. Thrombolytic therapy has the second highest impact on the dependent variable at 0.321; this indicates the effectiveness of the therapy and its impact in increasing the discharge rate from the cardiac care unit. Referral cases also have a positive impact of 0.137 on discharges, since patients are stabilised before being sent for further treatment.

The R^2 value is significant at 92.9 per cent ($F = 82.91$, $P = 0.000$) (Table 7.14). The Durbin-Watson statistic[17] value is 2.26. Since the data has been collected over a period of years, the DW statistic value of 2.26, indicates that an appropriate periodic function has been fitted to periodic data and therefore, the deviations from the regression are uncorrelated because the cycle of the data values is accounted for by the fitted function.

Analytical interpretation of the tests for Hypotheses: H8.1, H8.2, H8.3: Regression analysis is applied for identification of the impact of one or more variables on another variable and be able to predict the response. In the present case, the death of a patient, referral to the referral hospital for further treatment and thrombolytic therapy provided using Internet technology were considered and their impact measured on the discharge of patients from the critical care unit of the local hospitals. A positive coefficient in the regression equation as shown in the Table 7.13 indicates a positive impact. Further the parameters (beta values) indicate the variable with the greatest impact. Since this data has been collected over a period of years, the Durbin Watson statistic was necessary to be calculated to confirm that an appropriate periodic function has been fitted to the periodic data and therefore, the deviations from the regression is uncorrelated because the cycle of the data values is accounted for by the fitted function. Further, it was necessary to check the value of the variance and whether it was significant (R^2 value and its P value), so that the regression equation could be used for hypotheses testing. Based on these the hypotheses could be tested correctly on the data.

7.2.3 Discussion

The above study shows that the disease management by specialists from the referral center in RTIICS, during the period of hospitalisation in the local centers, using Internet as the medium, at all the three centers, are yielding satisfactory results by increasing the chances of survival amongst critically ill cardiac patients and providing sophisticated treatment at low costs and with less specialised manpower.

The findings confirm the benefit of using Internet technology based interventions on critical patients admitted in the local cardiac care units. The increase in their rate of discharge is positively related to the use of video-conference based consultations with specialist doctors from the referral center as well as thrombolytic therapy that is conducted using Internet technology. It is confirmed that its use has been effective in increasing the number of patients discharged from the cardiac care unit following improvement in health conditions. It has also been confirmed that teleconsultation is additionally an effective method of providing quality healthcare to remotely located patients and this model is effective in India. This technology enables remote stroke physicians to direct the local staff by telementoring, to administer TPA in rural settings where thrombolytics were not previously used. Telementoring is an educational technique that involves real-time guidance of a less experienced physician through a procedure in which he, or she has limited experience. This supports an endeavour to bring stroke expertise to rural community hospitals. Further, it is seen that telemedicine facilitated thrombolytic therapy for acute stroke patients was intended not to replace care provided by local providers but rather to address a time and spatially related emergency need. Similar inferences were drawn from the research[18] in community hospitals around Houston where telemedicine (video-teleconferencing) was deployed to provide acute stroke consultative services in case of brain strokes. An Internet based system like the above, thus facilitates the safe administration of thrombolytic therapy to patients within rural communities suffering an acute ischemic stroke.

Telemedicine can be used as a rapid consultation tool too that results in more accurate decision-making and may be used as a tool to provide the same quality of stroke care to patients in rural hospitals as is given in tertiary stroke centers. Similar conclusions were drawn in a research at the Medical College of Georgia where they have developed a telestroke evaluation system called REACH.[19] The success of using it as a rapid consultation tool when used in five rural hospitals in Georgia has also been reported.[20] In another study, where it was prospectively assessed whether telemedicine (real-time, two-way audio and video, and digital imaging and communications in medicine interpretation), or telephone was superior for decision making in acute telemedicine consultations, it was reported that stroke telemedicine consultations result in more accurate decision making compared with telephone consultations and can serve as a model for the effectiveness of telemedicine in other medical specialties.[21] A project that was established by The Ohio State University Medical Center (OSUMC) and the Ohio Department of Rehabilitation and Corrections (ODRC) to investigate the use of telemedicine in providing healthcare to Ohio's prison inmates reports the convenience and success of using telemedicine in prison set ups.[22] Thrombolytic therapy is the only proven therapy for acute ischemic stroke.[23] Use of Internet technology will thus enable greater use of thrombolytic therapy in strokes in a safe manner.

It can be concluded from this study that telemedicine can be a solution for emergency medical assistance, long-distance consultation, administration, supervision and quality assurance along with education and training for healthcare professionals and providers and this agrees with previous research. A study to construct a local telepathology network between the Department of Pathology, Tohoku University Hospital, and Koritu Kesennuma Hospital, about 150 km away in Japan cautioned against misdiagnosis due to poor quality of instruments, including the transmission cable and pictures, cost-benefit ratio, protection of patients' privacy, and overwork for pathologists. However, it concluded that despite the problems, telepathology is a promising technology.[24] Again a study has reported the success of telementoring by the Yale University School of Medicine using low-bandwidth in a surgery performed in a mobile surgery unit in Equador.[25] However, telemedicine needs to be implemented with care, supervision and administered well [26].

The impact of telemedicine on healthcare structures can then be significant. In this respect, telemedicine can be seen as a tool that can be used to build up new healthcare models and can be used in other specialties like head injuries.[27] When user satisfaction (i.e. that of patients, medical staff at a remote hospital and medical staff at a neurological centre) with realtime teleneurology consultations was studied prospectively, all of them reported confidence in the system and felt comfortable using it.[28]

7.2.4 Summary of the Findings

This study concludes that stroke and cardiology telemedicine consultations result in more accurate decision-making and can serve as a model for extending medical facilities. More appropriate decisions, higher rates of thrombolytic therapy use, low technical and manpower requirement, and timeliness of treatment, all support the efficacy of telemedicine for making treatment decisions, and might enable more practitioners to use this medium in daily stroke care and make treatment more available to the underserved population.

7.3 Internet in Agriculture and Rural Development

A quiet digital revolution is reshaping the lives of farmers in remote Indian villages. In these villages, farmers grow soyabeans, wheat and coffee in small plots of land as they have for thousands of years. A typical village has no reliable electricity and has antiquated telephone lines. The farmers are largely illiterate and have never seen a computer. But farmers in these villages are conducting e-business through an initiative called *e-Choupal*, created by ITC, one of India's largest consumer and agribusiness communities'.[29]

This research, which intends to study the impact of Internet in agriculture, is exploratory in nature based on a case study method with a background and research approach as detailed in section 6.7.1 in Chapter 6. By using analytical rather than statistical logic, cases studies help understand complex phenomena[30] better. This is a scientific research work based on different information gathered from various authentic sources. This exploratory study on ITC's *e-choupal* has been conducted by selecting five experts in this field. The researcher conducted personal interviews with these experts, to gain a better understanding of the linkages among Internet, participatory development and social development.

The interviews were conducted to obtain necessary information on existing systems, scalability, profitability and sustainability of the project, along with the range covered, new linkages formed and communication channels established. Further, the researcher visited two mandi and three *e-choupals* (Mograram, Barkhedanathu and Thumuda in Madhya Pradesh) to gain a first hand knowledge about the traditional methods of trade and the Internet impacted new method of trade.

The results of the study have been presented in three major sections. The first section presents a background study of agriculture in India, traditional methods of trade, ITC's agri-business unit and the *e-choupals*. The second section presents the analysis of the *e-choupal* model on the basis of Brown's[31] information based evaluation methodology and the last section draws a brief conclusion of the findings.

7.3.1 Contextual Framework

7.3.1.1 Agriculture in India

A large part of the Indian population lives in rural areas and is engaged in farming. Agriculture contributes to 23 per cent of India's Gross Domestic Product (GDP), employs 66 per cent of its workforce and feeds its huge population. Moreover, the share of agriculture products to exports is also significant, accounting for almost 15 per cent of export earnings. Years of good agricultural production have been the years of economic prosperity and those of lower output have been years of economic distress. India gained through its Green revolution in terms of self-sufficiency in food grains. However, the Indian farmer has continued to remain poor. Many reasons may be attributed for that-government regulations, small landholdings, lack of knowledge related to best farming practices, role of middlemen, corruption in the trading cycles, lack of proper storage facilities, limited media reach, illiteracy, unviable direct distribution systems and high dependence on weather to name a few. The World Bank's World Development Report 2000/2001: "Attacking poverty", identifies three main elements of income growth efforts in the rural economy: opportunity, empowerment and security.

The major problems that farmers have faced forever are lack of institutional support and lack of information on best farming practices, weather, quality and inputs, additionally the presence of middle men in the chain lead to incorrect pricing, quality and weightment, handling losses and waste of time.

The vicious circle of low incomes continues due to several reasons. The fragmentation of land adversely impacts productivity and quality of produce[32], thereby reducing the bargaining power of the farmer. Wide geographical dispersion results in limited or no real time access to information and also makes whatever information is delivered, very expensive. The heterogeneity of farmers imply, single farmer and multiple crops, so it becomes difficult to customise the land or other requirements like soil conditions and there is a perpetual need for investment and hence cash and finally the weak infrastructure-whether it is roads, telecommunication, power, irrigation or a distribution system leading the farmers to depend heavily on middlemen and money lenders.

Rural marketers on the other hand suffer a great deal due to fragmentation on account of low effort ratio, high cost of transportation due to the geographical dispersion, a customer base that can neither be customised nor is worth customisation on account of heterogeneity and a passive distribution system because of poor infrastructure.

Several efforts have been made to thwart these problems, but none have been able to deliver adequately. Institutional credit programmes have been constrained by difficult counter-party risk management; government agricultural extension workers have been high on cost but low on impact; agricultural input companies have been able to focus on only certain specific crops; cooperative societies have benefited only a few; *mandi* system had ideal price discovery, but the benefits were lost due to transportation costs, high transactions costs, middlemen and farmers were often forced to sell unwillingly.

7.3.1.2 Traditional Method of Trade

The traditional marketing route in the Indian farming system has been through traders, government authorised *mandi*'s, some cooperative societies and local bartering.

7.3.1.3 *Mandi* System

The *mandi's* were created through the Agricultural Products Marketing Act to ensure fair distribution of profit amongst the producers, consumers and traders. Each *mandi* serves a certain area, which varies from state to state. Farmers bring their entire produce to the nearest *mandi* on carts or tractors. There is always a big crowd in these *mandis*. The trading is conducted by agents who earn commissions, called *kachha ardatiyas* who buy on behalf of others, and *pukka ardatiyas* who buy for themselves or act as direct representatives of remote buyers. These *ardatiyas* are generally a close community who work in cartels and are very rich. The normal trade route is that the farmer sells his produce to a small trader called a *kaccha ardatiya*, who sells to a larger trader called *pukka ardatiya*, who in turn takes the produce to a local *mandi* or a market place, where a larger trader buys the same.

The produce is inspected only by sight and no scientific or formal method is applied. The *mandi* employee conducts the auction, through an open vocal method. The adatiyas start bidding incrementally and the produce is booked at a price. The farmer has to now get his produce weighed and bagged either in the weighing area or in the commission agent's house on a manual scale. After this the value of the transaction is computed and the farmer collects his cash from the agents office. The agent also has to pay a small percentage as *mandi* fees from the transaction.

7.3.1.4 *Mandi* System and the Farmer

The average poor farmer is hit hard by the existing *mandi* system in many ways. The farmer has no knowledge of market prices or trends and in most cases fails to get the optimum price for his produce. The farmer is restricted to one *mandi*. He has to transport his entire produce to the *mandi* resulting in loss of quality of his produce, wastage in transport and bagging due to spillage, which again forms part of the compensation to the *mandi* labourers, arbitrary judgement of quality, cost of transportation and bagging, and delay in receiving payments to name a few.

The *ardatiyas* are a close community different from the farmers and have always through history exploited the farmers and set up methods within the trade system to benefit their community. The farmers also have to face the harassment of long queues at the *mandis*, overnight stay - to be able to avoid the queues and traditional intimidation by the rich commission agent class. Further, the farmers do not receive any information related to soil conditions, weather or prevailing market prices and depend entirely on non-scientific methods for return on their produce.

7.3.1.5 *Mandi* System and Large Businesses

On the other hand, this system, abounding in inefficiencies, unscientific methods and harassment by the agents create huge problems in procurement for large corporations as well. Because of lack of standard practices, the commission agents pile up both good and bad quality produce together and sell it at higher prices. The agents inflate prices at the *mandis*, so that they earn higher commissions. However the profit is never really enjoyed by the farmer and the corporation that buys in large quantities also stands to lose. These companies never have a direct interaction with the farmers and there is always a problem related to supply-chain issues due to improper storage facilities, wastage and hoarding.

7.3.2.1 ITC

ITC was incorporated on August 24, 1910, under the name Imperial Tobacco Company of India Limited. The name of the company was changed from Imperial Tobacco Company of India Limited to India Tobacco Company Limited in 1970 and then to I.T.C. Limited in 1974. Since September 2001, it has been renamed ITC Limited.

The company focused mainly on its cigarettes and leaf tobacco business for the first sixty years before expanding to its current state. ITC's Packaging and Printing Business that was set up in 1925 as a strategic backward integration for ITC's cigarettes business is today India's most sophisticated packaging house. In 1975, the company launched its Hotels business with the acquisition of a hotel in Chennai that was rechristened 'ITC-Welcome group Hotel Chola'. The objective of ITC's entry into the hotels business was rooted in the concept of creating value for the nation.

In 1979, ITC entered the Paperboards business by promoting ITC Bhadrachalam Paperboards Limited, which today has become the market leader in India. In 1990, ITC acquired Tribeni Tissues Limited, a specialty paper manufacturing company and a major supplier of tissue paper to the cigarette industry.

In 1990, ITC set up the Agri-Business Division for export of agri-commodities. The division is today one of India's largest exporters. ITC's began its *e-choupal* initiative in 2000 with soya farmers in Madhya Pradesh. Today, it has expanded to 10 states covering over 4 million farmers. ITC's first rural mall, called *Choupal Saagar* was inaugurated in August 2004 at Sehore. On the rural retail front, 24 *Choupal Saagars* are now operational in the 3 states of Madhya Pradesh, Maharashtra and Uttar Pradesh.

In 2000, ITC entered the Greeting, Gifting and Stationery products business with the launch of Expressions range of greeting cards. A line of premium range of notebooks under the brand name "Paperkraft" was launched in 2002 and added another brand called "Classmate" in 2003. "Paperkraft" was launched in 2009 and marketed as the first environment friendly premium business paper.

ITC diversified into the Lifestyle Retailing business with the Wills Sport range of international quality relaxed wear for men and women in 2000 and added the brand John Players, in 2002.

In 2000, ITC converted its information technology business into a wholly owned subsidiary, ITC Infotech India Limited. ITC expanded in the business of Foods by launching its ready to eat Indian speciality dishes under the brand name 'Kitchens of India' in August 2001. In 2002, ITC entered the confectionery and staples segments with the launch of the brands mint-o and Candyman confectionery and Aashirvaad *atta* followed by Sunfeast and Bingo. ITC also markets popular safety matches brands and incense sticks. Further, ITC manufactures and sells premium range of Shampoos, Shower Gels and Soaps.

The ITC group of companies has a yearly turnover of Rs. 7.5 billion. Of these the Agri-Business Division is one of India's largest exporters of agricultural commodities.

ITC is well known for its corporate and social responsibility and it is this philosophy that initiated the *e-choupal* system, where the business model increased shareholders value as well as contributed to social development. ITC envisioned this project by using Internet as a medium.

7.3.3.2.2 Model of *e-choupal*

The model of *e-Choupal* was conceived by the Agri business division of ITC to make the supply chain more efficient and to be able to deliver value to all its customers on a sustainable basis through re-engineering and not re-construction. The model was specifically designed to overcome the characteristic features of Indian agriculture as discussed above, namely, fragmented farms, poor infrastructure, and the involvement of numerous middlemen.

Farmers have traditionally depended heavily on the local traders for procurement of seeds, fertilizers and pesticides, marketing his produce and also for borrowing money. The farmer benefits out of the low overall costs due to these linked transactions where he can defer payments or go in for barter, but it also increases his overall dependence on the trader and his vulnerability to be exploited.

Rural development efforts like the setting up of cooperatives, rural banks and *mandis* have all tried to help farmers in different ways. However, none of these have tried to provide help holistically and therefore the traders who continued to provide all services under one roof still continue to be popular.

The concept of *e-choupal* lay in an Information Technology driven solution based on Internet technology. The intention was to facilitate collaboration between the various stakeholders, scattered over large distances, through a medium of communication and deliver real-time information independent of a transaction.

7.3.2.3 Role of Internet in the Model

The idea of *e-choupal* was to be able to provide the farmer with real-time information on prices irrespective of whether the produce is sold, or not–unlike the *mandi* system, where the price is decided, produce is sold and also delivered. In the *e-choupal*, the farmer was empowered to decide whether or not to sell at a certain price. Further, Internet was used as a medium of communication, to be able to deliver real-time information on weather, soil testing, knowledge on best farming practices and also as a tool for procurement of other farming needs like pesticides, farming tools, seeds and fertilizers. E-mailing and Internet chat facilities were also utilised for two-way communication.

7.3.2.4 Farmer and *e-choupal*

The word, *Choupal* means 'village gathering place'[33] in Hindi. An *e-choupal* is a combination of an Internet *kiosk*, a village gathering place and an e-commerce hub. *E-choupals* utilise Information technology to virtually cluster all the different participants in the value chain. The Internet thus helps in reducing and controlling the role of various intermediaries when used as the medium. It uses the physical transmission capabilities of current intermediaries-aggregation, logistics, counter-party risk and bridge financing and disintermediates them from the path of information flow and market patterns.

Sanchalaks who are recruited from farmers, manage these Internet *kiosks*. They are trained at the nearest ITC plant on basic computer usage, working on the *e-choupal* website, basic business skills, and quality determination of crops. These *sanchalaks* are then able to provide information on weather, market prices and best scientific farming practices. They perform soil testing, facilitate the sale of farm inputs and also purchase farm produce from the farmer's doorstep through real-time information and embedded knowledge based decision-making.

The *e-choupal* system has been able to eliminate wasteful intermediation and multiple handling by virtually linking to the '*mandi*' and creating a direct marketing channel. This also significantly reduces the transaction costs.

E-choupals have been able to further benefit farmers by enhancing their farm productivity and better their selling prices.

ITC has been able to lower its net cost of procurement despite paying better prices to farmers by cutting down on the costs in the supply chain that do not add value.

7.3.3.5 The Trade Route at *e-choupal*

A farmer has to carry a sample of his produce to a *sanchalak* at a local *kiosk*. The *sanchalak* evaluates the sample and provides a spot quote. This evaluation is based on inspection of the produce and deductions if any made on some strong basis that has to explained and justified to the farmer. If the farmer accepts the price, the *sanchalak* gives him a receipt with his name, address, details of the test and its results and the conditional price and approximate quantity.

The farmer can now transport the produce directly to an ITC collection center, where a laboratory test is done to confirm the *sanchalak*'s opinion, but it does not alter the price. His produce is then electronically weighed and the farmer can get paid within two hours. These material receiving centers are equipped with state-of-the-art material handling systems to ensure minimum wastage and correct measure. The transportation cost is also reimbursed to the farmer. If the farmer is located in a remote area then he can sell his produce to the *sanchalak* or a nearby collection center. The farmer also does not have to incur any bagging cost.

The previous day's *mandi* closing price is used to decide the Fair Average Quality price at the *e-choupal*, which is valid for a day. This information is relayed to the *sanchalaks* through the ITC's portal. The commission agents at the *mandi*'s update the daily mandi prices into the *e-choupal* system.

It is important to note that even though ITC does not pay more for the produce, farmers prefer to sell to them because of the efficient system and transparency involved. There is monetary gain of around Rs. 400 per ton of soybean for a farmer and Rs 200 per ton for ITC by being able to circumvent the *mandi* and taking the crop directly to the collection center and other intermediary costs like bagging in the supply chain.[34] ITC also gains in terms of an assured supply. Farmers are experiencing greater yields due to various information available through the *e-choupals*. Moreover, the *e-choupals* also trade in good quality seeds, fertilizers and other products at prices that are much lower than the market prices.

7.3.2.6 Infrastructure of *e-choupals*

To set up an *e-choupal* a computer with a reasonable processor, printer and Internet connectivity using a dialup or a VSAT is required. ITC pays for the cost of equipment and the *sanchalak*, who is an educated and trained farmer, pays for the operational costs like electricity and Internet charges. The *sanchalak* also earns a commission of 0.5 per cent per ton of processed product, and therefore, acts as a salesman for ITC. ITC spends a small amount every year towards maintenance, repair, training and a helpdesk for each such *kiosk*.

To overcome the problem of rural electrification, ITC is providing battery backup and UPS (uninterrupted power supply) systems as well as venturing into solar powered batteries. The other practical difficulty is in providing telephone lines. These lines are mostly overhead and suffer a very high downtime.

Moreover, their transmission speed is very low and often renders Internet access impossible. Therefore, ITC has adopted a Satellite – based technology (VSAT) with a speed of 256 kbps. The operating system used is Windows 98.A Hindi word processor called Ankur is used. Short movies on *e-choupal* entitled *Sunehra-Kal* and videos on best farming practices like soil-testing, etc., are also available.

The website *http://www.e-choupal.com*[35] is the gateway for the farmer. The use is restricted to valid users having logging permission through login name and password verification. As of now, this permission is given to only the *sanchalaks*, who are given their username and password upon recruitment. The website provides link to weather reports and forecast, pricing, news related to agriculture, sports, local news and also entertainment, best farming practices and an interactive section.

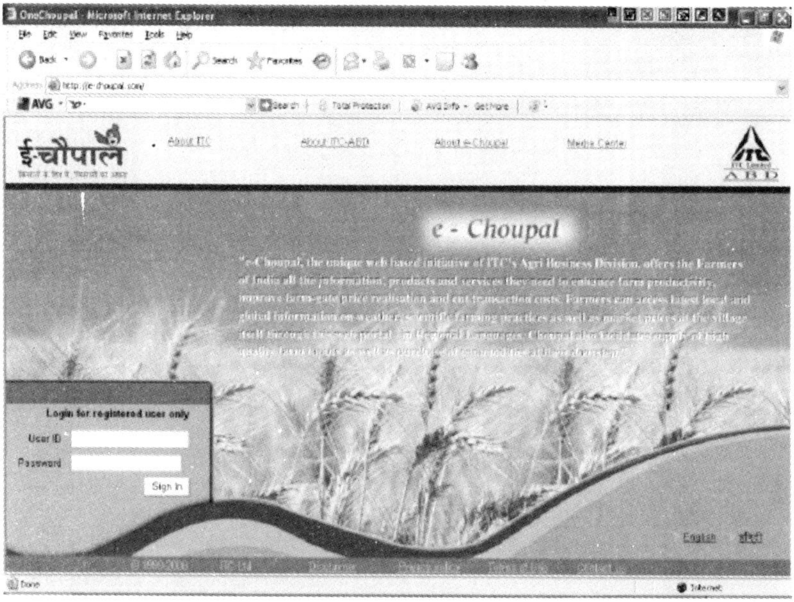

Exhibit 7.3: Homepage of *e-choupal.*

Exhibit 7.4: Picture of a sanchalak with the farmers.

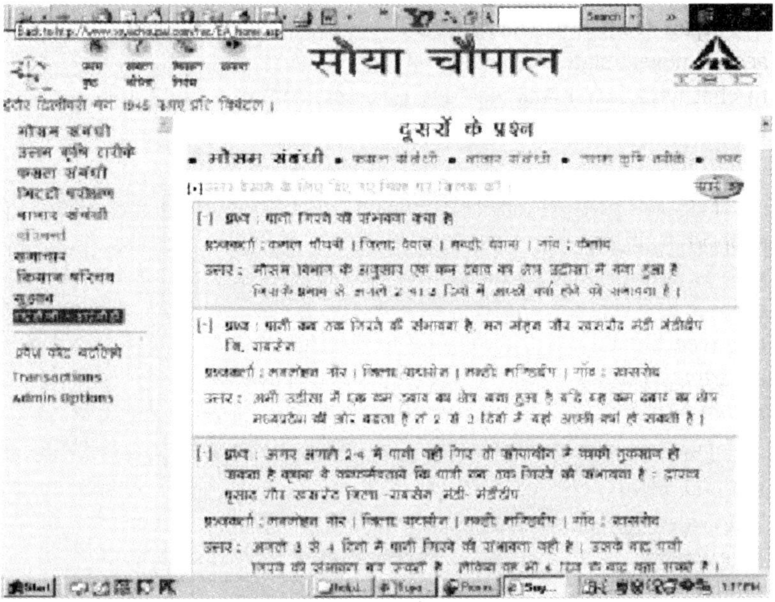

Exhibit 7.5: Homepage of soyachoupal.com

ITC coordinates with institutions of learning and departments like the meteorological department to develop useful and correct Internet content and also coordinate with companies selling agricultural raw materials like fertilizers, herbicides and seeds to enable greater e-commerce.

Localised weather data is available through the meteorological department, by clicking on the appropriate region of a map. These forecasts are for 24–72 hours. Advisories like instructions to farmers on when to sow are also provided. The *e-choupal* website displays clearly the ITC procurement rate and the *mandi* rates. ITC's following day's prices are clearly displayed as tickers on top of the page. These are updated every evening.

News related to crops, sports, local news and entertainment are also provided.

There is a section on the best practices followed for a certain crop. It provides information on the various fertilisers, etc., to use and also the method to be followed.

Finally, there is a question and answer section that allows users to post questions, which are replied by experts.

Apart from this, since Internet connectivity is available, *sanchalaks* access news related websites, sports related websites, use chat rooms to chat with ITC managers, and also use e-mail to communicate within themselves. Local students also use the Internet for checking their exam results.

ITC has also introduced the concept of a collaborator for logistic support from the local community called *samayojak*, into the system, who is able to provide local information like size of farms or preferred crops etc. They are the mediators from the old system who were not removed but their roles were revised in the value chain. They now act as *samayojaks,* or coordinators, who help ITC in setting up new *e-choupals* by identifying locations and selecting *sanchalaks.*

They manage the physical transportation of products sold through the *e-choupal*s, collect prices from local auctions and maintain records. They also get commissions. *E-choupals* help ITC to build long-term relationships with the farmers and thus ensure a regular supply of farm produce. Further, *samyojaks* and *sanchalaks* are able to provide ITC with tremendous grass-root level information on product quality, expected yields, soil conditions and also pricing.

7.3.2.7 Database and Information Building through *e-choupals*

The *e-choupal* system helps in building up informative databases through routine operations. Data regarding the farmers, like their location, financial condition, farming pattern, credit worthiness, spending patterns create the basis for an opportunity in rural commerce. Most of this information gets fed into the system either automatically based on transactions, or manually by the *sanchalak*. The Internet usage pattern at the *e-choupals* is also monitored remotely through the Internet. Thus peak usage periods, preferred *e-choupals*, most visited websites; interest areas of the local community can also be tracked. This is providing ITC with a huge benefit in terms of future diversification and planning.

This kind of information will also be useful for banks and lending institutions who are reluctant to operate in rural India due to lack of information about the credit history of farmers as well as the creditworthiness of an individual by utilising the information on holdings and transactions of the farmers.

7.3.3 Analysis of the Model

According to Brown's information based evaluation methodology, which is sensitive to context– specificity and seems appropriate in evaluating the success of a participative development project using Internet as a technology, the criteria of evaluation are based on linkage, coverage and direction. According to the author an information-based rather than a knowledge-based approach to evaluation of social development programs has two advantages: relative objectivity and equity. Increasingly equitable flows of information are one indicator of social development.

With the advent of *e-choupals* using Internet as the medium, farmers in remote rural settings have been brought in touch with the entire world. These Internet *kiosks* have been able to provide the farmers with information on best farming practices, weather, soil conditions, as well as current market prices. These linkages have also helped the farmer to learn about better fertilizers, herbicides and tools as also an easy way of procuring the same. These linkages have been created through Internet portals written in Hindi, the language mostly used by the farmers in that region. The language barrier has been overcome and as a result information is flowing more easily. Therefore, the farmers now have much better access to information than ever, due to this technology. The farmers have also been linked to the Chicago Board of Trade and thus also have an insight into the global prices. It is also relevant to note that *e-choupals* provide this information regardless of a transaction.

With the involvement of agricultural supplies companies in e-commerce, the farmers can now conveniently order agricultural inputs through the *e-choupals.*

The Web-enabled, real-time data on crop prices available at the *e-choupals* give farmers a correct idea of the price they can expect from ITC and from different *mandis*. This information enables them to take informed decisions, increase their bargaining power and thereby help them to sell their produce at a price that gives them a higher profit margin.

With the availability of the information on weather, soil conditions, scientific methods and use of fertilizers, farmers are getting educated and are being able to utilise their resources better. The farmers can get their soils tested and seek expert opinion form the *e-choupals*, too. This information also helps to check harvest failure, which was predominant earlier, due to lack of information, and with information on market trends being easily available, farmers can also align their agricultural output with the market demands.

The other element of empowerment for the rural population has been their inclusion and participation in this revolution. Farmers had actively contributed at the time of design of the project. Further the *sanchalak* is also a farmer. Moreover, the roles of the traditional intermediaries have been revised and some of them are now samayojaks or coordinators. The farmers using this facility do not have to face the high handedness of the wealthy traders or the harassment at the *mandis*. A renewed sense of pride and confidence has been thus enthused in them. The farmers have also been empowered by better and efficient accounting and weighing techniques. Also, due to the fewer number of hands that a crop changes the quality of produce is retained and wastage is lower.

The bagging charges and transportation costs are also reimbursed by ITC. Even though ITC does not pay more to the farmers than the prevailing price, the quick and correct recovery of the money post transaction from ITC has enabled farmers to be more self-sufficient and less dependent on money-lenders and other traditional agricultural intermediaries. Thus with the availability of these online real-time information and transaction systems the farmer has been more empowered than ever before.

This intervention has also generated the concept of a transparent and accountable system at the grass roots.

It must also be noted that this low technology has had a very high impact in terms of number of people addressed, money generated, loss reduction and gains achieved.

Due to the database and information building through *e-choupals*, banks and lending institutions are showing interest in operating in such areas as the records related to credit history, rating and holdings of farmers are being maintained properly. These links could have never been forged earlier. Just as local produce is being carried away from these villages in a reverse mode, fast moving consumer goods, durable products, automotives, banking and insurance services are also moving in to these villages. This is because connectivity of villages has increased and so have the spending power of the local community. This is thus providing the villagers a window to the outside world and the gap in opportunities between the urban and rural parts of India are reducing.

The introduction of *e-choupals* at numerous locations with an aim to make one available within 5 kms of any farmer has ensured a high coverage in the region. Moreover, by using technologies like VSAT and solar powered batteries for electricity and self-sufficiency in these *kiosks*, has made this coverage possible in spite of the absence of basic infrastructure. This model is easily replicable, too. According to ITC,

40,000 villages in 10 states have been covered through 6,500 *e-choupal*s, where 4 million farmers have already benefited.

The *e-choupal* web-portal provides a zone for direct communication. The fact that it is in the local language helps even further. Here farmers and other citizens as well as *sanchalaks* can post their questions and competent individuals reply to those within a short span. This exchange of communication is also in Hindi. This kind of two-way communication also helps in reducing the gap between the local community and the rest of the country. Moreover, it has also been reported by ITC, that websites on local news, cricket, entertainment and mobile phones are visited quite often, as are exam result sites. This indicates a new direction in the way the local farmers are beginning to think and learning to appreciate the value of information. *Sanchalaks* are in addition engaging in exchange of e-mails with ITC officials and participating in online chats amongst themselves and with ITC officials.

In other words, this application of Internet in rural India has been able to define a clear value proposition for all participants– farmers, ITC, *mandis*, *sanchalaks* and *samayoaks*. It has been able to empower the rural citizens with timely and accurate knowledge, thus also impacting the quality and quantity of crops. It has been able to organise the agricultural market in the villages under its domain despite having to fight the odds of infrastructure, illiteracy and traditional market intermediaries.

Based on Brown's theory of evaluation of social development programmes, we see that this model has in every way been successful in providing social development and empowerment to the rural population in a quick and easy way, which would normally have taken years to accomplish, if at all, by huge coverage, setting up linkages between the rural community and the rest of the country and world and setting up a bi-directional communication channel.

In terms of the project's sustainability, profitability and scalability, we have seen that ITC had started this as a measure to ensure a steady supply of quality farm produce for its agri-business division. The model was designed to be modular and experimental in nature. It was an easy model to replicate in a short time. The *e-choupal* model is not a subsidised model, neither does it have any government investment. The company is answerable to its shareholders for good returns.

Due to the re-structuring of the value chain the company has been able to reduce the transaction costs and wastages, thereby being able to provide better returns to the farmers, reducing its own costs of procurement, being able to sustain a steady inflow of quality produce and gaining farmer loyalty through this transparent and highly value-added model.

Thus in terms of sustainability, scalability and profitability as well, this model has been very successful.

7.3.4 Summary of the Findings

The social impact of introducing Internet based technology in agriculture has been tremendous. The *e-choupals* have been able to provide a window to the world and many opportunities. It has been able to structure and bring in a scientific edge to the old profession and old methods of trading and farming. The greatest contribution has been social empowerment of the villagers. Farmers have been empowered to take an informed decision through a transparent system. They have been able to introduce better farming practices, protect their crops from unexpected weather conditions and thus generate higher yields, better returns and finally earn a better living standard. All this has been possible due to Internet technology and the administration by the *sanchalaks*. Having built up a sizeable database on the rural markets, *e-choupals* have generated interest for other players to service this previously neglected but highly populated sector. Just as farm produce is being taken from villages, through a reverse process consumer durables and non-durables, banking and insurance services are moving in to villages.

For the poor farmers it has revived a sense of pride and confidence and has brought them out of the clutches of the commission agents and middlemen. With the local community showing interest in visiting websites other than *e-choupal*, it shows that the great divide between the rural and urban population as well as the global population has been reduced. Using the *e-choupal* as a medium of mass-communication socially relevant topics like soil erosion, sustainable development, conservation of energy, utilisation of alternate sources of energy are all being relayed easily to the huge rural community without additional cost or investment. Ideas and information are helping people to plan and dream of a better livelihood and future. People are learning to value knowledge and exposure. Finally, this model has also shown how large corporations can blend their commercial ventures with social development projects.

7.4 Internet on the Political Outcome

The relative backwardness of Andhra Pradesh and its aspirations to become a knowledge society provides an insightful case study of the impact factor of Internet in a backward state in India.

In a country plagued by poor infrastructure, high rural population, problems of electricity and water, illiteracy, lack of IT training and language barriers, it is difficult to convince the electorate of the concept of good governance through e-governance. People still rely more on hand written documents and are not satisfied with computerised copies. Further, most of the existing systems are inherently not adequate. A lot of restructuring and re-engineering of manual systems are required before implementing IT based systems. Information technology and Internet are only enablers; they can produce results only when the system is reengineered to be more efficient. Again the results and outcomes are also not visible immediately. Efficient systems are designed to maximise resources and avoid waste, they also make several processes redundant and thus the manpower involved in those processes become either surplus, or lacking in skills. This, too, does not go down well with people in a democracy. A lot of trust, awareness, understanding, conviction, willingness and hope are required to achieve this change. It is a process, most often a struggle that presents costs and risks– both financial and political. The challenges are enormous and more cultural than technical and have to be handled very sensitively.

N. Chandrababu Naidu's regime between 1995–2004 in Andhra Pradesh was a period that was marked by tremendous emphasis on information technology and communication. Inspite of a serious commitment by the Chief minister to make these technologies acceptable to the citizens, he seemed to have lost the bet at the next election when he was overthrown by an overwhelming majority. The researcher has tried to analyse through an exploratory case study based on a focus group interview with 7 knowledgeable members who had voted against the government at the 2004 elections. The study centers on the principal question of what was the impact of over emphasis on Internet on the political outcome in a democratic process.

7.4.1 *The Focus Group Interview*

A focus group interview method with the group comprising of educated individuals who had voted in the state elections in 2004, was felt to be the best method to address the following specific questions:

- Economic development under Chandrababu Naidu;
- Contributions of the Naidu government towards development of IT facilities and IT industry in the state;
- Did over emphasis on Internet have an impact on the way the electorate voted;

- Did the electorate benefit because of the introduction of Internet based services;
- Did this new technology bring in opportunities for employment ; and
- A summary for the reasons of failure.

The expert focus groups comprised of journalists, renowned academicians, software professionals, government officials and other residents from different parts of Andhra Pradesh. The role of the researcher was that of a moderator, to make the discussion one-dimensional. The group discussions continued for nearly an hour each and a consensus building approach had been taken to identify relevant dimensions in questions. Ten such focus groups were formed comprising of ten individuals in each interview. In all 100 people were interviewed.

No incentive, or remuneration was paid to the participants. However, the participants agreed to the discussion based on an informal agreement to keep their identities undisclosed. The interviews were held in Hyderabad and Vizag between 16th August and 31st December, 2008.

The interpretations of the outcome of the discussion have been presented below.

7.4.2 *Results of the Focus Group Interviews*

The context of the discussion was the regime of the Chief minister of Andhra Pradesh, Nara Chandrababu Naidu. Chandrababu Naidu brought with him a lot of hope and expectation to the citizens when he became the Chief Minister of Andhra Pradesh by declaring Andhra Pradesh a company, the citizens its stakeholders and himself the CEO, or Chief Executive officer of the same. This was in marked contrast to the populist attitude of past politicians specially the likes of N.T. Rama Rao. The new chief minister soon hiked the power tariff, water tariff, transport charges, land registration charges and also raised the price of rice under the subsidy scheme from Rs 2 per kilo to Rs 5 and then to Rs 6 per kilo. Moreover, he privatised several public sector undertakings during his tenure rendering over 10 lakh people jobless. Chandrababu Naidu, however, had introduced several populist schemes, too, like the *Janmabhoomi* programme in 1997, as a people centered development process aimed at achieving overall growth and improving the quality of life of the people; the Chief Minister's Empowerment of Youth programme launched in 1996; the *Adharana* programme in 1998 for providing improved hand tools, power tools and other equipments to backward class artisans; the Girl Child Labour Rehabilitation programme that was introduced for bringing attitudinal change in the society towards education of girl child; the Back to School programme for schedule caste working children was started in 1997, targeting those children who never attended schools or had been dropouts for re-admission to schools, the *Deepam* scheme was launched in 1999 to provide cooking gas connections to women below poverty line in the state; the *Mundadugu* was a programme specially packaged for citizens belonging to the schedule castes for their economic and social development; the *Roshni* project was the scheme for economic development and welfare of minorities. Then there were the Self-Help Groups created by the state government covering rural poor women for ensuring their financial security.

The *Neeru Meeru* programme was launched in April 2000 with the objective of sustainable utilisation of water. Priority was given to villages and mandals with water scarcity. The Clean and Green A.P. Campaign was started in 1998 with the objective of making every habitation and municipal ward clean and green that would enable every citizen of the state to lead a healthy life. The *Aptha Bandhu* programme was started to give rupees one lakh as compensation to families of accident victims.

7.4.3.1 *Economic Development under Chandrababu Naidu*

During the nine-year tenure of the Naidu government, the farmers were hard hit due to lack of power supply in the villages, drought and faulty policies of the past governments as revealed in the discussion.

Naidu did not concentrate much on rural development, especially in the agriculture sector on which more than 60 per cent of the population was dependent. According to the experts, 70 per cent of the population then resided in the rural areas where there was no proper infrastructure, no water facilities and drainage facilities. Due to depletion of the water tables in areas like Telengana, Rayalaseema and some other Costal regions, the farmers started depending on bore wells to supply water for their farms and crops, but there was no power supply to run these bore wells, moreover the power reforms in the state were not showing immediate results and crops suffered due to lack of water. Farmers started losing money and most of them were unable to pay back loans taken from banks, leading them to go back to the traditional money lenders, to borrow money at very high rates of interest, thus getting exploited and entering the vicious debt cycle. Added to that there was lack of strategy for marketing their products, non-availability of cheaper loans and dependence on power for irrigation. All this led to complete loss of trust in the TDP government by the rural population, which had been the backbone of support for the party in the past. The rural population was used to power supplied for free by the past government. The Naidu government on the other hand levied a nominal charge on the same. All this led to the very high rate of suicide amongst farmers.

The groups mentioned that the economics of the state was not good and kept fluctuating. The economy posted 6.3 per cent in 1996–97, 0.38 per cent higher than that of 1995-96 but fell by 1.37 per cent in the very next year, bouncing back to post 12.16 per cent in 1998–99. It slumped to 4.58 per cent in 1999-00 and then rose to over 8 per cent in 2000–01 to fall to 4.86 per cent and 3.83 per cent respectively in 2001–02 and 2002–03. In 2003–04, the final year, the growth rate settled at 8.98 per cent.

Naidu from the beginning had planned to develop the state under different plans and schemes. However, the state was already facing a monetary crunch. By supporting the BJP led, National democratic alliance (NDA) government in the center from outside he was able to mobilise lots of connections for funding in the state and also divert some money into the state from the centre. He was able to forge ties with the World Bank and the British led DFID.

The World Bank at that time was looking for involving itself at the state level to help the states, regions and provinces in developing countries. When Naidu approached the World Bank for funds for the development process in the state, the World Bank showed a special interest towards Andhra Pradesh, which was a first, since earlier all such projects and funds would be routed through the central government and no direct interactions were observed with state governments. Along with these ventures, the Naidu government also appointed the global consultant McKinsey to devise and design the road map of future reforms applicable for the state. When the Naidu government approached the World Bank along with McKinsey, the World Bank, based on their report entitled "Andhra Pradesh: Agenda for Economic Reforms" agreed to fund the state and that became the basis of the McKinsey's famous 'Vision 2020' document for Andhra Pradesh.

While these investment and development plans were being made, the World Bank and DFID jointly asked Naidu to create a separate entity, which would function above the state assembly and act as the principal consultant to the state. Naidu acceded the request and created the Implementation Secretariat, or IS, which included apart from Naidu, officials from the World Bank, DFID and experts from the British-Adam Smith Institute, which was also appointed the chief consultant for these projects.

Based on the reports, recommendations and suggestions of the World Bank, McKinsey and the Implementation secretariat, the Naidu government created its own 'Vision–2020: Swarna Andhra Pradesh' document, that was to set the goals for transforming the state into one of the most developed states in the world by 2020. The main focus of this document was on Information technology (IT) and Information Technology and Enabled services (ITES), biotechnology and other knowledge based services. It is clear because of these developments the expert groups opined, that the focus had clearly shifted out from the rural and agrarian policies of the past.

7.4.3.2 Contributions of the Naidu government towards development of IT facilities and IT industry in the state

All the members of the groups felt that Chandrababu Naidu was known for his strong affinity towards Information Technology. He initiated several e-governance projects during his tenure as he felt that Information Technology was a tool that opened up tremendous opportunities for providing basic government services to a much broader segment of the population at the optimal quality, time, place and cost and thus it should leverage its strength in IT to open up these services to all its citizens. Andhra Pradesh emerged as one of the leading states in India in e-government applications, with the State government implementing a comprehensive plan for the same.

In 1998, the state government along with a consortium of public sector IT companies from Singapore set up the APVAN or Andhra Pradesh Value Added Network to focus on revenue, commercial taxes, transaction charges, registrations and managing and maintaining the related data. This database was also meant to be utilised commercially by making it available on the Internet and thus became a revenue-earning project.

The APSWAN, or Andhra Pradesh State Wide Area Network was created to facilitate e-governance by acting as the basic information highway for all IT related applications of the Government. It had a backbone for data, voice and video communication threaded by a 2 mbps fiber optic link and connected the secretariat to 23 district head quarters, Tirupati and Vijaywada. It would help the government to have live interactions with the collectorates and other essential village officials and officers across the state on a regular and daily basis, ensuring regular and daily monitoring, during crisis and in emergency situations. These groups felt that this was a foray of the administration into e-governance.

The CARD project (Computer-aided Administration of Registration Department) was a comprehensive project of computerising one of the oldest departments of the Government "The Registration and Stamps Department". The project originally conceived in August 1996 was implemented at two test sites in August/September 1997. Since the project showed immense initial success and potential in transforming the concept of public service, the Government decided to replicate it all over the state, which was an intensive and dedicated effort.

E-seva started off as a pilot project in the twin cities of Hyderabad and Secunderabad and was, therefore, called TWINS, or Twin cities Integrated Network Systems. It started in 1999, funded by the Government of Andhra Pradesh. Initially, it provided registration of birth, death certificates, registration of vehicles and learner's driving licences. After its initial success in 2001 the project was renamed *E-seva*. A portal http: www.esevaonline.com was also launched.

The TWIN project or the subsequent *E-seva* projects were designed to serve all the citizens–rich-poor, urban-rural. The TWIN project gained lot of popularity and support across the state from all sections in the society. Through the TWIN project 19 basic services were made available at a single point service station. Bill payments–telephone bills, electricity bills, MCH bills, water bills, and many other bills was made easy using Internet at the *E-seva* places which were initially located in major junctions in the city of Hyderabad. These facilities were subsequently extended to municipal towns of the state as well. Apart from payment of bills many other services were offered in *E-seva* like issue of different application forms, submission of passport forms, payment of property tax, payment of certain examination fees. The groups concurred that this project too showed an initial urban bias for the place of start as well as the nature of initial services like driver's licenses or submission of passport forms.

The FAST (Fully Automated System for Transport) project again based on the Internet was well accepted, too, as it deals with issuing learner's licences, renewal of licences, payment of licence fees, registration of vehicles, transfer of ownership and allied documentation. Its popularity was based on the ease of the process that had evolved and also because of the short time in which these licences were issued–some took merely two hours and some only a day, or at most two.

A lot of media hype was generated around it in 2000 when the president of the United States Mr Bill Clinton was issued a driving license in record time. The computerisation of the department started in 1988 in phases. Several branch offices in Hyderabad, Vijayawada, Visakhapatnam, Chittoor, Mahabubnagar, Karimnagar, Warangal, Nalgonda and the Head Office were taken up for computerised transactions on a Unix operating system with Unify database. The services are based on the comprehensive database created and distributed through the APSWAN. The experts commented that this popular project was also available in mostly urban areas, even though Internet based data can be made available anywhere.

The APonline was a web portal developed to provide all basic information about the state. The website http://www.aponline.gov.in/ provided a link to several services and information related to the state. Several examination results, electricity service information and tourism related information was also made available through this site.

Chandrababu Naidu also initiated the SAPNET, or Society for Andhra Pradesh Network project, which was a major communication and infrastructure initiative of the department of IT and Communication, Government of Andhra Pradesh. It was essentially an education-oriented service, where experts from various renowned institutions conducted classes through satellite transmission and other distance learning technology. It was also meant to be a resource for e-governance, rural and agriculture development and telemedicine. SAPNET connected training schools of all types.

Another initiative in creating a socio-economic database of all residents and a database of all land records was done through a multi-purpose household survey that covered over a thousand mandals in several districts of the state. This reached e-governance facilities to the grass root level and at present it can in a matter of very short time issue- caste, birth and nativity certificates.

Apart from these projects, Naidu concentrated on developing the state in IT and allied areas. About 23 per cent of the total software professionals in the United States are from Andhra Pradesh and it has a strong number of skilled manpower in the area of IT. The state ranked third in India in terms of software exports in the year 2003. Established in 1992, STPI-H (Software Technology Park-Hyderabad) had a software export of about Rs. 2 lakh. And after the satellite earth station was established at Hyderabad with the support of Andhra Pradesh Government, the exports soared to Rs. 4.17 crore in 1992–93. For the next eight consecutive years the unit recorded 100 per cent growth every year. Also, the number of STP units grew several folds between 1992 and 2000. In the year 1999–2000, almost 800 units were registered, which was unprecedented and Hyderabad, a relatively late entrant, emerged as one of the fastest IT cities in the country with several multinational companies moving in. During 1999-2000, STPI-H alone had recorded exports of about Rs. 1,059 crore from its member units. The total exports of IT and ITES companies in the state by the end of the government's tenure stood at a whopping Rs. 7000 crores. Hyderabad was ranked fourth in Software Technology Parks in India only behind Bangalore, Noida and Chennai.

Chandrababu Naidu had also focused on developing both the Cyber city and the Hi-tech city. The Cyber City was meant for companies who wanted to invest in the state; they were provided land and necessary infrastructure. The Hi-tech city was built adjacent to the Cyber City at an estimated cost of 850 million USD. It was built jointly by Larsen and Toubro and the Andhra Pradesh Infrastructure Development Corporation and is a ten-storey building with state-of-the art technology and facilities available in it.

Chandrababu Naidu was able to bring software giants like Microsoft, Oracle and GE to the state and they all invested very heavily.

7.4.3.3 Problems with the Strategy

However, the groups concurred that the number of STP units in Andhra Pradesh grew very sporadically and the focus was mainly on big cities like Hyderabad and Vizag.

A great disparity in uniform growth in the IT industry was created. This was ascribed by the members as one of the reasons why IT failed to contribute to the rural sector in Andhra Pradesh. The CM had justified his stand by saying that if foreign investments were to be sought to develop a state then its main cities had to be showcased. Hyderabad being the capital city had to be thus developed first, since it was unlikely that foreign visitors would be initially keen to visit cities like Warangal, Tirupati, or Vijayawada. He felt that due to Hyderabad's development, the neighbouring areas of Ranga Reddy, Medak and Nalgonda could also ride the development wave. Further, he added that unlike what his critics felt he had just not spent on Hyderabad but had spent a lot of money in the villages on health, education, power, irrigation and infrastructure. He had built 50,000 school buildings and had launched several water schemes, but the plight of the poor has been so bad, with drought adding to their misery, that it was not possible to bring immediate relief and hence people felt he had not done enough.

Another observation of the groups was that, inspite of the rise of the IT and ITES sector in the state, it failed to generate adequate employment to its citizens. Further, the employments created were based on a basic education and knowledge of computers and software applications. Language was a major problem. This growth could therefore not offer much to the rural population in a state that had a high rural population and low literacy. For the urban youth as well, these investments by large multi-national companies did not bear direct benefits in terms of very high employment-less than a lakh jobs were only created and most of these were for technical and support staff.

Chandrababu Naidu had contributed to education by setting up the IIIT (Indian Institute of Information Technolgy), Nalsar Law University, Indian School of Business and many more large educational institutes of higher learning. These were expensive institutions and attracted students mostly from wealthier states. The local community could not directly benefit much.

7.4.4 Summary of the Findings

It would be worthwhile to analyse the Andhra experience of using the Internet for socio-economic development, improved governance, and generation of employment and as a change agent in the various government organisations.

In a state, where more than 73 per cent of the population resides in rural areas, 50 per cent are dependent on agriculture the sole focus on growth of the IT and ITES sectors at the cost of primary sectors like industry, agriculture and allied sectors proved to be very dear for Chandrababu Naidu. Most of the electorate viewed this expenditure as wasteful expenditure of public money.

His e-governance initiatives, though praise worthy have also been termed by many as a political gimmick. The public did not take kindly to his being directly involved in all these projects, with everything revolving around the CM. This apart, most of these initiatives of e-governance resulted in many retrenchments in government departments. Further, many employees found themselves lacking in skills to adapt to these changes with IT as the driving force. The public was also not so acquainted with the new medium and never realised the potential and the convenience of the Internet. Another reason for this could be that it was a concept still ahead of its times in an economy like India.

Further, most of the e-governance projects succeeded in the urban areas as people were better educated and had better access to the technology. This seems to have changed the perception of Internet as being elitist and created a further divide in the society between the users and non-users of the Internet.

While the Government had taken up a number of key initiatives for promoting the pervasive use for IT in the state, it is significant to note that technology appeared to be relatively less of a critical issue in these processes of change. Rather than introducing and using technology, it is the administration of the entire change management exercise that seems more critical in such cases.

Successes of projects of this nature and magnitude also depend on how well the government has been able to sell to the public and how well the public has bought it. Even though the CM used the platform of weekly live television programme–'Dial your CM' to emphasise the importance and relevance of IT for development, it still did not meet the desired level of public confidence.

When in 1998, the APVAN project started, McKinsey and Company, observed that several staff could be reduced and also relocated; in some cases the number was as high as 80 per cent. These suggestions naturally never go down well with employee associations, more so in a poor country like India. These also result in projects not delivering the required outcomes due to resistance, sabotage and fear. Further, when at the various stages of a project; the stakeholders are not involved in the planning, designing, implementation and maintenance of systems, they do not feel involved or develop a sense of ownership for the project and feel its only an imposition on them leading to resistance and apathy. These lead to incomplete projects, which are then, viewed as wasteful expenditure. When stakeholders were involved in the CARD project, it became a success since not only did the customers realise the convenience that it generated but also the employees felt empowered by little changes like not having to copy documents by hand only.

Most of the projects had an urban bias and even though this was mainly due to lack of infrastructure in the rural parts– the rural electorate felt discriminated. Further, due to lack of awareness most citizens were not able to utilise the Internet based services.

When such massive projects with such large number of stakeholders are to be handled, then a lot of political will and leadership is required. The Andhra government had both and yet the government failed to return to power. Many reasons were ascribed to the failure. One major cause assigned was that all the development projects using technology were centered around the Chief Minister. This contradicts the concept of a democracy where the public is only expected to follow. This can be a serious setback for a politician. This observation agrees with previous research.[36]

Inspite of all the utilities that Internet provided in establishing e-governance projects, its impact politically was very negative. The people were not comfortable using the medium. The reach was not adequate and the infrastructure requirements were also beyond the common man's means.

Therefore, in a country like India, several factors apart from the mere technology determine the spread and use of a new medium. With low level of literacy, huge urban-rural divide in terms of infrastructure, facilities and development and a large rural population such medium like the Internet is difficult to spread and replace existing mass medium.

The introduction of Internet technology for governance purpose in Andhra Pradesh was not only a complex and co-evolutionary process along with social changes but also with unintended and unpredicted consequences and ambiguous outcomes which may have endangered future socio-institutional and political changes. This observation too is supported by previous research.[37]

It may be concluded in agreement with the observations of Richard Sclove that the development of any new technology has broader social implications than those to which it was supposedly intended and these externalities are often overlooked. Sclove emphasises that "all technologies are associated with manifold latent social effects and meanings, and that it is largely in virtue of these that technologies come to function as social structures".[38]

References

1. Hair, J.F., Anderson, R.E., Tatham, R.L., and Black, W.C., Multivariate data analysis (5th edn.), Pearson education, Delhi, 2005, pp. 188–189.
2. *Ibid.*, pp. 220–221.
3. Anderson, D.R., Sweeney, D.J., and Williams, T.A., Statistics for Business and Economics, Cengage learning, 2009, UK, p. 563.
4. Fitzgerald, M., 1996, The effect of the Internet on print journalism, Editor and Publisher, Vol. 129, p. 72.
5. Outing, S., 1998, New media cutting into old media. Editor and Publisher, Vol. 131, p. 43.
6. Kayany, J., and Yelsma, P., 2000, Displacement effects of online media in the socio-technical contexts of households. Journal of Broadcasting and Electronic Media, Vol. 44(2), pp. 215–229.
7. Ngyuen, A., and Western, M., 2006, The Complementary relationship between the Internet and traditional mass media: The Case of Online News and Information, Information Research, Vol. 11(3), pp. 259–278.
8. Bring, J., 1994, How to standardise regression coefficients, American statistician, Vol. 48(3), pp. 209–213.

9. Gunther, A.C., 1992, Biased Press or Biased Public? Attitudes Toward Media Cover, Public Opinion Quarterly, Vol. 56(2), pp. 147–167.
10. Becker, L.B., and Shoenbach, K., When media content diversifies: Anticipating audience behaviors. In L.B. Backer and K. Shoenbach (Eds), Audience responses to media diversification: coping with plenty, Hillsdale, Lawrence Erlbaum Associates, NJ, 1989, pp. 1–27.
11. Dimmick, J., Chen, Y., and Li, Z., 2004, Competition between the Internet and traditional news media. The gratification-opportunities niche dimension, Journal of media economics, Vol. 17(1), pp. 19–33.
12. Li., S.C.S., 2001, New media and market competition. A niche analysis of television news, electronic news and newspaper news in Taiwan, Journal of broadcasting and electronic media, Vol. 45(2), pp. 259–276.
13. Bromley, R.V., and Bowles, D., 1995, Impact of Internet on Use of Traditional News Media, Newspaper research journal, Vol. 16(2), pp. 14–27.
14. Stempel III, G.H., T. Hargrove and J.P. Bernt, 2000, Relation of growth of use of the Internet to changes in media use from 1995–1999, Journalism and mass communication quarterly, Vol. 77 (1), pp. 71–79.
15. Fisher, M., Developing and implementing future stroke therapies: the potential of telemedicine, 2005, Annals of Neurology, Vol. 58(5), pp. 666–71.
16. Hair, J.F., Anderson, R.E., Tatham, R.L., Black, and W.C., Multivariate data analysis, Pearson Education, New Delhi, India, 1998, pp. 191–193.
17. Watson, G.S., and Durbin, J., 1951, Exact Tests of Serial Correlation using Noncircular Statistics, The Annals of Mathematical Statistics, Vol. 22(3), pp. 446–451.
18. Choi, J.Y., Porche, N.A., Albright, K.C., Khaja, A.M., Ho, V.S., and Grotta, J.C., 2006, Using telemedicine to facilitate thrombolytic therapy for patients with acute stroke, Joint commission journal on quality and patient safety/Joint commission resources, Vol. 32(4), pp. 199–205.
19. Switzer, J.A., Gross, H., Waller, J.L., Nichols, F.T., Wang, S., Adams, R.J. and Hess, D.C., 2009, A web-based Telestroke system facilitates rapid treatment of acute ischemic stroke patients in rural emergency departments, The Journal of Emergency Medicine, Vol. 36(1), pp. 12–18.
20. Wang, S., Gross, H., Lee, S.B., Pardue, C., Waller, J., Nichols, F.T., Adams, R.J., and Hess, D.C., 2004, Remote evaluation of acute ischemic stroke in rural community hospitals in Georgia, Stroke, Vol. 35(7), pp. 1763–68.
21. Meyer, B.C., Raman, R., Hemmen, T., Obler, R., Zivin, J.A., Rao, R., Thomas, R.G., and Lyden, P.D., 2008, Efficacy of site-independent telemedicine in the Stroke DOC trial: a randomised, blinded, prospective study, Lancet Neurology, Vol. 7(9), pp. 787–95.
22. Mekhjian, H., Warisse, J., Gailiun, M., and McCain, T., 1996, An Ohio Telmedicine System for Prison Inmates: A Case Report, Telemedicine Journal, Vol. 2(1), pp. 17–24.

23. Henninger, N., Chowdhury, N., Fisher, M., and Moonis, M., 2009, Use of Telemedicine to increase thrombolysis and advance care in acute ischemic stroke, Cerebrovascular diseases, Vol. 27 (4), pp. 9–14.
24. Sawai, T., Goto, K., Watanabe, M., Endoh, W., Ogata, K., and Nagura, H., 1999, Constructing a local district telepathology network in Japan. Diagnosis of intraoperative frozen sections via telepathology over an integrated service digital network and the National Television Standard Committee System, Analytical and Quantitative Cytology and Histology, Vol. 21(1), pp. 81–84.
25. Rosser, J.C., Bell, R.L., Harnett, B., Rodas, E., Murayama, M., and Merrell, R., 1999, Use of mobile low-bandwith telemedical techniques for extreme telemedicine applications, Journal of the American College of Surgeons, Vol. 189 (4), pp. 397–404.
26. Weaver, L. and Spence, D., 2000, Application of business case analysis in planning a province-wide telehealth network in Alberta, Journal of Telemedicine and Telecare, Vol. 6(l), pp. 87–89.
27. Goh, K.Y., Tsang, K.Y., and Poon, W.S., 1997, Does teleradiology improve inter-hospital management of head-injury? Canadian Journal of Neurological Sciences, Vol. 24(3), pp. 235–39.
28. Craig, J., Russell, C., Patterson, V., and Wootton, R., 1999, User satisfaction with realtime teleneurology, Journal of Telemedicine and Telecare, Vol. 5(4), pp. 237–41.
29. Sawhney Mohanbir, Fields of online dreams, CIO Magazine, October 15, 2002.
30. Yin, R.K., Case Study Research: Design and Methods, Sage Publications, Newbury, CA, 1994.
31. Brown, D., 1991, Methodological considerations in the evaluation of social development programmes—an alternative approach, Community Development Journal, Vol. 26(4), pp. 259–265.
32. Bardhan, P.K., Size, productivity and returns to scale: an analysis of farm-level data in Indian agriculture, The Journal of Political Economy, Vol. 81(6), pp. 1370–1386.
33. Sawhney Mohanbir, Fields of online dreams, CIO Magazine, October 15, 2002.
34. Bhatnagar S., Dewan A., Torres M.M. and Kanungo P., Case Study: E-Choupal: ITC's Rural Networking Project. Accessed and downloaded from http://siteresources.worldbank.org/INTEMPOWERMENT/Resources/14647_E-choupal-web.pdf on 10/12/2008.
35. Website of ITC's *e-choupal.*
36. Schudson, M., 1992, The limits of Teledemocracy, The American Prospect, pp. 41–45.
37. Bryan, C., Manchester: Democratic implications of an economic initiative. In R. Tsagarousianou, D. Tambini, and C. Bryan (Eds.), Cyberdemocracy: Technology, cities and civic networks, London: Routledge, 1998, pp. 152–166.
38. Sclove, R., Democracy and Technology, Guilford Press, London, 1995, p. 20.

8

Summary of the Research Work

Much research progress has been made in the field of communication with respect to Internet use, but many opportunities still exist. This study is a modest attempt to find the impact of Internet in India based on the following areas of focus:

- As a medium of news
- In healthcare services
- In agriculture and rural development
- In politics

This research is scientific and original, based on the objectives of the study and is exploratory, empirical, descriptive and qualitative in nature. To accomplish the objectives, twenty-six hypotheses have been framed and tested.

This book consists of eleven chapters.

The introductory chapter 1 (Introduction) tries to outline a general critique of the Internet and defines the dominant areas of focus in this study. It begins by discussing the traditional media, the print media, the electronic media and the Internet. The chapter has presented the various uses of Internet technology namely as a global broadcasting service, an instrument for distribution of news and information, a medium for collaboration and a means of communication between people regardless of the geographical divide. It has also discussed how the Internet, through its technology, presents great opportunities in the delivery of basic services like education and health information to far-flung regions. It has been argued that this revolutionary technology can be used as a tool by governments but there are considerable challenges to the state in terms of its acceptability and effectiveness.

This chapter also discusses the transformation of a new medium into a mass medium and how in the context of Internet some of these definitions will get altered and modified.

Finally, the chapter focuses on why the four areas namely news medium, health services, agriculture and rural development and political impact have been chosen for this research.

The second chapter (Objectives of the study) presents concisely but thoroughly the objectives and relevance of the study.

The third chapter (Previous research work) first presents a brief summary of relevant research work conducted in India and abroad. This chapter has summarised and explained what research has been done on the topic, citing the sources as and when they are mentioned, to show the different ways the researchers have treated the topic. Surveys, scholarly articles, books and other sources (e.g., dissertations, conference proceedings, news articles) relevant to the topic of research have been reviewed and a description, summary, and critical evaluation of each work to explain why the research question is significant have been provided.

The literature reviewed ranges between publications from 1987 to 2010 and covers studies in the United States of America, different European and Asian countries, Africa, Australia as well as India. They have been presented chronologically, with the more recent studies placed first.

This chapter consists of three main sections. The first section provides a brief summary of other relevant research work conducted in India and abroad. This section has five subsections, the first deals with studies related to news media, where twenty one studies have been presented, the second centers around healthcare, where four studies have been presented, the third focuses on rural development having two studies, the fourth on use of technology by governments and has nine studies and finally the fifth subsection presents five studies on Andhra Pradesh. Based on the literature review, the gaps in research have been identified and presented in the second main section of the chapter. Finally, based on these gaps the research questions have been framed and presented in the last section.

The fourth chapter (Research methodology) presents the theoretical framework of the study in the first section, followed by a broad description of the tools used in the second section. The third section describes the data.

The fifth chapter (Content analysis) has presented a background study based on literature review of evolution and history of printing and print newspapers, Internet and Internet newspapers in great detail. It has also traced the history of TV in India. This has been followed by a reasonable attempt to study the different theories and uses of news and media, credibility perception and credibility components of media as well as media displacement theory based on past research works of scholars. This was necessary to understand the medium of news in greater detail.

Further, a modest attempt has been made to review the existing literatures on telemedicine, infrastructure requirements, and telemedicine projects in India, cardiac diseases and their relevance along with the treatment technique of thrombolytic therapy to develop a better understanding of the history, use and other issues related to both telemedicine and critical cardiac care. The findings have been presented in this section.

Next, the concept of social development has been researched to understand how knowledge helps to achieve social development and how social development can be measured and presented in this context.

Finally, literature review has been done to gather a better understanding of democracy, use of technology by governments and about the state of Andhra Pradesh for the study on Internet and politics.

The sixth chapter (Methods of analysis) presents in detail the methods used and hypotheses tested for each of the four studies, namely, Internet as a medium of news, Internet in healthcare services, Internet in rural development and agriculture and Internet and politics respectively as each study is unique and the methods applied are also different.

For the first study (Internet as a medium of news), questionnaires were designed using factor analysis (principal component analysis). Validity was evaluated and reliability tested using Cronbach's alpha method. An initial pilot survey was done followed by the main survey with 481 usable sets of respondents' data. Statistical tests like ANOVA, t-test and paired t-test were performed on the data and additive form of multiple regression models used with ordinary least square algorithm to estimate the regression coefficients and test of hypotheses. Also, logistic regression method was applied on the data. The results have been discussed in the next chapter.

For the second study (Internet in healthcare services), secondary data has been collected and regression analysis has been done to estimate the parameters and test the hypotheses. The results have been presented later.

For the third study (Internet in agriculture and rural development) the study design has been provided in detail and the outcomes have been presented in the next chapter.

For the last study (Internet and politics), a qualitative analysis (focus group method) has been considered and the results have been presented in the following chapter.

The seventh chapter (Results and discussions) makes an attempt to present the results of the four studies in an organised and objective way separately. The results are followed by the related discussions and a summary of findings for each study.

The objective of this study was to explore the potentially growing effect of Internet news consumption on print and electronic news usage and *vice versa* in Indian metropolitan cities. Unlike previous analyses, this study has tracked the effect of Internet as medium of news. It has assessed the use of print and electronic news media such as print newspapers and TV news by identifying the relationship between the print and electronic media and new media in terms of the newsgathering habits of people in metropolitan cities of India who have access to print newspapers, TV news and Internet news. A one way ANOVA has confirmed that there is a significant difference amongst people in terms of their newsgathering habits from the three media. Results of the Tukey's HSD multiple comparative test between Print newspaper, TV news and Internet news have confirmed that there is significant difference in the news acquiring habits of people between Print newspapers and TV news, Print newspapers and Internet news and also between Internet news and TV news. It has thus been inferred that all these media are perceived to be distinct and people use them differently for different needs. However, no significant difference have been found when *t*-tests were done between the news gathering habits of readers and non-readers of Internet news with respect to news gathering habit from print newspapers or TV news and therefore it can be concluded that there is no significant difference between the groups with respect to news gathering habits from print newspapers and TV news. In order to test whether there is any significant difference between the groups of Internet news readers and non-readers in the way they acquire news from print newspapers and TV news, *t*-tests were again performed on the sample means, and it has been found that, even though there is no significant difference in the way non readers of Internet news gather news from print newspapers or TV news, there is a significant difference in the way the readers of Internet news treat these two media and hence print newspapers and TV news are competitors in the case of readers of Internet news.

To examine the relationship further, a logistic regression was performed to see whether acquiring news from print and electronic media have a negative impact on reading Internet news and the result has confirmed the negative impact. The results have further indicated that if the news gathering habit from print and electronic sources can be increased then the habit of reading news from the Internet will further reduce.

The study has then investigated the impact of the demographic variables of gender, age, education, profession and socio-economic variables like annual income, Internet connectivity at home, Internet usage patterns, credibility perception of Internet news, the credibility perceptions of print newspapers and TV news combined as well as the perceived change in dependence on Internet over the trend in print and electronic news media consumption. Regression analysis has confirmed that age has a negative impact, while higher education and profession both have positive impact. Further, when the credibility perception of Internet increases then that negatively affects newsgathering habits from print and electronic sources and when the credibility perceptions of print and electronic news media increase then it has a positive impact on the trend. It has also been found that number of days of Internet news weekly consumption and daily Internet usage in hours have a negative impact on collating news from TV news and print newspapers.

The study has been extended further to test whether there is any difference between respondents' perceived and observed utility perceptions with respect to Internet news. The three utility constructs for Internet news were, Information scanning and skimming utility construct, Entertainment utility construct and Interpersonal communication construct. Results of the paired t-tests between observed and perceived values of Internet news utilities confirm that that there is significant difference between the observed and perceived values in all the three utilities of Internet news and in all cases it was found that the observed values are less than the perceived values of all the utilities thus indicating that the Internet users are not fully satisfied. Therefore, it has been assumed that there is an impact of the perceived Interpersonal communication, Entertainment, Information scanning and Information skimming utilities of print newspapers and TV news on these identifiable gaps. For that reason, a regression equation, using ordinary least square method has been performed on the data. The results show that there are significant impacts on these identified gaps. This study has tried to analyse the displacement and complementary relationship of media in greater detail based on the above and has found that displacement relationship exists between the Internet news and print and electronic news in some utilities but a complementary relationship exists between the media in some other utilities.

The results have been presented in four sections. The first presents the descriptive statistics. The second presents the inferential statistics, the third documents the causal relationships and finally the fourth section presents the conclusions drawn from the study.

The next study has tried to assess the effect of using Internet in delivery of healthcare to critical cardiac patients amongst population, which are located in areas without proper medical facilities in India. For that the telemedicine project at the Rabindranath Tagore International Institute of Cardiac Sciences was chosen, for carrying out a case study based on qualitative analysis by observation, interviews through focused and non-directive methods as well as data collection. Three local centers at Bankura, Udaipur and Siliguri have been considered along with the referral centre at Kolkata. These centers are equipped to provide teleconsultation, transtelephonic electrocardiograph, consultation on medical reports and virtual rounds by doctors. The study has tried to estimate the success of providing thrombolytic therapy and referrals to the referral hospital in Kolkata based on video-consultation with specialists from the referral centers on the discharge of patients from the critical cardiac care units of the local telemedicine center to examine the impact of Internet technology on critical cardiac care by using a ordinary least square algorithm on the collected data. Results confirm the success of using thrombolytic therapy and video-consultation based on Internet technology on the patients of regions never exposed to such sophisticated treatment before. The study also shows how telementoring can be used as a tool for training healthcare professionals.

The results have been presented in four sections. The first section describes the case in detail. The second section analyses the causal relationships. The third section presents a discussion of the findings and the fourth section presents the conclusion drawn.

The third study has observed the effect of Internet in agriculture and rural development, based on a case study. This is a scientific research work based on different information gathered from various authentic sources. This exploratory study on ITC's *e-choupal* has been conducted by selecting five experts in this field and through field visits. The results have been presented in four major sections. The first section states the contextual framework and presents the research findings on agriculture in India and the traditional methods of trade in India. The next section presents the research findings on ITC and *e-choupal* in great detail by discussing the model, role of Internet in the model, the relationship between the farmer and *e-choupal*, the trade routes and infrastructure of *e-choupals* and database and information building through *e-choupals*.

The third section presents the analysis of the model. The study has analysed the *e-choupal* model on the basis of Brown's information based evaluation methodology. It is seen that this Internet based model has in every way been successful in providing social development and empowerment to the rural population in a quick and easy way by ensuring a very wide coverage, providing a scientific medium of trade, setting up linkages between the rural community and the rest of the country and world and setting up a bi-directional communication channel. The fourth section presents the conclusion drawn from the study.

In the end, the study has tried to analyse through an exploratory case study on Andhra Pradesh the principal question of what can be the impact of over emphasis on Internet on the political outcome in a democratic process. The scientific research is based on ten focus group interviews with 10 knowledgeable members in each who had voted in the 2004 elections. The interviews focused on the economic development under Chandrababu Naidu, contributions of the Naidu government towards development of IT facilities and IT industry in the state, whether over emphasis on Internet had an impact on the way the electorate voted, did the electorate benefit because of the introduction of Internet based services, did this new technology bring in opportunities for employment and a summary for the reasons of the democratic defeat of the government. The study concludes that inspite of all the utilities that the e-governance projects in Andhra Pradesh provided as well as the various popular projects that the government undertook; the focus on Internet technology had a very negative impact on the fate of the ruling party. The people were not comfortable using the medium. The reach was not adequate and the infrastructure requirements were also beyond the common man's means. Most of the electorate could not find any direct benefit and felt that the huge spending on the infrastructure was a huge waste and the government had neglected the cause of the common man in its pursuit of bringing in Internet. The findings have been presented in terms of the economic development under Chandra babu Naidu, contributions of the Naidu government towards development of IT facilities and IT industry in the state, the problems with the strategy and finally the summary of the findings.

9

Conclusion

The purpose of this chapter is to briefly outline the overall conclusion that may be drawn from this research. The second purpose is to discuss and present the implications of the study.

9.1 Conclusions

This study has made a modest attempt to examine the impact of Internet in the areas of news, healthcare services, agriculture and rural development and political outcome and has confirmed that Internet is a distinct medium of news that can also be used in tackling a wide range of healthcare, social and economic problems and can simultaneously contribute to rural development, but cannot be focused upon while neglecting the basic needs of the citizens in a developing country like India.

The study in the area of news has focused on Internet news and two other media—print and electronic news by choosing print newspapers and TV news. It has been found that Indians treat and use the three media differently. Internet newsreaders consume news differently from print newspapers and TV news. A negative impact of print newspapers and TV news on the news gathering habit from Internet is confirmed in this study suggesting a competition and displacement. Credibility perception of print newspapers and TV news has been seen to contribute positively and credibility perception about Internet news negatively on the news gathering habit from print and electronic media. Internet connectivity at home, number of days of Internet weekly use and number of hours spent on the Internet on an average also have a negative relationship with average number of days of TV news viewing and reading print newspapers. However, education, profession and increase in Internet dependence have been found to have a positive relationship with increased print and electronic media usage. Thus, it is concluded that media choice and usage is based on user's perception based on experience with the medium, and how well the different needs of the user have been satisfied. It has been seen that there are significant gaps between the perceived and observed utilities of Internet news and there is significant impact of perceived utilities of print newspapers and TV news on those identified gaps. The study has also identified both displacement effects and complementary relationship between Internet news and the print and electronic media.

From the study of the impact of Internet in the area of healthcare it is confirmed that Internet can be used as a medium successfully in providing emergency medical assistance, long-distance appropriate consultation, administration, supervision and quality assurance to remotely located patients along with education and training for healthcare professionals, and providers. It is seen to be an effective and affordable medium in saving the lives of critical heart patients and also providing consultations across large geographical distances without compromising on quality when it is administered well and implemented with care and supervision. The study has confirmed that disease management by specialists from the referral center in RTIICS, during the period of hospitalisation in the local centers, using Internet as the medium, at all the three centers have been effective over a long period of time, and is yielding satisfactory results by increasing the chances of survival amongst critically ill cardiac patients and providing sophisticated treatment at low costs and with less specialised manpower. This offers evidence that telemedicine can be a solution for emergency medical assistance over long–distances while being able to maintain quality standards. The impact of Internet on healthcare structures can then be very significant.

The findings of the current study on the use of Internet in agriculture have indicated several encouraging outcomes. Information related to scientific and better farming methods, weather, soil quality, fertilizers and pesticides has become more readily available to farmers. This information may possibly have helped increase the productivity of the cultivated land. Further, use of this technology by ITC as seen in this case study has enabled them to get a steady supply of good quality produce and their model has been easy to replicate. Farmers appear to have benefited by the new method of trade and the recovery of their costs have become faster leading to less borrowing. Since the different prevailing market prices are available on the website, the farmer is now able to make an informed choice of selling at a particular rate which was explained and provided by the social experts. Further, for running these Internet *kiosks*, new jobs–that of the *samayojaks* and *sanchalaks* have been created. These *sanchalaks* help the farmers by explaining the advantage of using the Internet for getting information and also provide the information to them. Many farmers may have possibly been empowered with better knowledge and greater choices. They may have also learned to value information and scientific methods of farming for improving their quality and quantity of produce with the help from the social workers who have provided them with the knowledge.

The study entitled 'Internet and politics' has indicated that the relationship is very complex that may have several unintended and unpredicted consequences and confusing outcomes in India. The study has confirmed that in a democracy it is necessary to involve people in the processes required to bring about such revolutionary changes in administration. People need to be educated about it and the advantage of using it instead of being compelled to use it from the beginning. Further, in a country like India, where the basic means of survival are not available to a large section of the population, investments in technology are viewed as wasteful and indulgent. It is necessary to be able to explain the gain to the various stakeholders successfully. Introducing new technology is more about managing change successfully than the technology itself and can have very serious implications for the administration.

Therefore, the Internet has the potential to be a mass medium in India if it can be made more easily available to the common educated man. The Internet can help further advance communication in the way television and radio did and make information more readily available to anyone who seeks it. This will reduce the difference between the common people and the educated people in getting information and thus contribute greatly to society. It can also be the key enabler in delivering various services to people.

9.2 Implications of the Study

As concluded from the study, the print newspaper and TV news industries should try to increase the perceptions of trustworthiness, current and in-time reporting, fairness, believability, balance, accuracy and timeliness of the print and electronic media to increase their readership and viewer ship, while Internet news portals should also try to increase similar credibility perceptions of Internet news.

Additionally, they will need to focus on reducing the identified gaps in the entertainment, information scanning and skimming and interpersonal communication utilities of Internet news by providing more funny, amusing, entertaining, enjoyable news that can be used in conversations, information gathering and sharing, while being easy to access and use in the news portals. If the Internet news portals can thus be able to increase the number of Internet newsreaders then that can also accelerate the rate of displacement of print and electronic media as observed in the study.

This study will also be useful for medical practitioners, hospital managers, policy makers, researchers and students who may like to consider the confirmed positive results of the study by using Internet in providing quality and critical healthcare to underserved population and remote areas.

For large corporations interested in discharging their corporate social responsibility, the study on the impact of Internet in agriculture could be relevant. These companies could implement a similar model that would ensure uninterrupted supply of quality raw material while bringing huge changes in the livelihoods of all its stakeholders.

In the case of administering e-governance, it will be vital for political leaders of the future to administer changes in technology in a more sensitive manner with greater emphasis on changing the perceptions of the electorate to that change.

There are several media in mass communication. Internet is the latest medium of mass communication. The other media like traditional, print, electronic, cinema, advertising etc are also popular media and are able to reach both the common as well as the educated people. While Internet has less access to the common and illiterate people it can still with help of social workers or the educators transmit the information through local dialect throughout the world to the common as well as the illiterate people. Internet as a medium of mass communication can provide more knowledge to the literate people and the young generation, specifically in the metro cities of India who are interested in social networking systems and in using this medium. Using this medium, people can get access throughout the world within a second through e-mail or by videoconference. Therefore, Internet is recognised as a powerful medium of mass communication.

10

Limitations of the Study

This study is not free of limitations. There are a few limitations as mentioned below.

This study has considered Internet in only four areas, namely, as a medium of news, in healthcare services, in agriculture and rural development and in politics. However, two other important areas—education and entertainment can be analysed to get more information.

There are various kinds of news media available for people to choose from. These include print newspapers, television news, radio, documentaries, magazines to name a few. Of these, only print newspapers and television news have been considered.

To accomplish the objectives of this research, data have been collected from four metropolitan cities in India to get the knowledge about the people living in metro cities.

The study on the telemedicine project has been conducted on only one referral centre located in Kolkata.

11

Scope for Further Research

This study can be extended to identify the impact of Internet on social communication centered around social networking applications like Facebook, Orkut and Twitter as they are emerging as an important and very popular tool in the present day.

The researcher would also like to replicate the study to find the impact of Internet on the political and social outcome in other states of India particularly the eastern states such as Bihar, Orissa and Jharkhand.

In case of agriculture, too, the researcher will design a questionnaire to measure the perception of the farmers towards the impact of Internet on their occupation and identify the relevant factors, which will enable the companies to perform their functions more efficiently in future.

In case of governance and administration aspects, the researcher will develop a questionnaire, collect data from a representative sample and analyse empirically to get a better insight as well as identify the relevant factors that impact e-governance.

Appendix

Please answer the following questions as directed—mostly by ticking.

Name: **Date:**

Profile Questions

1. Gender: M/F.
2. Age in years.
3. City of residence.
4. Educational qualification: Graduate/Post graduate/Others.
5. Annual family income: Less than or equal to Rs 4 Lakhs/more than Rs 4 Lakhs.
6. Are you a: Student/Professional/Unemployed/Teacher/Retired/Any other.
7. Do you have Internet connectivity at home? Yes/No

Descriptive Questions

8. How many hours on a typical day do you spend on the Internet?

<1	1–2
3–4	5–6
7–9	>9

9. On an average in a week, how many days do you work on the Internet?

   0 1 2 3 4 5 6 7

10. How many days per week do you read a print newspaper?

    0 1 2 3 4 5 6 7

11. How many days per week do your watch news on the Television?

    0 1 2 3 4 5 6 7

12. How many days per week do you access news online?

    0 1 2 3 4 5 6 7

13. Which medium do you compulsorily use when you want information on new products and services?

    Newspapers

    Television

    Internet websites/search engines/Social networking sites and blogs

    Radio

14. What do you do when you go online?

    E-mail

    Chat

    Read news

    Look for news updates

    Research a topic

    Trade shares

    Go to a social networking site like Orkut/Facebook to stay in touch with friends and family

    Upload and share photos with friends

    Send Instant messages

    Read Blogs

    Write/create/comment on Blogs

    Download/play music

    Reading reviews of films, new products, trends etc.

    Playing games

    Watch video

    Any other—please specify

15. Imagine that you are provided with both print newspapers and online newspapers with the same news content and at the same price. Which would you prefer without specifying the name of any newspaper?
16. Do you use a social networking site? Y/N
17. Do you prefer to read news from a newspaper, or from an online site? (Y/N)
18. Do you think that eventually newspapers will be replaced by online news? (Y/N)

Causal Questions

19. Has your Internet dependence increased over the years? Yes/No
20. I would like to know what you think about print newspapers/TV news/Internet news through some descriptive words. Please state your feeling by ticking one that you agree with most:

Newspapers are

Trustworthy	Strongly agree	Agree	Neutral	Disagree	Strongly disagree
Current	Strongly agree	Agree	Neutral	Disagree	Strongly disagree
Fair	Strongly agree	Agree	Neutral	Disagree	Strongly disagree
Believable	Strongly agree	Agree	Neutral	Disagree	Strongly disagree
Balanced	Strongly agree	Agree	Neutral	Disagree	Strongly disagree
Accurate	Strongly agree	Agree	Neutral	Disagree	Strongly disagree
Timely	Strongly agree	Agree	Neutral	Disagree	Strongly disagree

TV News is

Trustworthy	Strongly agree	Agree	Neutral	Disagree	Strongly disagree
Current	Strongly agree	Agree	Neutral	Disagree	Strongly disagree
Fair	Strongly agree	Agree	Neutral	Disagree	Strongly disagree
Believable	Strongly agree	Agree	Neutral	Disagree	Strongly disagree
Balanced	Strongly agree	Agree	Neutral	Disagree	Strongly disagree
Accurate	Strongly agree	Agree	Neutral	Disagree	Strongly disagree
Timely	Strongly agree	Agree	Neutral	Disagree	Strongly disagree

Internet News is

Trustworthy	Strongly agree	Agree	Neutral	Disagree	Strongly disagree
Current	Strongly agree	Agree	Neutral	Disagree	Strongly disagree
Fair	Strongly agree	Agree	Neutral	Disagree	Strongly disagree
Believable	Strongly agree	Agree	Neutral	Disagree	Strongly disagree
Balanced	Strongly agree	Agree	Neutral	Disagree	Strongly disagree
Accurate	Strongly agree	Agree	Neutral	Disagree	Strongly disagree
Timely	Strongly agree	Agree	Neutral	Disagree	Strongly disagree

Descriptive and Causal Questions

21. I would now like to know about your idea of Internet news based on certain qualifiers. There are two columns-observed and perceived-as the names suggest-please fill the former from your experience and the second with your expectation. You are requested to fill a number in the given columns between 1 and 7 of agreement, where 1 is lowest and 7 highest.

Internet News	*Observed (Experience)*	*Perceived (Expected)*
Finding stories that are fun to read		
Coming across amusing news		
Finding entertaining news		
Finding stories that are enjoyable		
Finding topics to use in conversations with other people		
Getting stories to share with other people		
Learning about things to discuss with other people		
Keeping up with what is going on in the news		
Getting a good overall picture of events in the world		
Learning what are the major news events of the day		
Following the major news stories of the day		
Going directly to important news stories		
Skipping the unimportant news		
Seeking out important news		

22. Finally, I would like to know about your expectations and idea of print newspapers and TV news based on certain qualifiers. You are requested to fill a number in the given column between 1 and 7 of agreement, where 1 is lowest and 7 highest.

Print Newspapers	*Perceived*
Finding stories that are fun to read	
Coming across amusing news	
Finding entertaining news	
Finding stories that are enjoyable	
Finding topics to use in conversations with other people	
Getting stories to share with other people	
Learning about things to discuss with other people	
Keeping up with what is going on in the news	
Getting a good overall picture of events in the world	
Learning what are the major news events of the day	
Following the major news stories of the day	
Going directly to important news stories	
Skipping the unimportant news	
Seeking out important news	

TV News	*Perceived*
Finding stories that are fun to read	
Coming across amusing news	
Finding entertaining news	
Finding stories that are enjoyable	
Finding topics to use in conversations with other people	
Getting stories to share with other people	
Learning about things to discuss with other people	
Keeping up with what is going on in the news	
Getting a good overall picture of events in the world	
Learning what are the major news events of the day	
Following the major news stories of the day	
Going directly to important news stories	
Skipping the unimportant news	
Seeking out important news	

Thank you for sparing your time.

Bibliography

Abbate Janet, Inventing the Internet, MIT Press, 1999.

Abdulla, R.A., Garrison, B., Salwen, M., Garrison, B., and Driscoll, P., Online news and the public, Routledge, 2005.

Abdulla, R.A., Garrison, B., Salwen, M., Garrison, B., and Driscoll, P., Online news credibility. In M.B Salwen, B. Garrison. and P.D. Driscoll (Eds.), Online news and the public, Lawrence Erlbaum Associates, Mahwah, NJ, 2005.

Adair, O.V., 2001, Cardiology secrets, Elsevier health sciences.

Agarwal, S., May 7, 2009, Connectivity, penetration keep IT away from rural India, *Financial Express*.

Althaus, S.L., and Tewksbury, D., 2000, Patterns of Internet and traditional news media use in a networked community, *Political communication*, Vol. 17(1), pp. 21–45.

American Anti-slavery society, Proceedings of the American Anti-slavery Society: at its third decade, held in the city of Philadelphia, Dec. 3rd and 4th, 1864 [i.e. 1863] Phonographic report by Henry M. Parkhurst, America Anti-slavery Society, 1864, p. 174

American Association for the Advancement of Science, Highwire Press and JSTOR, Science, Vol. 231, American Association for the Advancement of Science, 1986, pp. 945–949.

Amrita Bazar Patrika, dated May 13, 1931 (Cit. Basu Jitendra Nath, Romance of Indian Journalism, University of Calcutta, 1979, p. 21).

Anderson, D.R., Sweeney, D.J., and Williams, T.A., Statistics for Business and Economics, Cengage learning, 2009, UK, p. 563.

Andrew Alexander, The History of British Journalism, From the foundation of the Newspaper Press in England to the repeal of the Stamp Act in 1855, with Sketches of Press Celebrities, Vol. 2, Richard Bentley, New Burlington Street, London, 1858.

Andrew Pollack, America's answer to Japan's MITI, *New York Times*, March 5, 1989.

Atkin, D., 1993, Adoption of cable amidst a multimedia environment, Telematics and Informatics, Vol. 10, pp. 51–58.

Audebert, H J., Schultes, K., Tietz V., Heuschmann, P.U., Bogdahn, U., Haberl, R.L., and Schenkel, J., 2009, Long-term effects of specialised stroke care with telemedicine support in community hospitals on behalf of the Telemedical Project for Integrative Stroke Care (TEMPiS), Stroke,Vol. 40, pp. 902–908.

Backus, M., 2001, E-governance in developing countries, International Institute for Communication and Development Research, report, pp. 1–4.

Ball-Rokeah, S., and DeFleur, M., 1989, A dependency model of mass communication effects, *Communication Research*, Vol. 3, pp. 3–21.

Bardhan, P.K., Size, productivity and returns to scale: an analysis of farm-level data in Indian agriculture, *The Journal of Political Economy*, Vol. 81 (6), pp. 1370–1386.

Barnhurst, K.G., and Nerone, J., The form of news: A history, Guilford Press, New York, 2002.

Bashshur, R., Sanders, J., and Shannon, G., Telemedicine Theory and Practice, Springfield, IL: Charles C Thomas, 1997. In Darkins, A.W., Cary, M.A., Telemedicine and telehealth: principles, policies, performance and pitfalls, Springer Publishing Company, New York, 2000.

Basu Jitendra Nath, Romance of Indian Journalism, University of Calcutta, 1979, p. 22.

Beamish, R., The local newspaper in the age of multimedia. In B. Franklin and D. Murphy (Eds), Making Local News: Local Journalism in context, London: Routledge, 1998.

Bearden, W.O., and Netemeyer, R.G., Handbook of Marketing scales, Sage Publications (2nd ed), England, 1999.

Becker, L.B., and Shoenbach, K., When media content diversifies: Anticipating audience behaviors. In L.B. Backer and K. Shoenbach (Eds), Audience responses to media diversification: coping with plenty, Hillsdale, Lawrence Erlbaum Associates, NJ, 1989.

Becker, T., 2001, Rating the impact of new technology on democracy, Communication of the ACM, Vol. 44(1), pp. 39–43.

Bedi, B.S., 2008, Tele-medicine: Indian perspective and DIT initiatives, paper presented at United Nations/India Regional Workshop on Using Space Technology for Tele-Epidemiology to Benefit Asia and the Pacific Region, October 21st, 2008, at School of Telemedicine and Biomedical Informatics, Sanjay Gandhi Postgraduate Institute of Medical Sciences, Lucknow, U.P., India.

Bellamy, C., and Taylor, J.A., Governing in the information age, Buckingham, UK, Open University Press, 1998.

Belson, W.A., 1961, Effects of television on the reading and buying of newspapers and magazines, *Public Opinion Quarterly*, Vol. 25, pp. 366–381.

Benger, J., 2000, A review of telemedicine in accident and emergency: the story so far, *Journal of accident and emergency medicine*, Vol. 17(3), pp. 157–64.

Berman, J., and Witzner, D.J., 1997, Technology and democracy, *Social Research*, Vol. 64(3), pp. 1313–1320.

Berry, J.M., The Internet group society (3rd ed), Longman, New York, 1997.

Bhatnagar S., Dewan A., Torres M.M. and Kanungo P., Case Study: *E-Choupal*: ITC's Rural Networking Project. Accessed and downloaded from http://siteresources.worldbank.org/INTEMPOWERMENT/Resources/14647_E-choupal-web.pdf on 10/12/2008.

Bimber, B., 1998, The Internet and political transformation: Populism, community, and accelerated pluralism, *Polity*, Vol. 31(1), pp. 133–160.

Blumler, J.G., 1979, The role of theory in uses and gratifications studies. Communication Research, Vol. 6, pp. 9–36.

Boczkowski Pablo J., Digitising the News, The MIT Press, Cambridge, Massachusetts, USA, 2004.

Boczkowski, Pablo J., The development of online newspapers: What results tell us and what we might want to know. In Lievrouw, L. and Livingstone S., (Eds.): The handbook of new media, Sage Publications, London, 2002.

Bowles, K.H, Naylor, M.D., and Foust, J.B., 2000, Patient characteristics at hospital discharge and a comparison of discharge referral decisions, *Journal of the American Geriatric Society*, Vol. 50, pp. 336–42.

Bowles, K.H., Ratcliffe, S.J., Holmes, J.H., Liberatore, M., Nydick, and Naylor, R., 2008, Post-acute referral decisions made by multidisciplinary experts compared to hospital clinicians and the patients' 12-week outcomes, *Medical Care*, Vol. 46(2), pp. 158–66.

Briggs Asa and Burke Peter, A Social History of the Media, from Gutenberg to the Internet (Second edition), Polity Press, Cambridge, England, 2005.

Bring, J., 1994, How to standardise regression coefficients, American statistician, Vol. 48(3), pp. 209–213.

Bromley, R.V., and Bowles, D., 1995, Impact of Internet on Use of Traditional News Media, *Newspaper research journal*, Vol. 16(2), pp. 14–27.

Brown N., 1995, A brief history of telemedicine, *Telemedicine Information Exchange*, Vol. 105, pp. 833–835.

Brown, D., 1991, Methodological considerations in the evaluation of social development programmes–an alternative approach, *Community Development Journal*, Vol. 26(4), pp. 259–265.

Bryan, C., Manchester: Democratic implications of an economic initiative, In R. Tsagarousianou, D. Tambini, and C. Bryan (Eds.), Cyberdemocracy: Technology, cities and civic networks, London: Routledge, 1998.

Carlson, D., 2005, Online Timeline, Nieman Reports, Vol. 59(3), pp. 45–83.

Carlson, D., The history of online journalism, in Kawamoto Kevin's Digital journalism: Emerging media and the changing horizons of journalism, Rowman and Littlefield, USA, 2003.

Carveth, R., and Metz, J., 1996, Frederick Jackson Turner and the democratisation of the electronic frontier, American Sociologist, Vol. 27 (1), pp. 72–100.

Carveth, R., Owers, J. and Alexander, A., The Economics of Online Media. In A. Alexander, J. Owers and R. Carveth (Eds). *Media Economics—Theory and practice*, 1998, pp. 247–273.

Cassidy, W.P., 2007, Online news credibility: An examination of the perceptions of newspaper journalists, *Journal of Computer-Mediated Communication*, Vol. 12(2), article 7, pp. 1–24.

Cavender, S., 1998, Ray Tomlinson, *Forbes*, Vol. 162(7), pp. 126–127.

Census–1981: Census of India 1981 — Five per cent Sample Report, GOI, New Delhi, 1984.

Cerf, V., 1999, Requiem for the Arpanet, *Connexions*, Vol. 3(10), p. 27.

Chamberlain, M.A., 1994, New technologies in health communication, *American Behavioral Scientist*, Vol. 38, pp. 271–284.

Chan-Olmsted, S.M., Competitive strategy for media firms: Strategic and Brand management in changing media markets, Lawrence Erlbaum Associates Publishers, Mahwah, NJ, 2006.

Chaudhuri, A., Indian advertising: 1780 to 1950 A.D., Tata McGraw-Hill, 2007.

Chee Tham Seong (Eds), Essays on Literature and Society in Southeast Asia; *Political and Sociological Perspectives*, Singapore University Press, Singapore, 1981, pp. 83–84.

Choi, J.Y., Porche, N.A., Albright, K.C., Khaja, A.M., Ho, V.S., and Grotta, J.C., 2006, Using telemedicine to facilitate thrombolytic therapy for patients with acute stroke, *Joint commission journal on quality and patient safety/Joint commission resources*, Vol. 32(4), pp. 199–205.

Churchill, G.A., 1979, A Paradigm for developing better measures for marketing constructs, *Journal of Marketing Research*, Vol. 16, pp. 64–73.

Chyi, H.I., and Lasorsa, D., 1999, Access, use and preferences for online Newspapers, *Newspaper Research Journal*, Vol. 20(4), pp. 2–13.

Clarke, H.D., Sanders, D., Stewart, M.C., and Whiteley, P.F., 2003, Britain (not) at the polls 2001, *Political Science and Politics*, Vol. 36(1), pp. 59–64.

Clemens, E.L., and Hayes, H.E., 1997, Assessing and balancing elder risk, safety and autonomy: Decision-making practices of healthcare professionals, *Home Healthcare Services Quarterly*, Vol. 16 (3) pp. 3–21.

Cochran,W., 1995, Searching for the right mixture, Quill, Vol. 83(4), p. 36.

Connolly, T., and Thorn, B.K., Discretionary data bases: Theory, data, and implications, In J. Fulk and C. Steinfield (Eds.), Organisations and communication technology, Sage Publications, Newbury Park, CA, 1991, p. 221.

Cooke, B., and Kothari, U., The case for participation as tyranny, In B. Cooke and U. Kothari (Eds.), Participation: The new tyranny, New York, Zed Books, 2002.

Cowen, N., 2001, The future of British broadsheet newspaper on the world wide web, *Aslib proceedings*, Vol. 53(5), pp. 189–200.

Craig, J., Russell, C., Patterson, V., and Wootton, R., 1999, User satisfaction with realtime teleneurology, *Journal of Telemedicine and Telecare*, Vol. 5(4), pp. 237–41.

Craik, G.L., A manual of English literature and of the history of the English language, Oxford University, 1862, pp. 309–310.

Cresswell, J.W., Qualitative Inquiry and Research Design: Choosing among five traditions, Thousand Oaks, Sage Publications, California, 1998, pp. 27–228.

Cronbach, L.J., 1951, Coefficient alpha and the internal structure of the tests, Psychometrika, Vol. 16, pp. 297–334.

Cunningham, T. and Bartlett, K., 1996, Integrated telematic support for paediatrics: a practical model, *Journal of Telemedicine and Telecare*, Vol. 2 (1), pp. 50–54.

D., Shedden, 2006, New Media Timeline, Poynter Online, Poynter Institute.

Daniel, Stephen, James Ellis, and Tom Truscott, 1980, USENET—A General Access UNIX Network, Durham, NC: Duke University Press, In Quarterman, J.S., The Global Matrix of Minds Global Networks: Computers and International Communications (Eds.) Linda M. Harasim, MIT Press, Cambridge, 1993, pp. 35–56.

Dasgupta, D., 2006, E-governance in India: Global CEO, November, pp. 26–28.

David Carlson's virtual world, The Online Timetable, Accessed from http://iml.jou.ufl.edu/carlson/1995s.shtml on 10/4/2007.

Dewan, B.D., Malhotra, K.C., Gupta, S.P., 1974, Epidemiology study of coronary heart diseases in a rural community in Haryana, *Indian Heart Journal*, Vol. 26, pp. 26–68.

Diddi, A. and LaRose, R., 2006, Getting hooked on news: uses and gratifications and the formation of news habits among college students in an Internet environment, *Journal of Broadcasting and Electronic Media*, Vol. 50(2), pp. 193–210.

Dijk, J.V., Widening Information Gaps and Policies of Prevention. In K. Hacker and J. van Dijk (Eds.), Digital Democracy, Issues of theory and practice, London, Thousand Oaks, New Delhi: Sage Publications, 2000.

Dimmick, J., and Rothenbuhler, E., 1984, The theory of the niche: Quantifying competition among media industries, *Journal of Communication*, Vol. 34, pp. 103–119.

Dimmick, J., Chen, Y., and Li, Z., 2004, Competition between the Internet and traditional news media: The gratification — opportunities niche dimension, Journal of Media Economics, Vol. 17 (1), pp. 19–33.

Dimmick, J., Ecology, economics and gratification utilities. In A. Alexander, J. Owers, and R. Carveth (Eds.), Media economics, Lawrence Erlbaum Associates, Hillsdale, NJ, 1993, pp. 135–136.

Dimmick, J., Chen, Y., and Li, Z., 2004, Competition between the Internet and traditional news media. The gratification-opportunities niche dimension, Journal of media economics, Vol. 17(1), pp. 19–33.

Doctor, R.D., 1992, Social equity and information technologies: Moving toward information democracy, Annual Review of Information Science and Technology, Vol. 27, pp. 43–96.

Donohew, L., Palmgreen P., and Rayburn, J.D., II., 1987, Social and psychological origins of media use: A lifestyle analysis, *Journal of Broadcasting and Electronic Media*, Vol. 31, pp. 255–278.

Doyle, G., Understanding media economics, London, Sage Publications, 2002.

Dutta-Bergman, M., 2004, Complementarity in consumption of news types across traditional and new media., *Journal of Broadcasting and Electronic Media*, Vol. 48(1), pp. 41–61.

Dwyer Joseph, D., Russia the Soviet Union and Eastern Europe, Hoover Institution on Was Revolution and Peace, Hoover Institution Press, Stanford University, Stanford, California, 1980.

Elliot, W. and Quattlebaum, C.P., 1979, Similarities in patterns of media use: A cluster analysis of media gratifications, *The Western Journal of Speech Communication*, Vol. 43, pp. 61–72.

Ellis, I., 2004, Is telehealth the right tool for remote communities? Improving health status in rural Australia, *Contemporary nurse*, Vol. 16(3), pp. 163–168.

Emery E. and Emery M., The Press and America: An Interpretative History of the Mass Media, Fourth edition, Prentice-Hall, 1978.

Engst, A.C., Internet starter kit for Macintosh, Hayden Books, Michigan, 1993.

Ferguson D.A., and Perse, E.M., 2000, The world wide web as a functional alternative to television, *Journal of Broadcasting and Electronic Media*, Vol. 44(2), pp. 155–174.

Fern, E.F., 1982, The use of focus groups for idea generation: the effects of group size, acquaintanceship, and moderator on response quantity and quality, *Journal of Marketing Research*, Vol. 26 (February), pp. 1–13.

FICCI-PWC, 2006, Indian Entertainment and Media Industry — Unravelling the potential, Frames, 2006.

Fiser, D.H., 2000, Relationship of pediatric overall performance category and pediatric cerebral performance category scores at pediatric intensive care unit discharge with outcome measures collected at hospital discharge and 1 and 6 month follow-up assessments, *Critical Care Medicine*, Vol. 28(7), pp. 2616–20.

Fisher, M., Developing and implementing future stroke therapies: the potential of telemedicine, 2005, *Annals of Neurology*, Vol. 58(5), pp. 666–71.

Fitzgerald, M., 1996, The effect of the Internet on print journalism, Editor and Publisher, Vol. 129, p. 72.

Flanagin, A.J., and Metzger, M.J., 2000, Perceptions of Internet information credibility, *Journalism and Mass Communication Quarterly*, Vol. 77, pp. 515–540.

Flanagin, A.J., and Metzger, M.J., 2001, Internet use in the contemporary media environment, *Human Communication Research*, Vol. 27(1), pp. 153–181.

Fox, K.A., Steg, A., Eagle, P.G., Goodman, K.A., Anderson, S.G., Granger, C.B., Flather, M.D., Budaj, A, Quill, A, and Gore, J.M., 2007, Decline in rates of death and heart failure in acute coronary syndromes, 1999–2006, *Journal of the American Medical Association*, Vol. 297(17), pp. 1892–1900.

Franzen, A., 2000, Does the Internet Make Us Lonely, European Sociological Review, Vol. 16(4), pp. 427–438.

Frommel, D., May, 2002, Exporting health: Global market in medical workers, Le Monde diplomatique, p. 28.

Garrison, B.,1997, Online services: Internet in 1995 newsrooms, *Newspaper research journal*, Vol. 18(3), pp. 79–93.

Gartner Says Indian ICT Spending to Grow 14 per cent in 2010, Gartner Press release: Mumbai, April 28, 2010.

Gaski, R.M., and Etzel, M.J., 1986, The index of consumer sentiment towards marketing, *Journal of Marketing*, Vol. 50(3), pp. 71–81.

Gaziano, C., 1987, News peoples' ideology and the credibility debate. *Newspaper Research Journal*, Vol. 9(1), pp. 1–18.

Gaziano, C., and McGrath, K., 1986, Measuring the concept of credibility, *Journalism Quarterly*, Vol. 63 (3), pp. 451–462.

Ghosh, K.K., 2008, Telelmedicine initiative by DIT, paper presented at United Nations/India Regional Workshop on Using Space Technology for Tele-Epidemiology to Benefit Asia and the Pacific Region, October 21st, 2008, at School of Telemedicine and Biomedical Informatics, Sanjay Gandhi Postgraduate Institute of Medical Sciences, Lucknow, U.P., India.

Gillies James and Cailliau Robert, How the Web was born, Oxford University Press and CERN Accelerator School, 2000.

Giovas, P., Papadoyannis, D., Thomakos, D., Papazachos, G., Rallidis, M., Soulis, D., Stamatopoulos, C., Mavrogeni, S., and Katsilambros, N., 1998, Transmission of electrocardiograms from a moving ambulance, *Journal of Telemedicine and Telecare*, Vol. 4 (l), pp. 5–7.

Goh, K.Y., Tsang, K.Y., and Poon, W.S., 1997, Does teleradiology improve inter-hospital management of head-injury? *Canadian Journal of Neurological Sciences*, Vol. 24(3), pp. 235–39.

Gomez, R., 1997, Information society and civil society: NGOs and computer-mediated communication in Latin America, In J. Berleur and D. Whitehouse (Eds.), An Ethical Global Information Society: Culture and Democracy Revisited, London: Chapman and Hall.

Grant, A.E., Guthrie, K.K., and Ball-Rokeach, S., 1991, Television shopping: A media dependency perspective, *Communication Research*, Vol. 18, pp. 773–798.

Greer Jennifer D. and Mensing Donica, The Evolution of online Newspapers: A longitundinal Content Analysis, 1997–2003. In Internet Newspapers—The making of a mainstream medium (Eds) Xigen Li, Lawrence Erlbaum Associates, Publishers, Mahwah, New Jersey, London, 2006.

Grigsby, J., and Sanders, J.H., 1998, Telemedicine: Where it is and here it's going, *Annals of Internal Medicine*, Vol. 129(2), pp. 123–127.

Grigsby, J., Barton, P.L., Kaehny, M.M., Schlenker, R.E., Shaughnessy, P.W., and Beale, S.K., 1993, Analysis of Expansion of Access to Care Through Use of

Telemedicine and Mobile Health Services. Report 1, Literature Review and Analytic Framework, Denver: Center for Health Policy Research.

Grotta, G.L., and Newsom, D., 1982, How does cable television in the home relate to other media use patterns? Journalism Quarterly, Vol. 59, pp. 588–609.

Grzywa, M., Yurcik, W., and Brumbaugh, L., 2001, Application–level survivality: Resumable FTP, MILCOM, Vol. 1, pp. 107–112.

Guijt, I., 1999, Participatory monitoring and evaluation for natural resource management and research, Socio-economic Methodologies for Natural Resources Research. Chatham, UK, Natural Resources Institute, pp. 1–22.

Gunter, B., News and the Net, Lawrence Erlbaum Associates, Mahwah, NJ, 2003.

Gunther, A.C., 1992, Biased Press or Biased Public? Attitudes Toward Media Cover, Public Opinion Quarterly, Vol. 56(2), pp. 147–167.

Hafner, K. and Lyon, M., Where Wizards Stay Up Late: The Origins of the Internet. New York: Simon and Schuster, 1996, p. 10.

Hair, J.F., Anderson, R.E., Tatham, R.L., Black, and W.C., Multivariate data analysis, Pearson Education, New Delhi, India, 1998.

Haque, S.M., 2002, E-governance in India: Its impacts on relations among citizens, politicians and public servants, International Review of Administrative Sciences, Sage Publications (London, Thousand Oaks, CA and New Delhi), Vol. 68.

Harman, H.H., Modern Factor Analysis, 2nd edition. University Chicago Press: Chicago, 1976, pp. 1–362.

Hart, Michael, Ts'ai Lun: In 100 A Ranking of the Most Influential Persons in History, New York, Hart Publishing Co., 1978, pp. 36–41.

Hashim N.H., and Meloche J.A., 2007, Australian online newspaper: An exploratory study on Internet savvy users using Q-methodology, Research online, University of Wollongong, pp. 1–15.

Hawkins, R.P., and Pingree, S., 1981, Uniform messages and habitual viewing: Unnecessary assumptions in social reality effects, Human Communication Research, Vol. 7, pp. 291–301.

Hawley, A.H., Human ecology. In D.L. Sills (Ed.) International Encyclopedia of the Social Sciences, New York: Macmillan, 1968.

Healthcare in India, Emerging market report 2007, Pricewater House Coopers, pp. 1–26.

Heeks, Richard, 1999, Information and Communication Technologies, Poverty and Development. Development Informatics', Working Paper Series, Working Paper No. 5, Manchester: Institute for Development Policy and Management, University of Manchester.

Hendriks, P.C.J., 1998, Newspapers: a lost cause? Strategic management of newspaper firms in the United States and Netherlands, Doctoral thesis, University of Amsterdam.

Henninger, N., Chowdhury, N., Fisher, M., and Moonis, M., 2009, Use of Telemedicine to increase thrombolysis and advance care in acute ischemic stroke, Cerebrovascular diseases, Vol. 27(4), pp. 9–14.

Hibbing, J.R., and Theiss-Morse, E., Stealth democracy: Americans' beliefs about how government should work. Cambridge, UK: Cambridge University Press, 2002.

Himmelweit, H.T., Oppenheim, A.N., and Vince, P., Television and the child, London: Oxford University Press, 1958.

Hoffman Joel M., In the Beginning: A Short History of the Hebrew Language, New York University Press, New York, 2004, p. 18.

Hosmer, D.W., and Lemeshow, S., Applied Logistic Regression, Wiley, New York, 2000, pp. 1–259.

Hovland, C., and Weiss, W., 1951, The influence of source credibility on communication effectiveness. Public Opinion Quarterly, Vol. 15, pp. 635–650.

Hudson, F., Lee, A.M., and Mott, F.L., *American journalism*, 1690–1940, Vol. 1, Routledge, 2000.

Hulse Joseph H., Sustainable Development at Risk Ignoring the Past: Inc Net Library, International Development Research Centre, Canada, 2007, p. 316.

Hunt, C., TCP-IP network administration, O'Reilly Media, Inc., 2002, 3rd edn.

Indian Internet Subscribers up 215 per cent This Year, *India Telecom*, July 15, 2001.

Indian users grow to 71 million: IMRB, *The Times of India*, March 19, 2010.

Infante, D.A., The Construct Validity of Semantic Differential Scales for the Measurement of Source Credibility, *Communication Quarterly*, 1980, Vol. 28(2), pp. 19–26.

Internet History From ARPANET to Broadband, 2007, *Congressional Digest*, Vol. 86 (2), pp. 35–64.

Jacobson, H.K., 1969, Mass Media Believability, A Study of Receiver Judgements *Journalism Quarterly*, Vol. 46(1), pp. 20–28.

James K.L, The Internet: A user's Guide, Prentice Hall of India, 2004.

James, M.L., Wotring, C.E., and Forrest, E.J., 1995, An exploratory study of the perceived benefits of electronic bulletin board use and their impact on other communication activities, *Journal of Broadcasting and Electronic Media*, Vol. 39, pp. 30–50.

Janda, K., Berry, J.M., and Goldman, J., The challenge of democracy: Government in America (4th ed.), Houghton Mifflin, Boston, 1995, p. 42.

Johnson, T.J., and Kaye, B.K., 2000, Using is believing: The influence of reliance on the credibility of online political information among politically interested Internet users, *Journalism and Mass Communication Quarterly*, Vol. 77(4), pp. 865–879.

Johnson, T.J., and Kaye, B.K., 1998, Cruising is believing: Comparing Internet and traditional sources on media credibility measures, *Journalism and Mass Communication Quarterly*, Vol. 75(2), pp. 325–340.

Jones, A., Historical sketch of the electric telegraph: including its rise and progress in the United States, G.P. Putnam, 1852, p. 10.

Joseph, P.T., E-Commerce: An Indian Perspective 2nd Ed., PHI Learning Pvt. Ltd., 2006, p. 141.

Kaminow Ivan P. and Li Tingye, Optical Fiber Telecommunications IVB, Academic Press, 2002, p. 31.

Katz, E., 1959, Mass communication research and the study of culture, *Studies in Public Communication*, Vol. 2, pp. 1–6.

Katz, E., Blumler, J.G., and Gurevitch, M., Ulilisation of mass communication by the individual. In J.G. Blumler, and E. Katz (Eds.), The uses of mass communications: Current perspectives on gratifications research, Beverly Hills: Sage Publications, 1974.

Katz, E.M., Gurevitch, M., and Hass, H, 1973, On the uses of mass media for important things, *American Sociology Review*, Vol. 38(2), pp. 164–181.

Kayany, J. and Yelsma, P., 2000, Displacement effects of online media in the socio-technical contexts of households, *Journal of Broadcasting and Electronic Media*, Vol. 44(2), pp. 215–229.

Kesmodel, D., The domain game: How people get rich from Internet domain names, ISBN, 2008, p. 18.

Kestnbaum, M., Robinson, J.P., Neustadtl, A. and Alvarez, A., 2002, Information Technology and Social Time Displacement, IT and Society, Vol. 1(1), pp. 21–37.

Kettl, D.F., 2000, Public Administration at the Millennium: The State of the Field, *Journal of Public Administration Research and Theory*, Vol. 10(1), pp. 7–34.

Kiousis, S., 2001, Public Trust or Mistrust? Perceptions of Media Credibility in the Information Age, *Mass Communication and Society*, Vol. 4(4), pp. 381–403.

Kippax, S., and Murray, J.P, 1980, Using the mass media: Need gratification and 'perceived utility', *Communication Research*, Vol. 7, pp. 335–360.

Klein, Hans,1999, Tocqueville in Cyberspace: Using the Internet for Citizen Associations, *The Information Society*, Vol. 15, pp. 1–4.

Kling, R., and Callahan, E., 2003, Electronic journals, the Internet, and scholarly communication, *Annual Review of Information Science and Technology*, Vol. 37, pp. 127–177.

Kochen, M., 1983, Information and society, *Annual Review of Information Science and Technology*, Vol. 18, pp. 277–304.

Kraut, R., Patternson, M., Lundmark, V. Kiesler, S., Mukophadhayay, T., and Scherlis, W., 1998, Internet paradox: A social technology that reduces social involvement and psychological well-being? *The American Psychologist*, Vol. 53(9), pp. 1017–1031.

Kreuger, R.A., and M.A. Casey, Focus groups: A practical guide for applied research, 3rd edition, Thousand Oaks, Sage Publications, California, 2000.

Kuehn, S.A., 1994, Computer-mediated communication in instructional settings: A research agenda, *Communication Education*, Vol. 43, pp. 171–182.

Kwok, Y., 1998, August 21, Internet campaigns, Asiaweek.

La porte, T.M., Demchak, C.C., and De Jong, M., 2002, Democracy and bureaucracy in the age of the web: Empirical findings and theoretical speculations, *Administration and Society,* Vol. 34(4), pp. 411–446.

Landweber, L., 1979, Theory Net: An electronic mail system, Association for computer machinery, NY, USA.

LaQuey Tracey, The user's directory of computer networks, Bedford M.A, Digital Press, 1990, p. 194.

LaRose, R., Mastro, D., and Eastin, M.S., 2001, Understanding Internet usage: A Social-cognitive approach to uses and gratifications, *Social Science Computer Review*, Vol. 19(4), pp. 395–413.

Laudon, Kenneth C. and Laudon, Jane P., Essentials of Management Information Systems, Upper Saddle River, New Jersey, 2001.

Lazarsfeld, P. F., Radio and the printed page, New York: Dell, Sloan and Pearce, 1940, pp. 94–104.

Lee, A.M., *American journalism*, 1690–1940, Vol. 3, Routledge, 2000, p. 102.

Lee, W., Tan, T.M.K. and Hameed, S.S., 2005, Polychronicity, the Internet, and the mass media: A Singapore study, *Journal of Computer-Mediated Communication*, Vol. 11(1), pp. 1–18.

Leiner Barry M., Cerf Vinton G., Clark David D., Kahn Robert E., Kleinrock Leonard, Lynch Daniel C., Postel Jon, Roberts Larry G., Wolff Stephen, 1997, The past and future history of the Internet, *Communications of the ACM*, Vol. 40(2), pp. 102–108.

Lent, J.A., 1979, The evolution of development news: A brief history. In J.A. Lent and J.V. Vilanilam (Eds.), The use of development news: Case Studies in India, Malaysia, Ghana and Thailand, Singapore: Asian Mass Communication Research and Information Center, pp. 21–29.

Levy, Mark and Windahl, Sven, The concept of audience activity. In K. Rosengren, L.Wenner and P. Palmgreen (Eds.), Media gratifications research: Current perspectives, Beverly Hills, CA: Sage Publications, 1989, pp. 109–122.

Li., S.C.S., 2001, New media and market competition. A niche analysis of television news, electronic news and newspaper news in Taiwan, *Journal of broadcasting and electronic media*, Vol. 45(2), pp. 259–276.

Lichenstein, A., and Rosenfeld, L.B, 1983, Uses and misuses of gratifications research: An explication of media functions, *Communications Research*, Vol. 10, pp. 97–109.

Lievrouw, L., and Farb, S., 2003, Information and equity, *Annual Review of Information Science and Technology*, Vol. 37, pp. 499–540.

Lievrouw, L.A., and Livingstone, S.M., Handbook of new media: Social shaping and consequences of ICTs, Sage Publications, 2002.

Lin, C.A, 1999, Online service adoption likelihood, *Journal of Advertising Research*, Vol. 39(2), pp. 79–89.

Lin, C.A and Salwen, M.B., Utilities of online and offline news use. In Li, Xigen, (eds), Internet newspapers, Lawrence Erlbaum Associates, Mahwah, NJ, 2006.

Lindlof, T.R., and Taylor, B.C., Qualitative Communication Research Methods, 2nd Edition, Thousand Oaks, Sage Publications, California, 2002, p. 182.

Linkai Nihon Yunesuko Kokunai, Japan its land people and Culture, Printing Bureau, Ministry of Finance Japan, 1964, p. 354.

Liu, Z., 2003, Perception of credibility of scholarly information on the web, *Information processing and management*, Vol. 40, pp. 1027–1038.

Loges, W.E., and Ball-Rokeach, S., 1993, Dependency relations and newspaper readership, *Journalism Quarterly*, Vol. 70, pp. 601–614.

London, S., 1995, Teledemocracy vs. deliberative democracy: A comparative look at two models of public talk, *Journal of Interpersonal Computing and Technology*, Vol. 3(2), pp. 33–55.

Lu, H., and Andrews, J.E., 2006, College students' perception of the absolute media credibility about SARS-related news during the SARS outbreak in Taiwan, China, *Media Research*, Vol. 2(2), pp. 85–93.

Mackenzie, D., and Wajcman, J., (Eds), The social shaping of technology (2nd edn.), Buckingham, UK, Open University Press, 1999.

Madon, S., and Sahay, S., 2002, An information-based model of NGO mediation for the empowerment of slum dwellers in Bangalore, *The Information Society*, Vol. 18 (1), pp. 13–19.

Malhotra, N.K., Marketing research and applied orientation, Pearson Education Limited, England, 2007, pp. 369–473.

Mary, B., 1999, Ethernet emerges, Computer World, Vol. 33(25), p. 96.

Mashek, J.W., 1997, Lethargy 1996: How the media covered a listless campaign, Arlington, VA, The Freedom Forum.

Massey, B. and Levy, M., 1999, Interactivity, online journalism, and English-language web newspapers in Asia, *Journalism and Mass Communication Quarterly*, Vol. 76, pp. 138–51.

McCombs, M., and Shaw, D. L., 1972, The agenda-setting function of mass media. *Public Opinion Quarterly*, Vol. 36, pp. 176–187.

McDowell, S.D. and Pashupati, K., 1998, India's Internet Policies: New Media Ownership, Control and Purposes, *Media Development*, Vol. 15(4), pp. 18–24.

McIver, W.J., and Elmagarmid, A.K., Advances in digital government: Technology, human factors, and policy, Springer, USA, 2002, p. 4.

McLeod, J.M., and Reeves, B., On the nature of mass media effects. In Withey, S.B and Abeles, R.P., (Eds), Television and social behaviour: Beyond violence and children, Hillsdale, NJ: Lawrence Erlbaum Associates,1980, pp. 17–54.

McQuail, D., Mass Communication Theory (1st ed.), London, Sage Publications, 1983.

McQuail, D., The rise of media of mass communication. In D. McQuail (Ed.), Mass communication theory: An introduction, London, Sage Publications, 1994.

Mehrabi, D., Hassan, M.A., and Ali, M. S.S, 2009, News Media Credibility of the Internet and Television, *European Journal of Social Sciences*, Vol. 11(1), pp. 136–148.

Mehta, J.I, Advanced Study in the History of Medieval India, Vol. 2, Sterling Publishers Pvt. Ltd, Delhi, 1984.

Mekhjian, H., Warisse, J., Gailiun, M., and McCain, T., 1996, An Ohio Telmedicine System for Prison Inmates: A Case Report, *Telemedicine Journal*, Vol. 2(1), pp. 17–24.

Melville, A., 1923, The machine gun of commerce, *The Rotarian*, Vol. 23(4), p. 18.

Mendelsohn, H. (Ed.), Listening to radio, New York: Free Press, 1964.

Meyer, B.C., Raman, R., Hemmen, T., Obler, R., Zivin, J.A., Rao, R., Thomas, R.G., and Lyden, P.D., 2008, Efficacy of site-independent telemedicine in the Stroke DOC trial: A randomised, blinded, prospective study, *Lancet Neurology*, Vol. 7(9), pp. 787–95.

Meyer, P., 1988, Defining and measuring credibility of newspapers: Developing an index, *Journalism Quarterly*, Vol. 65 (3), pp. 567–574.

Million People Claimed to have used Internet in 2009, Internet and mobile association of India, Press release, 05 April, 2010.

Mings, S., and White, P.B., Profiting from online news: the search for viable business models. In Kahin, B. and Varain, H.R., (eds.) Internet publishing and beyond: The economics of digital information and intellectual property, The MIT press, Cambridge, MA, 2000.

Mockapetris, P.V., and Dunlap, K.J., 1995, Development of the domain name system, ACM SIGCOMM, *Computer Communication Review*, Vol. 25(1), pp. 112–122.

Molina, A., 1997, Issues and challenges in the evolution of multimedia: The case of the newspapers, *Futures*, Vol. 29, pp. 193–212.

Morris Merrill and Ogan Christine, Internet as a Mass Medium. In McQuail Denis, *McQuail's Reader in Mass Communication Theory*, Sage Publications, 2002, pp. 135–145.

Morris, M., and Ogan, C., 1996, The Internet as mass medium. *Journal of communication*, Vol. 46(1), pp. 39–50.

Morrone, A., and Zannella, L., 2004, IT and Mass media use among Italian youth, IT and Society, Vol. 1(6), pp. 59–67.

Mott Frank Luther, *American Journalism*, A History 1690–1960, Macmillan, New York, 1962.

Mueller, J., and Kamerer, D., 1995, Reader preference for electronic newspapers, *Newspaper research journal*, Vol. 16(3), pp. 2–13.

Mumford, E., Participation—from Aristotle to today, in T. Bemelmans (Eds.), Beyond productivity: Information Systems Development for Organisational Effectiveness, Amsterdam, the Netherlands, North-Holland Press, 1984.

Mutz, D.C., Roberts, D.F., van Vuuren, D.P., 1993, Reconsidering the displacement hypothesis: Television's influence on children's time use, *Communication Reseach*, Vol. 20(1), pp. 51–75.

Nadin Mihai, The Civilisation of Illiteracy, Dresden University Press, Dresden, Germany, 1997, p. 106.

National Readership Study, 2006 (NRS 2006).

National Research Council, Committee on Internet Navigation and the Domain Name System: Technical Alternatives and Policy Implications, Signposts in Cyberspace: The Domain Name System and Internet Navigation, National Academics, 2005.

Naughton, J., A brief history of the future: The origins of the Internet, Weidenfeld and Nicolson Ltd, London, 1999.

Navein, J., Fisher, A., Geiling, J., Richards, D. Roller, J., and Hagmann, J., 1998, Portable satellite telemedicine in practice, *Journal of Telemedicine and Telecare*, Vol. 4 (l), pp. 25–28.

Neuberger, C., Tonnemacher, J., Biebl, M., and Duck, A., 1998, Online—the future of newspapers, Germany's dailies on the World Wide Web, *Journal of Computer Mediated Communication*, Vol. 4(1), pp. 1–23.

Neustadl, A. and Robinson, J.P., 2002, Media use differences between Internet users and nonusers in the general social survey, *IT and Society*, Vol. 1(2), pp. 100–120.

Newhagen, J., 1997, The role of feedback in the assessment of news, Information Processing and Management, Vol. 33(5), pp. 583–594.

Ngyuen, A. and Western, M., 2006, The Complementary relationship between the Internet and traditional mass media: The Case of Online News and Information, Information Research, Vol. 11(3), pp. 259–278.

Nicholas D., Frossling I., Martin H., and Buesing P., 1997, (Really) getting to grips with the Internet: What it has to offer in the way of newspapers, *Vine*, Vol. 104, pp. 29–30.

Nie, N., Hillygus, D. and Erbring, L., Internet use, interpersonal relations and sociability: A time diary study. In Barry Wellman and Carolyne Haythorntwaite (Eds), The Internet in everyday life, Oxford: Blackwell, 2002, pp. 215–243.

NiedŸwiedzka, B., 2003, A proposed model of information behaviour, Information Research, Vol. 9. (1), pp. 1–17.

Noack, D., 1997, Off-line newspapers: Too small, too busy, or too unsure, some move slowly into cyberspace, *Editor and publisher*, Vol. 130(6), pp. 321–331.

Norris, P., (Eds), Critical citizens: Global support for democratic government, New York, Oxford University Press, 1999.

Norris, P., Who surfs? New technology, old voters and virtual democracy. In E. Kamarck and J. Nye (Eds), democracy.com? Governance in a networked world, Hollis, NH: Hollis Publishing, 1999, pp. 71–98.

Nozato, Y., 2002, Credibility of online newspapers, in Proceedings of the Annual Meeting of the Association for Education in Journalism and Mass Communication

(85th, Miami, Florida, August 5–8, 2002, Communication Technology and Policy Division, Collected Works - Proceedings; Reports–Research.

Number of Internet users in India reaches 37 million, *The Hindu*, Saturday, Sep. 23, 2006.

Nunnaly, J.L., and Bernstein, I.H., Psychometric theory, 3rd ed, McGraw-Hill, New York, 1994.

Ohinmaa, A., Hailey, D., and Roine, R., 2001, Assessing telemedicine: A systematic review of the literature, *Canadian Medical Association Journal*, Vol. 165(6), pp. 765–771.

Olver, I., and Selva-Nayagam, S., 2000, Evaluation of a telemedicine link between Darwin and Adelaide to facilitate cancer management, *Telemedicine Journal*, Vol. 6(2), pp. 213–218.

Otto, C. and Pipe, A., 1997, Remote, mobile telemedicine: the satellite transmission of medical data from Mount Logan, *Journal of Telemedicine and Telecare*, Vol. 3(1), pp. 84–85.

Outing S., 2003, Hold on (line) tight, Editor and Publisher, p. 41.

Outing, S., 1998, New media cutting into old media, *Editor and Publisher*, Vol. 131, p. 43.

Palmgreen, P., Wenner, L.A. and Rayburn, J.D. II., 1980, Relations between gratifications sought and obtained: Study of TV news, *Communication Research*, Vol. 7, pp. 161–192.

Park, K., Park's textbook of preventive and social medicine, Banarsidas Bhanot, Jabalpur, 2005.

Pathak, A., Public relations manager, Prabhat Prakashan, 2009.

Peng, F.Y., Tham, N.I., and Xiaoming, H., 1999, Trends in online newspapers: A look at the US web, *Newspaper Research Journal*, Vol. 20 (2), pp. 52–63.

Perse, E.M., and Courtright, J.A., 1993, Normative images of communication media: Mass and interpersonal channels in the new media environment, *Human Communication Research*, Vol. 19, pp. 485–503.

Pew Research Center for the People and the Press, 1999, The Internet News audience goes ordinary.

Picard, R.G., 2003, Cash cows or Entercôte: Publishing companies and disruptive technologies, *Trends in communication*, Vol. 11(2), pp. 127–136.

Plankers, S., 1994, Genealogy, A BBS, and You, Ancestry, Vol. 2(2), pp. 14–15.

Porter Beth, The net effect, Intellect books, UK, 2001, p. 45.

Porter, M.E., 2001, Strategy and the Internet, *Harvard Business Review*, pp. 1–21.

Pratiyogita Darpan, edited by Mahendra Jain, Upkar Prakashan, 2009.

Press Information Bureau, Government of India, *Press Release*, August 20, 2007.

Press Information Bureau, Government of India, *Press Release*, May 12, 2007.

Puskin, D.H., Brink, L.H., Mintzer, C.L., and Waseem, C.J., 1995, Joint Federal Initiative for Creating a Telemedicine Evaluation Framework, Letter to the Editor, *Telemedicine Journal*, Vol. 1(4), p. 394.

Putnam, R.D., 1995, Bowling alone, America's declining social capital, *Journal of democracy*, Vol. 6(1), pp. 65–78.

Quarterman John, The Matrix: Computer networks and conferencing systems worldwide, Bedford M.A, Digital Press, 1990, pp. 141–143.

Raatma, L., Thomas Edison, Compass Point Books, 2003.

Rafaeli, S. and LaRose R. J., 1993, Electronic Bulletin Boards and "Public Goods" Explanations of Collaborative Mass Media, *Communication Research*, Vol. 20 (2), pp. 277–297.

Rafaeli, S., Interactivity: From new media to communication. In R. Hawkins et al. (Eds.), Advancing communication science: Merging mass and interpersonal processes, Newbury Park, CA: Sage Publications, 1988, pp. 110–134.

Rainie L., Fox S., and Fallows D., The internet and the Iraq war: How online Americans have used the Internet to learn war news, understand events, and promote their views, Pew Internet and American Life.

Rajan, N., 21st century journalism in India, Sage Publications, 2007.

Rayburn, J.D., II., Uses and gratifications. In M.B. Salwen and D.W. Stacks (Eds.), An integrated approach to communication theory and research, Mahwah NJ: Lawrence Erlbaum Associates, 1996, pp. 15–163.

Rimmer, T., and Weaver, D., 1987, Different questions, different answers. Media use and media credibility, *Journalism Quarterly*, Vol. 64 (1), pp. 28–36.

Robinson, J.P., Barth, K., and Kohut, A., 1997, Social impact research: Personal computers, mass media and use of time, *Social Science Computer Review*, Vol. 15(1), pp. 65–82.

Robinson, J.P., Kestnbaum, M., Neustadtl, A., and Alvarez, A., 2000, Mass Media and Social Life among Internet Users, *Social Science Computer Review*, Winter, Vol. 18(4), pp. 490–501.

Robinson, J., 1981, Television and leisure time: A new scenario, *Journal of Communication*, Vol. 31, pp. 120–130.

Rogers, E., Communication Technology: The new media in society, 1986, Free Press, New York.

Rosser, J.C., Bell, R.L., Harnett, B., Rodas, E., Murayama, M., and Merrell, R., 1999, Use of mobile low-bandwith telemedical techniques for extreme telemedicine applications, *Journal of the American College of Surgeons*, Vol. 189 (4), pp. 397–404.

Rubin, A.M., and Perse, E.M., 1987, Audience activity and television news gratifications, Communication research, Vol. 14, pp. 58–84.

Rubin, R.B., Palmgren, P., and Sypher, H.E., Communication research measures: A sourcebook, Vol. 2, Routledge, 2004.

Rubin, R.B., Perse, E.M., and Barbato, C.A., 1988, Conceptualisation and measurement of interpersonal communication motives, *Human Communication Research*, Vol. 14, pp. 602–628.

Ruggiero, T., 2000, Uses and gratifications theory in the 21st century, *Mass Communication and Society*, Vol. 3(1), pp. 3–37.

Sahay, S., and Avgerou, C., 2002, Introducing the special issue on information and communication technologies in developing countries, *The Information Society*, Vol. 18, pp. 73–76.

Sakai, M., Imai, T., Kuboki, K., Maeda, S., Ueda, S., Kuwajima, I., Ohkawa, S., and Matshushita, S., 1999, Usefulness and safety of intravenous thrombolytic therapy for elderly patients with acute myocardial infarction: relationship with cardiac rupture, *Journal of cardiology*, Vol. 33(3), pp. 153–61.

Salwen, M.B., Garrison, B., and Driscoll, P.D., Online news and the public, Routledge, 2005.

Sawai, T., Goto, K., Watanabe, M., Endoh, W., Ogata, K., and Nagura, H., 1999, Constructing a local district telepathology network in Japan. Diagnosis of intraoperative frozen sections via telepathology over an integrated service digital network and the National Television Standard Committee System, *Analytical and Quantitative Cytology and Histology*, Vol. 21(1), pp. 81–84.

Sawhney Mohanbir, Fields of online dreams, CIO Magazine, October 15, 2002.

Sawyer, S., and Eschenfelder, K.R., 2002, Social informatics: Perspectives, examples, and trends, Annual Review of Information Science and Technology, Vol. 36, pp. 427–467.

Schroth, P.W., Sharma, P., 2003, Transnational law and technology as potential forces against corruption in Africa, *Management decision*, Vol. 41(3), pp. 296–303.

Schudson, M., 1992, The limits of Teledemocracy, *The American Prospect*, pp. 41–45.

Schwamm, L.H., Rosenthal, E.S., Hirshberg, A., Schaaefer, P.W., Little, E.A., Kvedar, J.C., Petkovska, I., Koroshetz, W.J., and Levine, S., 2004, Virtual telestroke support for the emergency department evaluation of acute stroke, *Academic Emergency Medicine*, Vol. 11(11), pp. 1193–97.

Schweiger, W., 2000, Media credibility or experience or image: A survey on the credibility of the World Wide Web in Germany in comparison to other media, *European Journal of Communication*, Vol. 15, pp. 37–59.

Sclove, R., Democracy and Technology, Guilford Press, London, 1995, p. 20.

Severin W.J., and Tankard, J.W. (Eds.), Communication Theories: Origins, Methods, and Uses in the Mass Media (3rd ed.), New York: Longman. 1992, pp. 272–275.

Simon, L., Type and Type Founding, I.B. Tauris, 2004.

Singh, S., 1999, India ISP licenses pickup, Infoworld, 23/08/1999, Vol. 21(34).

Singhal, A. and Rogers, E.M., 2001, India's communication revolution: From bullock carts to cybermarts, New Delhi, Sage Publications.

Singhal, A. and Sthapitanonda, P., 1996, The role of communication in development, Lessons learned from a critique of the dominant, dependency, and alternative paradigms, *The Journal of Development Communication*, Vol. 7(1), pp. 10–25.

Sinha B.C., 1970, Ischaemic heart diseases in India, *Journal of Indian Medical Association*, Vol. 55, p. 171.

Site Statistics for Telegraphindia.com. Accessed and downloaded from http://www.alexa.com/data/details/main/telegraphindia.com on 23/7/2008.

Sloan, W.D., and Parcell, L.M., *American journalism: history, principles, practices*, McFarland, 2002.

Smil, V., Creating the twentieth century: technical innovations of 1867–1914 and their lasting impact, Oxford University Press, US, 2005.

Smith, J.N., 2007, Great moments in World Trade: The making of the Internet, *World Trade*, Vol. 20(6), p. 62.

Society for promoting Christian knowledge, The History of printing, W. Clowes and Sons, London, 1855.

Special website on National task force on IT and Software development. Available at http://it-taskforce.nic.in/ accessed on 26/12/2008.

Speech by Rupert Murdoch to the American Society of Newspaper Editors, American Society of Newspaper Editors, April 13, 2005, available at http://www.newscorp.com/news/news_247.html, accessed on 12/10/2006.

Srikantaiah,T.K., and Xiaoying, D., 1998, The Internet and its impact on developing countries: examples from China and India, Asian Libraries, Vol. 7(9), pp. 199–209.

Stempel, G., Hargrove, T. and Bernt, J., 2000, Relation of growth of use of the Internet to changes in media use from 1995 to 1999, *Journalism and Mass Communication Quarterly*, Vol. 77(1), pp. 71–79.

Stromer-Galley, J., 2000, On-line interaction and why candidates avoid it, *Journal of Communication*, Vol. 50 (4), pp. 111–132.

Sunden, S., and Wicander,G., 2006, Information and communication technology applied for developing countries in a rural context: Towards a framework for analysing factors influencing sustainable use, *Karlstad University Studies 2006*, Vol. (69), pp. 18–34.

Switzer, J.A., Gross, H., Waller, J.L., Nichols, F.T., Wang, S., Adams, R.J. and Hess, D.C., 2009, A web-based Telestroke system facilitates rapid treatment of acute ischemic stroke patients in rural emergency departments, *The Journal of Emergency Medicine*, Vol. 36(1), pp. 12–18.

Tambini, D., 1999, New media and democracy: The civic networking movement, *New Media and Society*, Vol. 1 (3), pp. 305–329.

Tether, T., 2008, DARPA Fifty years of inventing the future 1958–2008, Aerospace America, Vol. 46(2), pp. 30–43.

Thakur Kiran, Internet Journalism, Department of Journalism, Pune University, Pune.

Thalhimer, M.,1994, High-tech news or just "shovelware", *Media studies journal*, Vol. 8, pp. 41–51.

Thogmartin, C., The national daily press of France, Summa Publications Inc., 1998, pp. 12–14.

Tseng, S., and Fogg, B., 1999, Credibility and computing technology, *Communications of the ACM*, Vol. 42(5), pp. 39–44.

UNDP, 1999, Human Development Report 1999, New York: Oxford University Press.

United States Congress, House Committee on Science and Technology, Task force on Science policy, A history of Science Policy in the United States, 1940–1985, For sale by the Superintendent of documents, US GPO, 1986.

Uslaner, E.M., 2004, Trust, civic engagement, and the Internet, *Political communication*,Vol. 21, pp. 223–242.

Vaishnav, A.G., Pettigrew, L.C., Ryan, S., 2008, Telephonic guidance of systemic thrombolysis in acute ischemic stroke: safety outcome in rural hospitals, *Clinical Neurology and Neurosurgery*, Vol. 110 (5), pp. 451–454.

Valente, T.W., 1993, Diffusion of innovations and policy decision-making, *Journal of Communication*, Vol. 43(1), pp. 30–45.

Verba, S., Schlozman, K.L., and Brady, H.E., Voice and equality: Civic voluntarism in American politics, Harvard University Press, Cambridge, MA, 1995.

Verba, S., Schlozman, K.L., Brady, H., and Nie, N.H., 1993, Race, ethnicity, and political resources: Participation in the United States, *British Journal of Political Science*, Vol. 23(4), pp. 453–497.

Vinne, T.L.D., The Practice of Typography, Biblio Bazaar, LLC, 2008, pp. 133–142.

Vyas, R.S., Singh N.P., and Bhabhra, S., 2007, Media displacement effect: Investigating the impact of Internet on newspaper reading habits of consumers, *Vision: The journal of Business Perspective*, Vol. 11(2), pp. 29–40.

Walravens, H., International newspaper librarianship for the 21st century, Vol. 118, Walter de Gruyter, 2006, p. 235.

Wang, S., Gross, H., Lee, S.B., Pardue, C., Waller, J., Nichols, F.T., Adams, R.J., and Hess, D.C., 2004, Remote evaluation of acute ischemic stroke in rural community hospitals in Georgia, *Stroke*, Vol. 35(7), pp. 1763–68.

Watson, G. S., and Durbin, J., 1951, Exact Tests of Serial Correlation using Non-circular Statistics, *The Annals of Mathematical Statistics*, Vol. 22(3), pp. 446–451.

Weaver, D.H, 1980, Audience need for orientation and media effects, *Communication Research*, Vol. 7, pp. 361–376.

Weaver, L. and Spence, D., 2000, Application of business case analysis in planning a province-wide telehealth network in Alberta, *Journal of Telemedicine and Telecare*, Vol. 6(l), pp. 87–89.

Website of The Hindu, http://epaper.thehindu.com/ accessed on 02/07/2008.

Website of Indiapress–Indian Newspapers Links and India News, http://www.indiapress.org/, accessed on 22/07/2008.

Website of ITC's *e-choupal*.

Webster, F., Democracy and information in a network society. In S. Criddle, L. Dempsey, and R. Heseltine (Eds.), Information landscapes for a learning society: Networking and the future of libraries, Library Association, London, 1999.

Weiss, W., The impact of mass media, In G. Lindzey and E. Aronson (Eds.), *Handbook of Social Psychology,* Vol. 5, Reading, MA: Addison-Wesley, 1968.

West, M. D., 1994, Validating a scale for the measurement of credibility: A covariance structure modeling approach, *Journalism Quarterly*, Vol. 71(1), pp. 159–168.

Whitten, P. S., and Allen, A., 1995, Analysis of Telemedicine from an Organisational Perspective, *Telemedicine Journal*, Vol. 1(3), pp. 203–14.

WHO Director-General Highlights Potential of Telemedicine, 1997 Press Release WHO/65 accessed from http://www.who.org/inf-pr-1997/en/pr97-65.html on 10.1.2007.

Williams, F., Rice, R.E., and Rogers, E.M., Research methods and the new media, Free Press, New York, 1988.

Williams, T.M., The impact of television, New York: Academic Press, 1986.

Wilson, T.D., 1998, Information behaviour: an interdisciplinary perspective, *Information processing and management*, Vol. 33(4), pp. 551–572.

Wilson, T.D., 1999, Models in information behaviour research, *Journal of Documentation*, Vol. 55(3), pp. 249–270.

Windahl, S., 1981, Uses and gratifications at the crossroads, *Mass Communication Review Yearbook*, Vol. 2, pp. 174–185.

Woo, K.S., Tse, K.K., Mak, Y.K., Chung, H.K., 1992, The impact of thrombolytic therapy on hospital mortality from acute myocardial infarction in the Chinese in Hong Kong, *International journal of cardiology*, Vol. 37(2), pp. 169–175.

Yin, R.K., Case Study Research: Design and Methods, Sage Publications, Newbury, CA, 1994.

Zhang, J., 2002, Will the government serve the people? The development of Chinese e-government, *New Media and Society*, Vol. 4(2), pp. 163–184.

Index

D

I

J

T

U

V